From Bonn to Berlin

From Bonn
to Berlin

German Politics in Transition

Lewis J. Edinger and Brigitte L. Nacos

New York   Columbia University Press

Columbia University Press
Publishers Since 1893
New York   Chichester, West Sussex

Library of Congress Cataloging-in-Publication Data

Edinger, Lewis Joachim, 1922–
    From Bonn to Berlin : German politics in transition / Lewis J.
Edinger and Brigitte L. Nacos.
        p.   cm.
    Includes bibliographical references and index.
    ISBN 0–231–08412–9 (cl). — ISBN 0–231–08413–7 (p)
    1. Germany—Politics and government—20th century.   I. Nacos,
Brigitte Lebens.   II. Title.
JN3971.A58E35   1998
320.943'09'049—dc21   97–51253
                                                            CIP

Printed in the United States of America

c 10 9 8 7 6 5 4 3 2 1
p 10 9 8 7 6 5 4 3 2 1

Contents

Acknowledgments

We owe large debts to many individuals and institutions in the United States and in the Federal Republic of Germany who supported us in many ways. Most of all we are grateful to Robert Y. Shapiro, our colleague and friend at Columbia University, for reading the manuscript in its entirety and for making many useful suggestions to improve the text. We also appreciate greatly the constructive criticism offered by Gisela Knight and Peter Johnson, who read parts of the manuscript. The German Information Center (GIC) in New York provided us with material and most of the photographs used to illustrate the book. The center's informative publications (*Deutschland Nachrichten* and *The Week in Germany*) were valuable sources. Ingeborg Godenschweder, Hannelore Köhler, and Werner Koep-Kerstin were especially helpful at the GIC. Manfred Küchler at Hunter College gave us access to useful poll data.

In Germany several institutions and their officials were generous in sharing information and ideas during our several visits in and travels throughout Germany. The federal press office (*Bundespresseamt*) was extremely supportive during the last phase of the 1994 federal election campaign, when Brigitte Nacos was among a group of invited American professors. We are grateful to Inter Nationes for providing us with book material. The Konrad-Adenauer-Stiftung and the Friedrich-Ebert-Stiftung gave us generous access to their information resources as did the Institut für angewandte Sozialwissenschaft in Bad Godesberg and the Allensbach Institut fuer Demoskopie.

Many individuals in Germany deserve to be singled out for illuminating our understanding of German politics in the 1990s: In Bonn: Hanne Pollmann and Peter Pollmann, Karl Kaiser and Hanns W. Maull, Dorothea von Stetten, Karl Dietrich Bracher and Dorothea Bracher, Hans-Adolf Jacobson and Dorothea Jacobson, Hans-Peter Schwarz, Ursula Lehr, Dieter Piel, Gerhard Stümpfig, Ferdinand Protzman, Randolph Walerius, Rosemarie Callmann, Klaus Liepelt, Wolfgang Hartenstein, Wolfgang Bergsdorf, Ursula Jaerisch, Hans-Joachim Veen, Peter Gluchowski; in Cologne: Fritz W. Scharpf, Helene and Rolf Meyer, Hans Eberhart and Ursula Ehlers; in Konstanz: Jens Alber; in Essen: Brigitte and Thorsten Scharnhorst; in Dortmund: Joachim Westhoff; in Hagen: Ursula and Horst Kniese, Inge, Guenter and Ralf Schlasse; in Schwelm: Friedhelm Felsch and Klaus Balve; in Dresden: Heidrun Mueller, Otfried Weiss, Manfred Stüting; in Dessau: Peter Petsching, Klaus and Inge Skerra, Ursula Böhne.

We thank Kate Wittenberg, editor-in-chief of Columbia University Press, for her interest in our work, and manuscript editor Leslie Bialler for his superb editing job.

Last but not least we thank our spouses Hanni Edinger and Jimmy Nacos for traveling with us to and in Germany and for supporting us and our book project in many important ways.

While we are indebted to many, the buck stops at our desks and at our computers: we are entirely responsible for the content of the book.

Lewis J. Edinger, Dobbs Ferry, N.Y.
Brigitte L. Nacos, Sands Point, N.Y.
January 1998

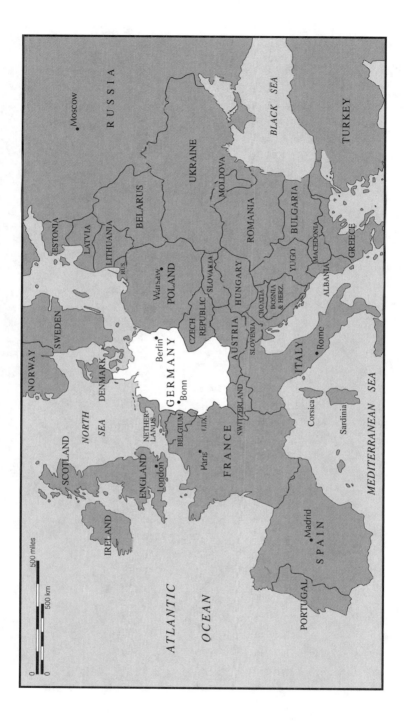

From Bonn to Berlin

Introduction: At the Crossroads

In the summer of 1995, when the conceptual artist Christo and his wife Jeanne-Claude covered the 101-year-old German *Reichstag* (Parliament) in Berlin with more than a million square feet of silver-colored fabric and transformed the building temporarily into a colossal gift-box, they presented Germans with one of the most spectacular outdoor projects of this sort and with a powerful metaphor for the country's transition from West Germany's Bonn Republic to reunited Germany's Berlin Republic. Moreover, as one American observer put it, "If the architecture of the Reichstag represents a kind of Prussian hardness—Germany as it was—the wrapped version can almost be seen as an ideal symbol of the new Germany struggling to emerge from unification."[1]

Two years earlier, when the federal diet (*Bundestag*) had debated and narrowly approved the wrapping, many deputies had opposed the project as trivialization of the country's perhaps most famous landmark. One deputy had warned that the wrapping would not bring people together but polarize them. But contrary to such strong reservations millions of joyful East and West Germans viewed and perhaps understood the symbolic meaning of the wrapped landmark. The veiling and unveiling of the monumental building signified the country's enduring and changing features: Just as the Reichstag's foundations, bearing walls, and facades reemerged unchanged and strong when Christo's gift-wrapping was taken off, the Bonn Republic's democratic roots, solid structures, and institutional framework remained the underpinnings of a slowly emerging Berlin Republic. Just as the gutted interior of the Reichstag required significant remodeling to house the Bundestag, Germany's political, economic, and social arrangements needed meaningful modifications to deal with the realities of the 1990s and the dawn of the new century. And just as the surroundings of the Reichstag looked dramatically different since the fall of communism, the external environment of the Federal Republic also had changed since the end of the Cold War in both political and economic terms.[2]

Several years after German reunification, Columbia University Press asked Lewis Edinger to consider another revision of his widely used textbook *German Politics*. Recognizing that the dynamic internal and external changes after the fall of the Berlin wall and the collapse of communism raised new and different questions about the political process in the Federal Republic, Edinger concluded that a revision would not do. The idea of a new book—this book—and of our collaboration took shape during our conversations in the political science department at Columbia University. Although working in different fields (American-raised Lewis Edinger in comparative politics with special expertise in Western Europe and especially Germany; German-raised Brigitte Nacos in American government and politics), we shared a profound interest in Germany—and still do.

Most mass-media organizations in the United States tend to cover the Federal Republic of Germany sparsely unless major events unfold. Consequently, most Americans see, read, and hear very little about German politics and policies. For this reason we decided against writing a textbook on German politics and collaborated instead on a book that gives the interested general public an opportunity to learn about politics in the Federal Republic at a time when the reunified country faces formidable challenges within its own borders and in the European and global setting. With a broad audience in mind we tried to refrain from political science jargon—probably without fully succeeding.

We do not claim to address all pertinent political problems and issues in present-day Germany; instead, we have concentrated on what we believe are some of the most important and interesting factors and issue areas. Our work is *primarily* about German politics on the road to the twenty-first century with special attention to the patterns of continuity and change in the country's governmental process. Whether the German democracy can adapt to and cope with the rapidly changing domestic and international conditions and whether the country remains a model of stability in the heart of Europe, is of vital interest to Germans, Europeans and Americans. Our *secondary* theme concerns comparisons between German and American political traditions, structures, institutions, actors, processes, and issues—but only to the extent that they illuminate the similarities and differences and help American readers to understand German politics better and perhaps their own as well.

To be sure, writing about German politics after the end of the Cold War is like aiming at a moving target. More than half a century after the fall of Hitler's Third Reich the political patterns established in the first four decades of the Federal Republic are undergoing endurance tests under dynamic new conditions. Politics and policies are in flux, and it is now far more difficult than in the preceding decades to pinpoint continuing and changing trends. But the challenges prompted by the reunification of the two Germanys, the move toward increased economic and political integration in Europe, and the intensifying global interdependence of the economic and monetary markets are precisely the reasons why we have examined German politics at this critical time.

In choosing *From Bonn to Berlin: German Politics in Transition* as the title of our book, we hope to convey the fluid mode of German politics in the 1990s and conceivably in the early part of the twenty-first century. Some observers have argued that contemporary Germany is at a crossroads and expressed doubts about the future direction of German politics; others have proclaimed the collapse of the socioeconomic "German model" altogether. Although we, too, were somewhat pessimistic at the outset, we have become more optimistic as we researched and wrote this book.

We have arranged our work in two distinct parts. In Part I, "Continuity and Change" (Chapters 1 through 3), we describe the basic attributes of German politics and the degree of constancy and change found in the country's political institutions, actors, values, and realities. In Part II, "Problems, Issues, and Prospects" (Chapters 4 through 7), we look at specific problems and issues in several policy areas and examine whether the political realm will be able to cope with the significant challenges it is facing now and will face for some time to come.

After reviewing several German motion pictures in 1994, film critic John Rockwell concluded that the overwhelming majority of Germans "are eerily like centrist-left-liberal Americans of the middle and upper-middle classes. . . . They dress like us, they talk like us, they behave like us, much of the time. . . . But they aren't us, and the differences lurk just beneath the familiar surface."[3] In many respects, German politics and the major political issues, too, resemble contemporary American politics and issues a great deal. But there are distinct differences as well. In Chapter 1 we address features that are peculiar to the Federal Republic, namely the consequences of reunification, the legacy of the Nazi past, and the country's enhanced role in Europe. In one way or the other these factors touch upon contemporary German politics.

For the reader not familiar with politics in the Federal Republic, in chapter 2 we explain the basic governmental design of Germany's representative democracy, the electoral system, and the central role of political parties. The institutional order that existed in West Germany long before the two Germanies reunified in 1990 has remained the framework for government and politics. But apart from this continuity in the basic political arrangements, this chapter also addresses some of the notable changes in the party system and within the major parties.

The founders of the Federal Republic designed a representative democracy where voting was the only feature for mass participation. But declining party loyalty and diminishing trust in what Germans call the political class has put pressure on the major parties to reconnect with their members as well as with citizens and voters in general and enact reforms that foster greater participation. Chapter 3 traces these still fairly modest shifts and the recent changes in the German mass media that favor a move toward more direct mass participation in the electoral and governmental process.

German reunification has accelerated the pace of societal changes that had already been underway in West Germany at the time reunification took place. Thus, Germans have become less religious, narrowed the gender gap in society and politics, and encountered the aging of their society as people live longer and birthrates decline. As Chapter 4 explains, Germans and German politics have far greater difficulties coming to terms with the fact that immigrants replenish their declining population and strengthen their economy and welfare state than with the changing role of women and churches in society and in politics.

Since the early 1990s, Germany's social market economy with its "capitalism with a human face" (Chapter 5) and its expansive social safety net (Chapter 6) has been under more pressure than ever to reform in ways that curtail some of the costs in order to safeguard the system itself. Because cooperation, not conflict, has guided the politics of economic and social policymaking in the Federal Republic before, during, and after the "economic miracle" era, we explore the German model itself and whether it will be able to adapt to the more recent internal and external challenges without risking social peace and political stability.

Foreign policy has not been high on the agenda of German politics in the 1990s, as we explain in Chapter 7. Just as public officials and experts in the United States have been preoccupied with domestic politics and policies in the years following the collapse of communism, German leaders also have shown so little interest in rethinking the country's role and importance in the post-Cold War era that some critical observers have asked whether the Federal Republic is at all interested in foreign policy in the 1990s.

We conclude with a summary of our findings and take a look at the road ahead in order to speculate about Germany's and the emerging Berlin Republic's politics and policies in the next century.

PART ONE
Continuity and Change

1

German Questions
Old and New

On June 20, 1991 the parliament of the Federal Republic of Germany, the Bundestag, resolved to move the capital from Bonn, its "temporary" location for some 40 years, to Berlin, the traditional capital until the Cold War had split the country into two parts. The day-long, passionate debate that preceded a very close decision was in the judgment of observers the greatest in the Federal Diet's history. With the advocates of Berlin and the champions of Bonn divided across party lines, the deputies were not shackled by the usual party discipline but free to express and vote their own convictions. The outcome of the late-night ballot was uncertain until the Bundestag's President, Rita Süssmuth, announced the result: 338 deputies voted for Berlin and 320 for Bonn.

In the end, an emotional speech by Interior Minister Wolfgang Schäuble, who had been instrumental in negotiating the unification treaty between the governments of East and West Germany in 1990, was credited with swinging the decisive votes for Berlin. For four decades Germany's largest city, divided like the rest of the country and completely surrounded by the territory of the East German socialist state, had been the symbol of Germany's partition and the quest for unity—even in the face of the mutually recognized political reality of the two sovereign German states. In 1949, when the Bundestag made Bonn the capital of the new Federal Republic, the deputies tied this decision to an explicit promise to move the leading institutions of government to Berlin as soon as free elections could be held in what was at the time the Soviet zone of occupation. Not to live up to this promise now, the supporters of Berlin argued, would deepen the sense of abandonment, distance, and alienation that many East Germans felt in the wake of unification. "What is at stake today is not Bonn or Berlin but the future of us all," Interior Minister Schäuble said in his plea. Others argued that the move from Bonn to Berlin would help to demolish the psychological wall between East and West Germans and cement unification. "For me," Chancellor Helmut Kohl said, "Berlin has always meant the opportunity to overcome division."

But the supporters of Bonn rejected a change of venue to Berlin just as passionately by summoning the light and the dark chapters of the country's past. For them Bonn stood for the years preceding reunification, when the small town on the Rhine River was the center of the German politics that had built a sound democratic society and steered the ship of state away from the troubled past during which Berlin had been the capital city.

Willy Brandt, the former West German Chancellor who had also been the Mayor of Berlin, chided speakers who alluded to Berlin as a symbol of German aggression, arrogance, and failure; he took exception to what he labeled "nonsense" aimed at blemishing the city as the stronghold of criminal Nazism and fanatic nationalism. But the young and middle-aged deputies did not share their elders' attachment to Berlin; they wanted to keep the capital of united Germany in Bonn, the birthplace of Germany's stable democracy and the city most closely linked to the longest peaceful chapter in Germany's history.

These arguments aroused also anxieties among Germany's neighbors for whom Berlin had symbolized Prussian and Nazi expansionism. During the most chilling periods of the Cold War Germany's Western allies had come to view and defend West Berlin as the bulwark of freedom and democracy, but when the communist bloc disintegrated and the two Germanys reunited, old fears reemerged in Europe. One French observer pointed out that

> the emergence of the German colossus is bringing under our noses what we did not like to see. Over and above that, it [German reunification] moves the center of gravity away from us—from the Rhine towards Prussia and from Bonn to Berlin. From the top of the Reichstag that has been regained, the German eagle nests equidistant from Strasbourg and from Warsaw. Germany, a big nation, is again becom-

ing a great nation: all it lacks is the military arm. From the height of its power, its industrialists and merchants are looking far beyond the West, at the wide world. And France looks at Germany. It is the season of suspicion—thoroughly foreseeable after all.[1]

Thus, the Bonn-or-Berlin issue also dramatized questions as to the future role of a unified German state in the new European and world order.

The political significance of the decision was not lost on either the legislators, who made the close call, or on domestic and foreign observers, who interpreted it. For Germans and their neighbors the vote in favor of Berlin—more so than the legal unification of the two Germanys on October 3, 1990—signaled the end of the post-World War II period and the dawn of a newly united, sovereign Germany.

The openness, setting, and rules of the Berlin-or-Bonn debate confirmed the widely held view that politics in the Federal Republic resembled in many respects politics in any other major democracy—including the United States. But this particular issue highlighted also the uniquely German factors that affect politics in the Federal Republic at the threshold of the twenty-first century. After all, the issue and the debate were caused, shaped, and fueled by three unique features of German politics: (1) the consequences of German unification after more than four decades of division, (2) the lingering legacy of the country's Nazi past, and (3) Germany's geographic uniqueness as a country in the middle of Europe *(Land der Mitte)* that was restored after the collapse of the Soviet-dominated Eastern European bloc.

The Consequences of Division and Unification

When joyous East and West Germans embraced and danced on top of the Berlin Wall on November 9, 1989, nobody was more surprised than political leaders and average citizens in the Federal Republic of Germany (FRG). Just a year before the Iron Curtain crumbled in Berlin and along the border between the two Germanys, Chancellor Kohl had publicly stated that he did not expect a united Germany during his lifetime. More than 70 percent of the West German public were of the same opinion while only 9 percent believed that they would live to witness the reunification of their divided land. Neither the West German nor the American nor any other Western intelligence services anticipated the events in the Communist German Democratic Republic (GDR).

If Erich Honecker, East Germany's aging leader, had a hunch about things to come, he did not tell. In January 1989, he still insisted that the Berlin Wall would stand tall in 50 and even in 100 years.

Nobody in the West questioned that prediction. On the contrary, when the 40th birthday of the Federal Republic was celebrated in May 1989, none of the prominent West German speakers bothered to connect the political developments in Central and Eastern Europe to possible consequences for the two German states. Instead, they were preoccupied with renewing their commitment to strengthen economic and political cooperation within the Western European Community. A month later, in a speech commemorating the "Day of German Unity," Erhard Eppler, an astute Social Democrat, urged his fellow-Germans to think about what should and shouldn't be done if the Iron Curtain fell. No one seemed to listen because such a development seemed too remote.

Such attitudes were hardly surprising. Most West Germans simply accepted the country's partition as reality and unification as an impossible dream. The "Day of National Unity," for example, established as a West German legal holiday after the unsuccessful East Berlin uprising in 1953, became just another day off from work, not a time to reflect on the country's division. In the East, too, unification lost its salience, especially after Willy Brandt forged a new German-German relationship based on mutual recognition and cooperation in the early 1970s.

Politicians and experts in the West considered the East German economy sound and its politics much more stable than the systems in other Eastern bloc countries. Hailed as the "economic locomotive" of the socialist bloc, the German Democratic Republic provided its citizens with a higher standard of living than other socialist countries in the Eastern bloc. When economic problems became obvious in the 1980s, Western observers explained them as temporary difficulties similar to the cyclical downturns in capitalist market economies instead of diagnosing them as the symptoms of a terminal disease in East Germany's centrally planned economic structure.

The West failed to recognize that external developments had the potential to topple even the most Stalinist state in the Soviet orbit and that the reform efforts in the Soviet Union and the peaceful changes in Poland and Hungary had paved the road for East Germany's own gentle revolution. But above all, Mikhail Gorbachev's de facto repeal of the Brezhnev doctrine, the Soviet Union's claimed right to intervene in the domestic matters of Eastern European states, should have signaled that the stage was set for the Soviet Empire's dominoes to tumble. Neither West German politicians nor business leaders nor experts in the country's publicly financed think-tanks had prepared contingency plans for the East's rapid collapse.

The unraveling of the GDR began with the flight of tens of thousands of its citizens in the summer of 1989. "Vacationing" East Germans in Hungary, Czechoslovakia, and other Eastern bloc states either escaped through holes these countries had punched into the Iron Curtain or pushed into the West German embassy compounds in Prague, Warsaw, Budapest, and East Berlin to demand free passage entry into West Germany. When Hungary opened its borders with Austria, 50,000 waiting East Germans crossed into the West. In the five months preceding the dismantling of the German-German border some 100,000 East Germans fled, most of them young men and most valuable workers.

By fall, millions of those who stayed behind took to the streets of Leipzig, Dresden, and East Berlin and demonstrated for an opening up of their system: for a German version of the Soviet's recent perestroika. Even then virtually no one in either Germany foresaw the sudden and dramatic events that would begin in mid-October 1989. After stubbornly ignoring the demands expressed by millions of demonstrators and Gorbachev's personal warning that "life will punish those who delay," Erich Honecker was forced to resign. Within days other members of his hardline leadership clique were ousted. Less than three weeks later, in a sudden chain reaction of bureaucratic confusion and improvisation, the East German border police unlocked the checkpoints along the Berlin Wall opening the flood-gates for spontaneous East-West celebrations.

It is still not known, and it may never be, what exactly transpired behind the scenes and who was involved in the fateful decision to lift the German part of the Iron Curtain. But after Guenther Schabowski, a member of the still ruling Socialist Unity Party's (SED) politburo, announced plans to allow East Germans to travel freely across the borders to the West, events spun out of control: Alerted by reports in the Eastern and Western media, East Berliners rushed to checkpoints at the wall, where the border police—without explicit orders—allowed them to pass into West Berlin. During the next few days, several million GDR citizens visited West Berlin and West German towns close to the borders.

After the hesitant reign of an interim leadership, the first free elections in the German Democratic Republic were held in March 1990. This was a momentous event for a region that had not experienced free elections

since 1932. East Germans had to be at least 79 years old to have participated in the last democratic elections before Nazi and then Communist
rule. Other equally important events—the agreement on a monetary, economic, and social union between the two Germanys in May, and the
actual replacement of East Germany's *Ost-Mark* by West Germany's
Deutschmark or *D-Mark* on July 1, were like hasty pit-stops in a high-
speed race toward Germany's full-fledged political unification. Negotiations between the four World War II allied powers—the United States,
Great Britain, France, and the Soviet Union—and the two Germanys produced agreements on the external relationships of a united Germany.
Both German parliaments and former allies approved the final compact
of formal unification on October 3, 1990: The German Democratic
Republic ceased to exist by acceding to the Federal Republic whose ten
states were joined by the five newly established East German states and
Berlin, a city state combining its formerly separated eastern and western
parts. Germans henceforth drew a distinction between the "old" and the
"new" *Bundesländer* or federal states—even though historically speaking some of the "new" states (i.e., Saxony) had existed long before most
of the "old" *Länder* (i.e., North Rhine-Westphalia).

Ironically, the resolution of what had until then been called "the German Question" created a new and potentially much more difficult one:
how to integrate East and West Germany and their respective citizens
who had lived for nearly half a century under fundamentally different
and hostile systems and alliances. What Germans in the East and West
came to recognize as "inner separation" or "the wall in our heads" after
unification was in large part the result of the problems associated with
the sudden merger of two incompatible political, economic, and social
systems that had developed in the two Germanys between 1945 and
1990.

The two German states were the ultimate result of Nazi Germany's
defeat and unconditional surrender on May 9, 1945 and the ensuing disagreements between the Western allies and the Soviet Union over the
future of Germany and Eastern Europe. These disagreements escalated
into the Cold War. Even before the Federal Republic of Germany in the
West and the German Democratic Republic in the East were established
in 1949, the civic institutions and arrangements that were reconstructed
in the three Western occupational zones (the American, the British and
the French) were strikingly different from those in the Soviet-dominated
Eastern zone.

The Federal Republic was designed in the tradition of Western-style democracies and free market economies. It flourished into an open, pluralist polity that enjoyed political stability and economic prosperity. As a member of the North Atlantic Treaty Organization (NATO) and the European Economic Community (EEC) West Germany became a reliable partner in the U.S.-led Western military bloc and a major player in the drive for economic and political cooperation among Western European democracies.

In stark contrast, East Germany was remade in the image of the Soviet Union's Marxist-Leninist model. The absolute rule of the Communist Party was established along with a state-run command economy. After Soviet troops helped to crush an uprising of East German workers in 1953 and the East German regime built the Berlin Wall eight years later to stop its citizens from going West, the Communist system stood unchallenged for nearly four decades. It displayed political stability and showed more economic strength than the rest of Eastern Europe. Throughout those years, East Germany's foreign relations were firmly anchored in the Soviet-led Eastern bloc with membership in the Warsaw Pact military alliance and the Council for Mutual Economic Aid (COMECON).

During the Cold War, and especially during periods of heightened tensions, the location of the two Germanys put Germans squarely on top of the bipolar world's nuclear powder keg and made both countries a likely East-West battle ground. West German Chancellor Willy Brandt's bold "Deutschlandpolitik" initiative to relax tensions between the two antagonistic German states led to the Basic Treaty of 1972 in which the two governments recognized each other and normalized their relations. Unification became more elusive.

When both German states joined the United Nations, however, Willy Brandt emphasized the goal of unification and declared, "My people live in two states but continue to think of themselves as one nation." This assessment in 1973 was apparently confirmed when East German demonstrators in the late 1980s changed their initial outcry for democratic participation within the socialist structure ("We are the people!") to an emotionally charged demand for unification ("We are one people!") that was echoed by West Germans. But then the experiences after unification did not restore the indestructible common bonds, which Chancellor Brandt and most observers had assumed. This period uncovered, accentuated, and deepened the differences between the old and the new Federal Republicans. Perhaps the idea of one nation, two states that

Brandt had expressed had been an illusion all along; a few years after unification the new reality was better characterized as two societies, one state.

One Plus One Does Not Add Up As Expected

In 1992, for the first time since 1936, a single German team competed in the Olympic games. For the German sports fans the results were utterly disappointing: The merger of the East and West teams did not add up to the combined gold, silver, and bronze medals that the separate German teams had routinely won in international competitions. Few had anticipated the problems, controversies, and resentments that arose when the sports stars, coaches, and officials of the two completely different athletic systems with different methods, attitudes, goals, and ethics were thrown together.

Similarly, the merger of the world's third largest (West Germany) and supposedly seventh largest (East Germany) industrial powers did not automatically produce an economic superpower once unification occurred. Rather, East Germany's actually decayed industrial infrastructure and the loss of its major export partners in the disintegrating Communist world precluded the quick economic miracle that Chancellor Kohl had promised and that many East and West Germans expected.

These examples are representative for the high and unrealistic expectations that prevailed among East and West Germans in the hectic months before unification and for a short while thereafter. Such expectations were bound for disappointments, frustrations, and resentments in all areas.

The majority of East Germans who supported unification wanted the political freedom and a standard of living of West Germany's affluent society. Indeed, once the Communist rulers were gone, liberty was quick to follow as East Germans learned when they participated in their country's first free election. They expected that Western style affluence was not far behind once they were united with their wealthy cousins in the Federal Republic. East German intellectuals, who did not want to dismantle but reform the system in the East by combining the best features of socialism and capitalism into a democratic "third way," never had a chance to sell their vision. After more than forty years of Communist dictatorship most East Germans were not tempted by another utopian experiment but by the promise of Western affluence. As a student in

Leipzig put it, "Almost nobody wanted another unrealistic ideal, almost everybody wanted a car, a dishwasher, a trip abroad. . . ."

Deeply disappointed, the reformers lamented that East Germans were not as hungry for freedom as they were for an assortment of consumer goods when they opted for unification and that they would have continued to live under the communist rule if it had provided them with a better standard of living. Actually, East Germans wanted freedom and affluence. Once they had won their civil liberties, they looked for a better life and believed that unification guaranteed it—just as Chancellor Helmut Kohl and his party promised. "Helmut, take us by your hand and lead us into the land of the Economic Miracle," East German placards begged, when the Chancellor visited the GDR. Public opinion polls confirmed what the sound majority of East Germans expected from a united Germany most of all: a Western standard of living. Kohl promised that the desolate areas of the East would become "flourishing landscapes" in but a few years.

At the same time, West Germans also looked upon unification in terms of its economic and fiscal advantages and disadvantages. But unlike East Germans, they were more inclined to focus on the possible drawbacks in form of tax increases, shrinking incomes, and a deterioration of the social safety net for them.

While both publics were nevertheless overwhelmingly supportive of unification, the personal expectations of East Germans were far more optimistic than those of West Germans. Similarly, East and West Germans looked with different eyes at the overall political, socioeconomic, and cultural effects of unification: East Germans were more confident than West Germans that their united country would be stronger than before in all aspects of public life.

Still, the majority of Germans believed Chancellor Kohl's promise that unification was a "winners only" proposition and would not require sacrifices. Two-thirds of West Germany's political and business leaders shared this comforting pre-unification outlook predicting an "economic miracle" for East Germany within three years. Social Democrat Oskar Lafontaine, Chancellor Kohl's opponent in the first federal elections of the reunited Germany, warned that a hasty merger would have serious consequences. In December 1990, when voters went to the polls to elect the first Bundestag of the reunited Germany, they punished Lafontaine and his Social Democratic Party (SPD), for his gloom and doom vision.

Whether based on poor information, error of judgment, opportunistic election year politics, or all of these, the lofty predictions and expectations were bound for disappointments after a seemingly exciting and promising start. The monetary union of July 1, 1990 allowed East Germans to exchange part of their currency against West Germany's *Deutschmark* at a 1–1 conversion rate even though one East German Mark was valued only at 23 Pfennigs at the time.[2] With Deutschmarks in their hands, East Germans had instant access to their consumer paradise. They embarked on a nonstop shopping spree in West German cities and towns closest to the open borders. Even large department stores were hard-pressed to keep their shelves stocked. Used car lots were swept clean by eager East German buyers who acted like children under the Christmas tree. Under communist rule, they had waited a dozen years or more to buy a model of the GDR-built "Trabant," an ugly duckling in comparison to Western cars. At first, many East Germans preferred shopping across the border, but Western consumer goods were available in the East, too, as soon as the currency union was established. Eager to keep their dream alive even when they ran out of Deutschmarks, East Germans learned in a hurry about the instant gratification and the lasting pain of giving in to the "buy now—pay later" offers that they were unfamiliar with.

While the currency union triggered an unprecedented shopping frenzy and a quick economic boom in the West, its architects in Bonn had different objectives in mind: to prevent most of all the complete collapse of the GDR's economic sector, to stem the exodus of skilled East German workers to the West, and to stop West Germans from buying highly subsidized and therefore very cheap products in the East for a fraction of what they cost in the Federal Republic.

Once forced to compete under the West's free market conditions, East Germany's already weak economy deteriorated. Within three years the East German workforce shrank to nearly half its size (from 9.7 to 5.0 million). Many of those who lost their jobs were forced into early retirement; men and women in their fifties, even in their late forties, were left without hope of ever working again. As the rapid change from a centrally planned command economy to a market economy occurred, the costs of living skyrocketed. While prices rose quickly to West German levels, the per capita income in East Germany was significantly lower than in West Germany. This was a shocking experience for people who were used to living very modestly but nevertheless with a sense of security. The East German state had guaranteed full employment and the rudimentary necessities of life like housing and basic food for nominal costs. Once united with West Germany, East Germans overlooked that the German Democratic Republic had subsidized jobs, rents, mass transportation, and many consumer staples and that this feature of Communist economics had significantly contributed to the GDR's growing problems.

East Germans' belief that unification meant to partake from the outset in the good life of West Germany was quickly shattered. They felt betrayed and abandoned by their affluent brethren in the West. "Deceived and Sold Out"—one of the slogans, painted on buildings, bridges, and fences—expressed those sentiments well.

West Germans, too, had a sobering awakening when they recognized that the "winners only" promise was a myth and that the costs for rebuilding the East had been grossly underestimated. Most West Germans were prepared to make some sacrifices and accepted the first round of tax surcharges without noise. But while the government pumped more than $100 billion each year into the new states, the Federal Republic experienced an economic crisis accompanied by the highest unemployment rate in its history. Many in the West began to resent that they were forced to carry the growing burden for rebuilding the East and its industrial sector while their own plants closed or struggled for survival. As they felt increasingly the pinch of belt-tightening measures to finance the reconstruction in the East, West-Germans' sympathies for the plight of fellow-Germans in the new states dwindled. "We have reached the outer limits of what we can pay for the reconstruction of the East," they said. Easterners were increasingly perceived as demanding and unthankful whiners.

These and other attitudinal differences between East and West Germans were not temporary features but emerged as enduring and major factors in German politics. In public debates and in their private emotions and frustrations many old and new Federal Republicans found themselves on opposite sides on many issues that touched on the real or perceived consequences of unification and the East's reconstruction. It was no coincidence that a number of years after the formal merger, public opinion was still routinely broken down to compare the attitudes of Germans in the old and in the new states. This practice continued for one simple reason: East and West Germans' political views and policy preferences obviously differed significantly on a wide range of issues from legalized abortion to the proper role of the German military in the post–Cold War era.

There was agreement in both parts of the country that much went wrong when the two Germanys became one country. So far, "Unity Day," a national holiday established to commemorate the formal unification of October 3, 1990, has not been an occasion to celebrate national unity and sovereignty like the Fourth of July holiday has long been for Americans. On the contrary, the day stirred resentments and frustrations associated with the merger costs. In East and West Germany, the third anniversary of unification, for example, was conspicuously chosen for angry protests against mass unemployment and widening gaps in the social safety net. According to pollsters, when faced with government demands to give up one of their legal holidays (to pay for a new, long-term nursing care insurance), the overwhelming majority of Germans picked "Unity Day" as their first choice because two in three believed that unification had triggered enormous problems and disadvantages.

When West Germans were frustrated and offended during the post-World War II reconstruction of their badly destroyed country, they could blame the occupational powers, and they often did. This time, East and West Germans faulted each other for the numerous post-unification problems.

Demands for Socioeconomic Equality

The German constitution, the *Grundgesetz* or Basic Law, requires the government to equalize the conditions of life in all parts of the Federal Republic to the greatest extent possible. The massive transfers from West Germany to the Eastern states in the years after unification surpassed by far anything that could have been accomplished by the traditional transfers between the West German states before unification. East Germans expected from the outset a standard of living that equaled the conditions in West Germany. East Germans never regarded the massive transfers of resources from the old to the new states as a matter of good will, charity, or routine fiscal equalization between rich and poor states but rather as a moral obligation to rectify past injustices.

Some aspects of the arguments and issues raised in this context resembled those frequently made in disputes over affirmative action policies in the United States. For example, just as American proponents of affirmative action with respect to African-Americans have justified this concept as an appropriate remedy to correct past injustices against this group—even at the expense of contemporary whites—East Germans, too, framed their demand for affirmative action in terms of past injustices and corrective measures.

East Germans felt all along that they had paid disproportionately for Hitler's lost war simply because "the fate of geography" had placed them into the Soviet occupational zone. The occupiers of their land dismantled and transported to Russia whatever was left of East Germany's industrial plants. Altogether, the Russians extracted more than 50 billion Marks in reparations from the region. Meanwhile, West Germans received generous American Marshall Plan aid, rebuilt their industrial infrastructure, and laid the foundation for the legendary "Economic Miracle" and decades of increasing affluence. Nearly half a century later, East Germans expected their cousins in the West to repay belatedly their share of the price for Hitler. "All Germans lost the war—not only those of us who happened to live in the East," they said. They discounted the argument that West Germany made restitution payments to the state of Israel and to individual survivors of the Holocaust after the war and argued that those expenses were negligible in comparison to the heavy costs East Germans paid, when the Russians stripped their factories of machines and other equipment.

West Germans did not buy such arguments but blamed the East Germans' mentality for the different standards of living in the Eastern and Western parts of the country. When Westerners remarked, "Working as under the communists and living as under the capitalists is impossible," they implied that they worked harder than their East German kin. The average citizen—the taxi driver, the steelworker, the shopkeeper—was more explicit with remarks like, "We have worked damned hard for more than forty years, Ossis [East Germans] must work just as hard, if they want what we got. . . ." Such reasoning was reminiscent of U.S. foes of affirmative action, who have long insisted that the substantial differences in the socioeconomic status of American whites and blacks are the result of disparate work ethics, not of previous and current discriminatory conditions and practices.

Within a few years enormous progress was made toward the eventual equalization of incomes in terms of wages, social security benefits, and so on. By 1995 the standard of living in the East had surpassed for example that of Greece, wages were at about 85 percent, public pensions at 80 percent of the Western levels. But there was no prospect for the same standard of living in the foreseeable future. While Westerners could spent their disposable income to sustain (or improve further) their established life styles, Easterners had a long way to go to simply catch up to Western levels. The wealth that many West Germans acquired during the pros-

perous last decades had been inherited already by the postwar generation, or was to be soon. This was a source of enduring inequalities in the
socioeconomic playing field and the cause for resentments and frictions.
Easterners resented that Westerners had the capital to invest in the East
while they themselves lacked the financial resources.

Unification or Colonialization?

The bulk of the investments in East Germany for buying, restoring, or
constructing hotels, office buildings, restaurants, supermarkets, shopping centers, factories, and other projects were made in the years since
unification (and will be in the future) by West Germans and Americans
or other foreigners. State and local governments went out of their way to
attract investments from West Germany and abroad; they often complained that not enough Western investments were forthcoming. Enterprising young Easterners, who tried to set up their own modest businesses, like auto repair shops, beauty parlors, restaurants, or guest
houses, were unable to get start-up loans because they had neither sufficient income nor collateral to meet borrowing requirements. Many Easterners resented that "West Germans criticize us for lacking creativity, initiative, and the will to take risks, but their bankers here in the East refuse
to take chances with us."

Even more than five years after unification it was not unusual for Easterners to speak of "robber barons," when they characterized Westerners.
They pointed to the hectic building and restoration activities in the business and historic sections of cities and towns where Westerners expected
excellent returns on their investments, in contrast to the lack of funds for
the rehabilitation of poorly built apartment houses that had been put up
during the communist rule. Many plans to acquire, renovate, and convert
these buildings into condominiums or cooperatives were dropped
quickly, when potential investors recognized that for the foreseeable
future East Germans were unlikely candidates to buy their own apart-
ments; most Easterners lacked the necessary financial resources. Public
money was primarily used to fix and expand the Eastern infrastructure
(e.g., highways, mass transit, communication) and historic landmarks
(e.g., churches, castles, museums), not to overhaul apartment buildings
that literally fell apart. Public officials defended these priorities as ultimately serving the public interest. In the words of one official in Dresden,
"Unless we rebuild our infrastructure, our inner cities, and our land-

marks, we can't attract the investors nor the tourists we need to build a viable economy." This did not appease tenants who lived in decaying quarters for which they paid much higher rents than during GDR times. The blame was largely laid at the doorstep of Westerners who were and still are the architects and the financiers of the reconstruction process.

There were many other sources of friction early on. For example, a number of Western investors who had acquired state-owned factories with the promise to transform them into viable companies with secure jobs instead shut them down. They were attempting to get rid of firms that were competing with their companies in the West. In the eyes of East Germans it was just as despicable when Westerners bought plants in the East, mortgaged them to the hilt, used the bank-loans and tax writeoffs for the benefit of their companies in the West, and abandoned the acquired factories. When East Germans learned of these cases, they tended to generalize. Altogether, Eastern indignation over the behavior of Westerners can be compared to the outrage American Southerners felt toward Northern carpetbaggers who invaded the defeated South after the Civil War and profited from the political, economic, and social reconstruction dictated by the victorious North.

While the two Germanys, unlike the American North and South, did not go to war against each other, they were on opposite sides and enemies during the Cold War. Their soldiers faced each other along the Iron Curtain, and there was the prospect that Germans might have to fight Germans. After the fall of the wall, the hope tied to unification evaporated, and East Germans frequently compared themselves to a defeated people in an annexed and occupied territory which was reconstructed in the image of the victorious power by West Germans, whom they called "Wessis" for short. They came to resent them as *Besserwessies* (know-it-all-wessis). Even years after unification such feelings were shared by many average people and intellectuals alike. It was as if united Germany were on the way to develop two distinct languages—one West German, one East German—without developing bilingual people who could understand each other and overcome their differences.

Once such resentments took over, two important factors were ignored: First, when unification was agreed upon, the decision was made to replace the East German state apparatus with West Germany's political, administrative, economic, and social institutions and arrangements. Second, the "knowhow" of West Germans was indispensable if the dissolution of the existing socialist system and the establishment of a capitalist democracy was to be achieved without seriously disrupting the lives in East Germany and in the West as well.

East Germans who won local and state offices in the 1990 elections realized quickly that they needed help from the West to organize the administration of the five newly established states and the municipal governments in ways that made them compatible with the federal government—with its agencies, laws, and procedures. Tens of thousands of Western civil servants were dispatched (few volunteered) to assignments in the East. Although Eastern politicians and administrators had no idea about West German policies and their implementation at the various levels of government, they resented that Westerners were in charge while they were cast in supporting roles. "For half a century we were not able to make our own decisions," they complained, "and now, after unification, we must do everything the West German way."

West German state, county, and city governments that forged partnerships with East German governments made great efforts and financial sacrifices to help their counterparts get organized and learn how governments work in a democracy. It was a major task to replace the centralized, authoritarian GDR system with a decentralized, democratic governmental structure. The working conditions in the East were very difficult, especially in the early months and years: There were not enough telephone lines, computers, nor even basic office furniture and equipment. Much of what was needed to set up functioning administrations was donated by so-called partner states, counties, and cities in the West. Western governments also made available significant numbers of their own officials.

But if West Germans expected that Easterners would be grateful, they were disappointed. While Easterners realized how much they needed all the help they could get, they still resented that they had to depend on others. The relationship between officials from North Rhine-Westphalia, a Western state, and their colleagues in the government of the Eastern state of Brandenburg was a case in point. No other Western state did as much for a partner state in the East as North Rhine-Westphalia. Nevertheless, a study conducted by a member of the North Rhine-Westphalian state assembly and designed to explain the interactions between East and West Germans in Brandenburg's government concluded, "The westerners are the chieftains, the Easterners the Indians. But the Indians want to decide for themselves." At the time, nearly 1,000 administration officials of the North Rhine-Westphalian government were working in Potsdam, Brandenburg's capital; thousands of others, on loan from North Rhine-Westphalian cities and counties, directed and trained the administrations of Brandenburg's local governments. More than half of the Brandenburg government's cabinet members and all state secretaries were from the West. Western visitors were repeatedly told by Brandenburgers that they were determined to resist "becoming a colony" of their Western "partners."

Obviously, East Germans did not buy the notion of being full partners in these relationships but considered them unequal associations in which West Germans were the superiors and "haves" and East Germans the subordinates and "have-nots." It did not help matters that West German public servants received higher salaries than their East German colleagues in the same or similar jobs. This inequality was justified on the ground that Westerners needed incentives to work in the Eastern part of the country. Some level-headed Westerners waved their right to extra pay. But most of them collected everything they were entitled to, and some proved outright greedy. In late 1993 the cabinet of Saxony-Anhalt was forced to resigned after it was revealed that the governor of the East German state and three of his ministers—all imported from the West and three of them members of Chancellor Kohl's Christian Democratic Union—had overpaid themselves a total of about 900,000 German Marks. When the political scandal broke, East Germans reacted with outrage. After all, the four who had been caught with their hands in the state's cookie jar, were not even—as the British weekly *The Economist* observed—the West's best and brightest but had either failed to win political offices or lost public jobs before coming to power in one of the poorest regions of Eastern Germany.

The already existing distrust between Easterners and Westerners deepened. In most instances, East and West Germans who did work closely together during the week were not able—and perhaps did not even try—to bridge the gap that was much deeper than the obvious difference in their appearances—with West Germans wearing more expensive and fashionable clothes than East Germans. Westerners who went out of their way to fit in and understand their Eastern colleagues were often written off at home as having been coopted; upon their return to the West they often found their career opportunities diminished.

These conditions and the uneasiness they created lingered on as the reconstruction process continued, and not only in Brandenburg but also in the other Eastern states and in practically all areas of the public sector as well. West German prosecutors and judges, police experts, and educators revamped the judiciary, law enforcement agencies, and the educational system. The task of retraining judges, police officials, and teachers to function in a democratic society required far more time and continued guidance by Western experts. Zealous and unscrupulous supporters of the Communist regime lost their positions. In this respect, the judiciary was a compelling example: many GDR judges had served the communist state by handing out harsh sentences for political crimes. Therefore, any judge who wanted to remain on the bench had to pass a litmus test administered by peer committees as to his or her fitness to adjudicate the legal code in a democracy. Those who passed the reviews had to undergo extensive retraining. As a result, West Germans came to hold many key positions in the East German judiciary and took responsibility for many unpopular decisions.

Many East Germans who were forced out of their jobs complained bitterly that under the Communist regime they had been given no choice other than to conform. And many of those who were allowed to stay on struggled to make the switch from an authoritarian to a democratic working environment. For teachers who up to 1989 had been forced to explain to their students the superiority of communism and the decadence of capitalism, it was certainly not easy to tell the same students the exact opposite once the West German brand of democracy and capitalism was extended to the East.

The courts in the East were flooded with property cases that were oil on the fire of one of the most divisive East-West issues and the "them-against-us" attitude among Easterners. According to the unification treaty, anyone whose property in the East had been confiscated during the Hitler period (1933–45) or the GDR era (1949–1990) had a right to the real estate or adequate compensation. More than a million people laid claims on more than 2.5 million titles. Because most of these cases ended up in litigation, it took years before all the files could be closed. In addition, legal battles were fought over the rights of persons whose properties had been confiscated in the years between the end of the war and the establishment of the GDR (1945 and 1949). East German families who had already lost, or feared that they would lose, the homes they had lived in and taken care of for thirty or more years blamed West German authorities for providing the legal basis of these claims and they blamed the original owners, most of them West Germans and American Jews, for dispossessing them. On this issue, too, many East Germans felt exploited and violated by ruthless and greedy intruders from the West.

East Germans: Strangers in Their Own Land

Whether filling out their tax returns, applying for unemployment benefits, registering their cars, or dealing with the sales pitches of aggressive
West German insurance agents, East Germans had to learn the ropes of
a way of life completely different from what they had grown used to. By
pointing out that the *grüne Pfeil*, the green arrow traffic sign placed at
intersections where right turns on red are permitted, was the only relic
left of their GDR past, East Germans illustrated their enormous disori-
entation and alienation in an environment that emerged once the steam-
roller of West Germany's massive and rapid reconstruction measures had
crushed everything they were familiar with. Many East Germans felt like
strangers in their own land. For more than forty years they had lived
under a communist dictatorship that had demanded conformity and told
them what they could and could not do. They had developed qualities to
cope under difficult circumstances and to help each other with the tribu-
lations of everyday's life; many escaped into the nonpolitical niches of
their private spheres and activities.

But the attributes well-suited for life under an authoritarian system
were not helpful in an open, competitive society that rewarded individualism, initiative, and risk-taking. While a small number of East Germans
made the transition very quickly by, as fellow-Easterners noted sarcasti-
cally, "learning West German" and becoming "turncoats," most were
unable to function effectively in their new surroundings. Having become
accustomed to a system under which the state and the party did all their
thinking and made all their decisions for them, they were unable to take
charge of their own affairs and become self-reliant. Men and women
who worked all their lives in the noncompetitive state-run system could
not readily adjust to the vastly different rules of the game in a competitive market-economy.

Years after unification, Western visitors to Eastern Germany were still
struck by the inferior services in stores, restaurants, hotels, and elsewhere. Whether salespersons or waiters or busdrivers—most did not try
at all to please their customers or guests but were rather indifferent if not
outright unfriendly and uncooperative. This is hardly surprising, if one
recalls that there were chronic shortages of consumer goods in the GDR
and that citizens were used to standing in line at stores and restaurants.
In contrast to Western countries, where lines of people tend to get shorter
and shorter, when people queued up in East Germany or elsewhere in the

Eastern bloc, the lines got longer and longer as the word spread that a shipment of oranges or bananas or whatever had been received by a neighborhood store. Under these circumstances, there was no need for efficient and friendly services; on the contrary, customers and guests expected to be treated rudely.

These and other attitudes and habits were not easily changed. The idea that job security and the level of compensation depend on the competitiveness of the products or services offered by one's employer—and thus on one's own contributions as well—was alien to employees who never worried about their jobs and competitors. West Germans who took over or established businesses in the East were daily confronted by East German employees' behavior that could not be understood without knowing and sympathizing with their past experiences.

Thus, the East German editors and reporters of a daily newspaper in a city with several competing dailies, who did not cover major events in order to pick up their children from school or to run a personal errand, shocked the West German editor-in-chief but not their East German colleagues. The East German manager of a resort hotel at the Baltic Sea, who insisted on her extensive mid-day rest at the beach even during the peak season, shocked the West German owner of the resort but not her fellow-Easterners.

In these instances the employees' inability to change their ways contributed to the fiscal problems of the newspaper whose editor had to fire part of his staff, and to the decision of the West German resort owner to replace the East German hotel manager by one from the West. Both cases are fairly typical illustrations of the great differences between the East and West German people—far greater in fact than between citizens of Western Germany and France or Italy or the United States. Both cases illuminate as well why and how East and West Germans blame each other for the many disappointments and frustrations that spring from their different experiences. Thus, the East German worker who lost the job he had held for thirty years and refused to apply for openings in a neighboring town was perceived as lazy and useless in the eyes of West Germans, who could not understand someone who insisted that the government "must find me a job near home." On the other hand, West German bosses who demanded Western attitudes and performances from East German employees were considered "arrogant" and "inhuman capitalists" in the eyes of "Ossis," who could not understand their bosses' desire for productivity and competitiveness.

In this climate, East Germans were increasingly resentful of the complete annihilation of whatever they had been used to during their GDR past while everything remained the same for their West German brethren. They took offense at explicit or implicit suggestions that nothing in their own past was worthy while everything in West Germany's past was, and that they had been forced to "block out our own biography of the last 45 years." In their eyes, West Germans did not want integration but rather the complete assimilation of East Germans. Whether they were willing to assimilate or not, most adult East Germans, especially the older generation, believed that they could not be like West Germans for a long time, if ever. East Germans said frequently and in a tone of defiance, "I will always be an Ossi." Others expressed more resignation than indignation. "Perhaps my grandchildren will be like West Germans one day," elderly East Germans remarked often in these or similar words, "as for us, we will always be East Germans." Given this mindset and the enduring socioeconomic discrepancies between East and West, most East Germans were convinced that they were and would remain for quite some time "second class citizens."

By the mid-1990s, according to opinion polls, two in three East Germans were convinced that the inner separation (*die Mauer in den Koepfen* or the wall in the heads) between East and West Germans was growing higher.[3] Polls also revealed consistently that most West Germans thought of themselves first and foremost as "Germans," not "West Germans," while most East Germans defined themselves increasingly as "East Germans," not Germans. Whereas nearly two-thirds of the East German identified as "Germans" in 1990, only one-third did in the following years.[4]

All of this underscored a point that East German critics of the unification process made frequently: Public officials and the population of the Federal Republic considered their part of the country as "whole" long before the events of the late 1980s. For West Germans the FRG was "Germany" and they were the Germans while the GDR was "East Germany" and its citizens were East Germans. Indeed, before unification it was a common practice in the West to speak and write of "German" and "East German" embassies abroad, "German" and "East German" sports teams, the "German" and the "East German" currency. When the two states' national soccer teams met, as far as West Germans were concerned, it was a match between the best kickers of "Germany" and "East Germany."

With this in mind, East Germans argued that for West Germans the merger of the two Germanys meant only the enlargement of what they had considered Germany all along and the eradication of everything that existed in East Germany. The fact that following unification most West Germans never bothered to visit East Germany while West Germany was the preferred destination of traveling East Germans was cited as proof of West Germans' arrogant attitude toward the East.

The era of bad feelings kindled among East Germans a nostalgia for the past they had been familiar with. While they had recognized a superiority of their Communist state in only three of nine specific policy areas in 1990, five years later East Germans believed that they had been better off in seven of nine: protection from crime, gender equality, social security, education, vocational training, health care, and housing. They gave the edge to the Federal Republic only with respect to the standard of living and science and technology.[5]

Coming to Terms with East Germany's Past

This is not to say that East Germans yearn for the return of the Socialist Unity Party (SED), its leaders, or the reign of the secret police (*Staatssicherheitsdienst or Stasi*). The SED regime and its leading figures were once and for all discredited and disgraced. East Germans looked back in anger at their former leaders who preached egalitarianism, which meant that they themselves were more equal than the rest; it took the dismantling of the old regime to expose this double standard. While certainly not especially lavish in comparison to Western lifestyles, the comfort enjoyed secretly by the GDR's leadership starkly contrasted with the average East German's sparse existence.

As much as East Germans felt betrayed by their former leaders in this respect, they had a harder time still coming to terms with the darkest chapter of their GDR past: the sinister activities of one of the most extensive secret service system designed by a police state. Many were shocked when they learned of the Stasi's intrusive surveillance apparatus and its physical and psychological state terror. But nothing had a more traumatic effect than the files stored on 125 miles of Stasi shelves that contained 6 million intelligence dossiers—one for every two East German adults. Nearly 100,000 full-time Stasi agents and an even greater number of "informal informers" compiled those files. When the SED regime unraveled, a portion of the files were stolen by former Stasi officials and sold to West German publications even before the authorities decided to open them in early 1992.

It was not only people implicated by the Stasi records who wished that the files had not been made accessible to the public. In hindsight, others wondered whether the Poles were wiser when they sealed their own files in 1989. The content of the Stasi dossiers caused countless human tragedies and shattered many lives once their content became known. Informal informers spied on their acquaintances, friends, colleagues, parents, spouses, and children. People once thought to be critics of the regime turned out to be Stasi collaborators—the author who spied on fellow authors, the physician who prescribed harmful drugs for his trusting patient, the supportive husband who reported on his dissident wife. Several of the East Germans who had been active in the "gentle revolution" of 1989/90 and won public offices after the breakdown of the SED regime resigned when their cooperation with the Stasi was revealed; some committed suicide.

Others, like Brandenburg's governor Manfred Stolpe, refused to resign and explained his contacts with the secret police as necessary and prudent for an official of the Protestant Church, an organization that managed to survive under the Communists and tried to help people who were in trouble with the regime. In Stolpe's case, East Germans showed a great deal of understanding and compassion; following accusations that the former church official had been an important Stasi informant, two of three Ossis sided with him and rejected calls for his resignation. He remained in office.

East Germans had not forgotten that life in the GDR allowed them two basic choices: (1) to adapt, get along, and live quietly or (2) to dissent, resist, and suffer. Most chose the first option which meant access to higher education, careers, and retreats to a private niche in society. This could also mean contacts with the Stasi even if no damaging information was passed along. Appalled by West Germans who were quick to pass moral judgment on the East German society of spies, East Germans countered that West Germans in the same situation would have acted no differently. Moreover, East Germans argued that only those who had experienced the conditions in the GDR could understand and speak to the issues arising from their past—just as African-Americans have argued at times that even their white compatriots with the best intentions cannot understand them and their plight since they lack the black experience.

In 1990, only one in four East Germans wanted to close the book on the forty years of communist past, but five years later every second Easterner shared this view. A majority opted for destroying the Stasi files or use them exclusively for investigating specific crimes.[6]

Their understanding the pressure to get along and to make the best of tough circumstances hardly meant that East Germans were inclined to forgive the offenses committed by the Stasi. They did, however, question the wisdom of a judiciary (dominated by West Germans) that let the "big fish" off the hook while being tough on the "small fry." Although indicted, Erich Honecker, who subsequently was allowed to go to Chile into exile, and Willi Stoph, a former prime minister, were spared long trials because of their poor health. The notorious GDR security chief Erich Mielke was tried, convicted, and sentenced for two murders committed in 1931 and not, as East Germans would have preferred, for the many crimes he orchestrated more recently against them. In contrast, young border guards who followed orders and shot East Germans trying to flee into the West, were tried and in some instances sentenced to prison terms. Little wonder that most East Germans came to believe that there was no equality before the law in the Federal Republic.

The judiciary was in a quandary in that it could not prosecute actions that breached the Federal Republic's law but had been lawful under GDR law. For this reason prosecutors first indicted Mielke for the two murders he was linked to more than 60 years earlier. GDR law had permitted border guards to shoot, but the prosecution argued nevertheless that the subordinates should not have obeyed their superiors and an evil law.

However, by 1997 dozens of ordinary border guards and a number of high officials in the GDR's Defense Council, Defense Ministry, and Border Guard Command had been found guilty of shooting fleeing East Germans or giving the order to kill and sentenced to prison terms. Dozens of additional trials were taking place or scheduled for the future.

One Germany—Two Distinct Communities

In hindsight, the crucial 1989 decision against a gradual reunification in favor of an immediate one has been questioned. Would a confederate interim solution (as some East German reformers and some West German voices had suggested before and after the merger) have prevented or eased the post-unification pains? In politics, as elsewhere, Monday morning quarterbacking is tempting. But even in retrospect it is hard to fault Chancellor Kohl for taking advantage of the opportunity that opened toward the end of Gorbachev's reign before the political circumstances in the Soviet Union might have changed.

There is no doubt that in the years following the fall of the Berlin Wall, East and West Germans have grown further apart. East Germans have come to suspect that many West Germans regret the merger. Forced to live in and cope with a fundamentally different political, socioeconomic, and social environment, East Germans, experiencing democracy after more than a half-century of dictatorship became increasingly dysfunctional and discouraged. West Germans, too, lost heart as they saw their comfortable personal way of life and the social security of their system threatened by the high costs of rebuilding the East. To negotiate and sign the unification agreements was easy; to unite East and West German societies into an integrated political, socioeconomic, and cultural community proved to be far more complex. Unification would have an affect on all aspects of German politics throughout the 1990s. The unified Germany would remain a state with two distinct communities and two diverging political cultures.

Before they could grow together and forge an inner unity, East and West Germans needed to agree on common values, ideals, and goals that would make the inevitable sacrifices in the wake of unification worthwhile. Efforts to rediscover shared ideas and a national purpose in the distant past—as Americans can and do, when they trace their widely agreed upon creed back to the Declaration of Independence and the Bill of Rights—have proven unproductive because the history of Germany and the Germans is mostly one of division, not unity.

Few foreign visitors to Germany who come to see the country's castles and churches and other historic landmarks that predate the Pilgrims' landing at American shores realize that for most of their history the German people lived in separate political entities rather than in one German state. Up to 1871, when Prussian Prime Minister Otto von Bismarck combined most of these states into a German Reich or Empire, the territory had been divided among a multitude of small principalities, several kingdoms, and two large powers, Prussia and Austria. Thus, before postwar East and West Germany were separated for 45 years, a unified Germany had existed for merely 74 years—a rather short span in comparison to the age of most European nation states and even the United States.

As a result, regional idiosyncrasies and prejudices rooted in Germany's political fragmentation before 1871 and in the rift between overwhelmingly Roman Catholic and Lutheran Protestant areas have not disappeared. In their mentality, customs, and identity the outgoing Bavarians and the jolly Rhinelanders, for example, seem to belong to different "tribes" than the reserved natives of Hamburg or the stubborn people of Westphalia. Indeed, the Weimar constitution (*Reichsverfassung*) of 1919 described the German nation as united German tribes. But none of the traditional differences and rivalries that survived the first unification of 1871 have been as great as the differences and lasting resentments between East and West Germans that surfaced after the short period of good feelings immediately after the fall of the Berlin wall.

In spite of all the difficulties between the old and the new Federal Republicans, one must keep in mind that vast majorities in East and West Germany believe that the decision to reunite the two Germanys was unquestionably the right one. Indeed, public opinion polls revealed that this support for the decision has grown significantly over the years.[7]

Still, the consequences of unification compelled Germans to search for their identity and to define a national purpose and interest that could unite and guide them in both domestic and foreign matters. Inevitably, this quest included not only the reexamination of the Nazi past and its relevance for contemporary Germany's politics and policies, but also the reunited Germany's role in post-Cold War Europe.

The Legacy of Hitler's Germany

At the beginning of contemporary German politics was the end—the end of the Nazi regime in 1945. Ever since the so-called Year Zero the legacy of that regime has been a unique element in German domestic and foreign affairs. The era of Adolf Hitler's spectacular rise and absolute rule was quite brief. But the enormous imprint left by the twelve years of his "Third Reich" has remained in evidence to this day, most notably with reference to Weimar, World War II, and Holocaust.

The Nazi regime was built on the wreckage of the Weimar Republic, Germany's first and failed experiment with liberal democracy. Established in the wake of the defeat and collapse of autocratic Imperial Germany in World War I, the Weimar regime was plagued by insurrections, assassinations, and widespread subversion in high places and rocked by politically destabilizing socioeconomic crises. While the ill-fated regime formally lasted fourteen years, in reality its precarious existence ended even sooner. Weimar's all too feeble and disunited adherents were overwhelmed by more determined opponents who, in many respects, had little or nothing in common. Among these Hitler proved to be the most ruthless and astute in the pursuit of power. By promoting as well as exploiting the political turmoil of the last years of the Weimar Republic he managed to come to power "legally" and obtain "temporary" dictatorial powers under the terms of its constitution.

Hitler became Germany's leader at the very moment that Franklin D. Roosevelt assumed the presidency of a United States that was also caught up in a severe economic crisis. Both leaders promised economic recovery, more jobs, and greater social security. But whereas Roosevelt promoted his "New Deal" in the gradual ways of America's well-established democracy, the Nazi dictator's so-called National Revolution of 1933 was dedicated to more rapid economic and more far-reaching political changes." Give me four years time and you won't recognize Germany" Hitler promised the millions who had come to associate Weimar democracy with political anarchy and economic misery. He more than kept his promise. The "new order" soon took the form of a totalitarian dictatorship, and the impressive pace of economic recovery was fueled by a tremendous rearmament program.

When Hitler came to power the chief of his new Ministry for Propaganda and Enlightenment, Joseph Goebbels, immediately declared: "The people shall begin to think uniformly, react uniformly, and put themselves at the disposal of the Government with full sympathy." Most of them did so very quickly. A dramatic shift in public opinion gave enormous and enthusiastic popular support to a leader who had never obtained the endorsement of a majority of the voters in a free election. People from every walk of life believed that they and their country were now better off than under the discredited "system of Weimar" with its squabbling, ineffective party politicians. Such sentiments did more to consolidate Hitler's rule in those early years than the far-reaching repressive measures of the Nazi regime. He and his cohorts identified the Third Reich with the mythical notion of a "Community of the German People" from which Jews and other "inferior non-German races" were excluded. Belligerent nationalism, anti-Semitism. and radical romanticism became part of a rather vague National Socialist ideology based on Hitler's speeches and writings and focused on the secular godhead. "Hitler is Germany and Germany is Hitler" was the slogan chanted in unison by thousands at huge, carefully staged rallies and echoed all over the country from millions of loudspeakers. The Berlin Olympic Games of 1936

were a highpoint that brought people from all over the world to the capital of Hitler's Germany decked out with Nazi swastikas.

The firmly established absolute ruler was now ready and able to take
the Germans down the road that ended in death and destruction for millions of people. His "leadership state" gave him the military force for the
conquest of most of Europe and the disciplined organization for the efficient extermination of almost all of its Jews.

For the last six of the twelve years of the Nazi era Germany was at
war. The spectacular military triumphs in the first phase of the war
boosted Hitler's popularity enormously; the catastrophic defeats in the
second failed to destroy it. Though bombing attacks devastated German
cities and German soldiers suffered enormous losses, Germans continued
to the bitter end to kill and to die in compliance with Hitler's wishes. A
few abortive attempts to assassinate him involved no more than a handful of conspirators. The obvious and increasingly brutal persecution of
the Jews was accepted, if not supported, by most Germans from the outset and the effective participation of many thousands of them was
required to put into effect the deadly horrors of the "final solution of the
Jewish problem." Hitler committed suicide when the Third Reich finally
collapsed, leaving it to future German leaders to come to terms with the
Reich's legacy.

For the leaders of contemporary Germany the Nazi legacy is not so
much of a problem as it was for their predecessors. For some three to
four decades after Hitler—far longer than he ruled—German politics
reflected in large part the consequences of what he had wrought. In the
Eastern part of the defeated and divided country the Nazi past provided
a new dictatorship with the "anti-fascist" ideological underpinnings for
Communist rule under Soviet sponsorship. In the Western part it
induced the initiators of a new democratic regime to enact constitutional safeguards against the rise of another Hitler. Political leaders in
the West rejected the victors' arguments that Germans bore a collective
guilt for Nazi crimes and therefore were required to pay dearly in terri-
torial concessions and reparations. But they accepted a collective German responsibility for compensating Jews and other Nazi victims, and
they accordingly committed the Federal Republic to make sizable restitution payments to surviving victims or to surrogates such as Israel and
Jewish relief agencies. This obligation, embedded in law, remained in
effect and was also applied to East Germans, whose rulers had never
accepted it.

With the passage of time and the coming of new generations, however, the once so heavy political burden of the Third Reich's legacy came to rest more lightly on German shoulders. The poisonous fruits of the Nazi harvest were no longer in evidence as a reminder that the Germans who willingly danced to Hitler's tune had to pay dearly for it. Coming to terms with an "unresolved" Nazi past was no longer the political problem it had been, when it involved such troublesome issues as denazification, retribution, and restitution. Abroad Germans no longer faced widespread hostility and suspicion, and the country's leaders were less preoccupied with polishing up their country's image.

Yet, long after the end of the Third Reich, the legacy of the Hitler past continued to figure prominently in political calculations. In the wake of brutal attacks against foreigners in the early 1990s, for example, Chancellor Kohl and other politicians seemed far more concerned with countering negative publicity abroad than with publicly condemning and stopping this sort of violence.

Half a century after the end of the war, what most people inside and outside Germany make of its Nazi legacy is based on received rather than personal knowledge, on hearsay rather than experience. After all, not many remain who are old enough to have lived through Hitler's rise and rule as adults. What most contemporary Germans knew about the Third Reich is not so much what they have learned from their elders as what they have been told in school and the media by anti-Nazi teachers, preachers, journalists, and politicians who have upheld the present democratic order. As the turn of the century approached, one in five Germans was, however, relatively new to this order: they were taught earlier in East Germany or some other Communist country to consider the Third Reich the product of a pernicious capitalist system that had been eradicated in the east but still thrived in the west. Moreover, for such individuals, indirect knowledge of the Nazi dictatorship has far less significance than their own experiences under another authoritarian government. On the whole most Germans are fully aware of the Nazi past, at least in a general way, and have no desire to return to it.

Opinion polls show that in the United States—as in other countries once at war with Germany—most ordinary people have come to believe that the Nazis could not come to power again in the Federal Republic. Some American observers of German politics, however, are less sanguine. History, they warn, has a way of repeating itself; therefore, manifestations of intolerant nationalism and skinhead violence in Germany must

be considered more menacing there than elsewhere. For someone supposedly cured of a respiratory disease, a cough should not simply be dismissed as a harmless tickle in the throat. The trouble with such analogies
is however that for German, as for American politics, they provide
appealingly simplistic interpretations of the present in terms of the past.
These explanations, then, are often more of a hindrance than a help to
understanding complex current developments.

In Germany itself there is substantial disagreement about the lessons
to be derived from the Nazi past. To some that past has little or no bearing on the here and now; to others, what happened then is most relevant
today. Politicians and journalists are correspondingly more or less prone
to invoke memories of Weimar and the Third Reich in supporting or
opposing a particular controversial course of action.

The imagery of Weimar as prelude to ultimate disaster under Hitler
serves all sorts of arguments. In the early 1990s, for example, the startling growth of radical right-wing groups and skinhead violence brought
demands for drastic counter-measures so that, this time, the Nazis would
be crushed in good time. "The state must bare its teeth," it was said,
because "Weimar is closer than many realize." When left-wing demonstrators roughed up deputies on their way to a critical vote in parliament,
one of the members proclaimed that this brought to mind that "dark time
in German history—Weimar," when force had also been employed to
prevent the people's representatives from doing their duty. For another
deputy the lesson of history was that "Weimar failed because its democrats could not unite." On a more mundane level, time and again, the
politically destabilizing effects of hyperinflation in the Weimar period
have been invoked both to justify the tremendous authority wielded by
the unelected governors of Germany's Central Bank (*Bundesbank*) and to
counter criticism of their sometimes politically problematical monetary
policies.

However, it is not the prelude but the catastrophic climax that is the
politically most potent memory of the Nazi regime for most Germans. If
they are too young to recall the ravages of war and the miseries of defeat,
they are likely to have lived through them vicariously by vivid accounts
of such hardship. In reunified Germany, as earlier in its separate parts,
the evocation of such unpleasant memories has served the political purposes of many individuals and groups.

Recollections of suffering inflicted by Nazi aggression and conquests
on other countries, as well as the unforgotten consequences for Germans,

continue to be significant in contemporary politics—as will become evident in chapters to follow. At this point it may be noted that it is in large part due to these remembrances that Germans are exceptionally averse to military ventures—far more so than Americans who do not have such memories and much like the Japanese who do. No longer confronting each other on the frontlines of a Cold War that many feared might turn into a nuclear conflagration, Germans now show more than before that the most impressive and enduring lesson of the Nazi legacy has been that their country must not engage in the use of force in foreign lands.

For Germans and other Europeans it is Hitler's war that casts the deepest shadow, but for Americans it is the Nazi Holocaust—perhaps partly because they suffered less from the war and partly because the number of Jews traumatized by the Holocaust is so much greater. For decades most German leaders subscribed to the official position that the "need to deal with the Holocaust" was—in the words of a 1991 government publication—"of crucial significance for the credibility of the Federal Republic of Germany as a free democratic state based on the rule of law." Accordingly, Germans were instructed never to forget the Holocaust and to accept their exceptional responsibility for those Jews who survived it. Auschwitz, the Nazis' most notorious extermination camp, was symbolic of this commitment. In the fall of 1993, however, the leading candidate for the Presidency of the Federal Republic called the Holocaust a historical episode in abnormal times that should cease to be a taboo subject in German politics. In his view it was high time to discard this legacy of the Nazi past because it served to put Germany "forever in a special position" among the nations. Not forever, responded a prominent journalist, but certainly as long as the spectres of Hitler's Holocaust and Hitler's war continue to loom large for German politics.

At the end of the twentieth century, Germany still has a "Jewish Problem" although it has almost no Jews. While there were more than 500,000 before Hitler, there are now only about 50,000, and many of these are quite old.[8] German laws no longer serve to persecute Jews, but to safeguard them like exotic greenhouse plants kept under carefully controlled climatic conditions. In Germany there are few, if any, people who do not know in some detail what happened to millions of Jews and other victims of Nazi racial policies. Indeed, majorities or pluralities even among those Germans under thirty believe that there is a continued need to deal with the Nazi past.

German leaders' sensitivity to manifestations of anti-Semitism that might harm foreign relations has produced periodic pulse-taking studies of popular attitudes about Jews. These studies indicate that anti-Semitism is not particularly widespread in present-day Germany, and is in fact a good deal less common than in the United States; they also show that more or less anti-Jewish views are more prevalent in long-democratic West Germany than in recently Communist East Germany and more among the old, who lived in Hitler's days, than among younger people. And in a Federal Republic that has become less prosperous since unification, West Germans are more likely to reject and East Germans to accept the official position that the Nazi legacy continues to obligate them to restitution payments to Jewish survivors of the Holocaust.

The politics of history are a familiar element of national and international conflicts all over the world. In the United States different versions of the Civil War and, more recently, the Vietnam War have provided ammunition for bitter political battles. In Germany, as indicated by the presidential candidate's controversial remarks about the Holocaust, disputes regarding the Nazi past have surfaced in a new politics of history.

Unification boosted what in previous decades had remained minor objections to the prevalent condemnation of the Nazi regime in all its aspects. The most conspicuous challenge has come from outspoken Neo-Nazis and radical nationalists who have laid claim in the most virulent and extreme fashion to all sorts of "good" things in the legacy of the Third Reich. Less obvious, but over the long run probably more significant, are the revisionist arguments of conservative scholars, journalists, and politicians who object to the continuing propagation in schools and media of what they hold to be outdated and simplistic "doctrines" of dogmatic anti-Nazis. They maintain that such one-sided presentations give a distorted view of the Third Reich by oversimplifying the diversity in a highly complex regime and by slighting its good features—recovery of the German economy and German national pride, for example. Some hold that strongly anti-Nazi views have been compromised by the totally discredited anti-Fascist ideology of Communist East Germany. Conservative revisionists also contend that with unification the old problem of coming to terms with a distant Nazi past has taken on a new meaning now that so many Germans are confronted with the need to come to terms with a very recent Communist past.

One argument holds that the negative picture of the Nazi past obstructs the restoration of an integrated version of national history that will provide East and West Germans with a unifying sense of collective identity. The other is that the "normalization" of German politics after the postwar era requires an end to lessons that confuse healthy patriotism with pernicious nationalism and the proper employment of police and military power by democrats with the illegitimate use of brutal force by autocrats. Revisionists prefer a view of the Third Reich that explains it as less exceptional in terms of German history or in comparison to totalitarian Communist regimes. They push for a new, less moralistic and more sober consideration of the Nazi legacy that will put a dark chapter in German history in what they believe is an appropriate perspective for the conduct of present-day politics at home and abroad. This may, however, create new problems for German governments, if conflicting versions of the Nazi past are employed in foreign and in domestic politics.

United Germany and Europe

From the time of the westward expansion of the United States in the nineteenth century to the days of Germany's eastward drive for living space in the twentieth century, the notion that a country's destiny was shaped by its geography provided political leaders in both countries with justification for pushing frontiers outward. That sort of geopolitical determinism will no longer do in either the United States or Germany. But a comparative examination of their geographic features reveals one more element of the exceptional aspects of contemporary politics in the Federal Republic. American politics are set in a spacious country that is much larger than the entire continent of Europe. German politics take place in a crowded country that is half the size of Texas and sits in the middle of Europe. And because of this location the Germans are now, as they have been in the past, more deeply engaged than other Europeans in relations with countries to their west as well as to their east.

The most remarkable aspect of these relationships is that they are entirely peaceful and not, as in the past, shaped by force. For more than a thousand years Germans gave little peace and were given little in return. They were usually either at war or between wars, and never far from the possibility of war. From the time of their first unification in 1871 to their second in 1990 the Germans were central to the preliminary arms build-up, the savage warfare, and the high-tension aftermath of the devastating continental conflicts in the First and the Second World Wars. At the high-tide of Hitler's conquests Germany controlled almost all of Europe. And after Hitler had fallen and the defeated country had been divided and dismembered, the countries that had been the victims of German power shared a fear of its restoration, even as they stood on opposite sides in the new East-West conflict in Europe. Both superpowers played on these fears, and German leaders in the West as well as the East did their best to reassure their respective allies on this score.

In the postwar era of a divided Germany in a divided Europe the opposing camps were united in ruling out the re-creation of a country in Central Europe that might once again dominate the continent. The Western powers and the Soviet Union each sought to contain as well as use restored German military and economic power—the Western allies by anchoring West Germany firmly in Western Europe through the NATO alliance and the European Community, the Soviet Union by making East Germany a cornerstone of the East European Communist bloc. But with the disintegration of the Eastern bloc, the door was open for a united Germany in the "House of Europe"—as Mikhail Gorbachev called it, when there was still a Soviet Union and he at its helm.

In today's Europe the expanded Federal Republic is second only to Russia in population and second to none in economic power. Berlin, the once and future capital, is closer to its new Eastern border with Poland than Bonn is to its old Western one with Belgium. Germans, along with other Europeans, have found it difficult to adjust to these changes. "I know Europe stretches to Moscow," said a university student in Bonn to an American reporter after reunification, "but I still think of Europe as Western Europe." Both young and middle-aged West Germans consider themselves closer in lifestyle and cultural values to their Western neighbors than to their fellow Germans in the eastern portions of their country. East Germans, for their part, have more affinity than West Germans with their eastern neighbors.

Elsewhere in Europe some prominent people found the sudden and unexpected geopolitical shift toward Germany hard to accept. Writing in her memoirs of her unsuccessful efforts to prevent reunification and "check the German juggernaut," former British Prime Minister Margaret Thatcher considered the prospect of eventual German hegemony over Eastern Europe particularly worrisome. German leaders sought to still such fears with assurances that in this new age of entirely peaceful relations their country's central location made it a bridge rather than a menace in inter-European relations. Chancellor Kohl, Germany's most fervent advocate of an ever closer European Union described the reassuring vision of "a European Germany, not a German Europe" in response to fears that Germany might once strive to become the overbearing power on the European continent. Yet, even politicians like Kohl could not help but deal with the uncertain implications of Germany's unprecedented geopolitical situation. Nobody doubted that Europe needed Germany and that a weak Germany in the heart of Europe would be just as disconcerting as a German superpower eager to flex its muscles.

In the forefront of relations with the liberal democracies of western and southern Europe are the intimate economic links with fellow members of the European Union, above all France. In the common market for capital, goods, and services, Germany is the principal buyer and seller and its *Deutschmark* the dominant currency. The basic patterns were established over four decades by the step-wise economic integration of former enemies thrown together by the postwar division of the continent. They did away with all restrictions on trade and migration between them and set up joint institutions for making and enforcing common rules and regulations on economic as well as social policy issues. While Germany was divided, what then was the European Community afforded the Federal Republic its best opportunities for the gradual recovery of German political influence on the continent. Beginning in 1952, after France and Britain ended their military governments of defeated Germany, economic integration served to make West Germany the equal of these two in European politics and first among equals in European economic affairs. No wonder, then, that West German governments consistently embraced this sort of "Europeanization" with a good deal more enthusiasm and public support than the French and, especially, the British governments. The Germans did not have to yield national independence in the bargain.

In the 1990s, under radically altered conditions on the continent, earlier hopes and plans for a more thorough merger of economic and monetary systems and for some kind of United States of Western Europe seemed to some less realistic than before. What seemed to be emerging in the new Europe instead was a wider but shallower form of economic integration that would take in countries that heretofore would not or could not join the common market. For the people of the country in the middle this development posed exceptional political problems, some for economic reasons and some because a weakening of integrative "Europeanist" sentiments around Germany accentuated the particularly weak sense of national identity within it.

Before unification opinion polls indicated that West Germans were more intensively and extensively committed to European integration than the French or the British. While most were never as enthusiastic about it as many of their leaders, they came to like it more when they realized that the economic and political benefits for the Federal Republic exceeded the costs. This attitude, however, changed quickly. After unification the benefits and costs of European integration seemed to many Germans far less attractive. The free migration of labor that allowed professionals from any other European Union country to practice in Germany, the right of "citizens" of the European Union to vote in local German elections, and the imposition of common European Union standards on German business establishments were not appreciated as much the promoters of Europeanization wished. And the high costs of integrating East Germany into the Federal Republic made Germans, perhaps temporarily only, far less willing than in the past to shoulder most of the financial burdens of the European Union's budget.

Popular hostility toward European economic integration was most intense in the enlarged Federal Republic, when it seemed to threaten the collective good Germans hold most dear—the sanctity of their hard currency. Polls revealed consistently that majorities or pluralities in West and East Germany did not want the German Mark to be replaced by a common European currency. Surveys established also that the number of people who thought that membership in the existing common market brought them advantages dropped in both parts of the country. There was significantly greater support for economic and monetary integration among German leaders, but more so among politicians than businessmen.

For Germany's position in Europe the shift in political focus from Bonn to Berlin was most striking on the other side of the continent. Before unification, the Federal Republic had already become the most important Western trading partner for the Communist countries of Central and Eastern Europe, but political relations were constrained by Cold War conditions. That has drastically changed. Berlin replaced Moscow as the center of a new network of power for this part of Europe. Its principal strands were close and extensive economic ties between Germany and its eastern neighbors. The Czech Republic, Hungary, and Poland depended on German technology, capital, services, and markets. For them, as for Russia and other ex-Communist nations, economic necessity made it all but impossible to resist the extension of German influence in cultural as well as political matters.

The 1992 amendment to the Constitution's basic law deleted from the Federal Republic's declared objectives the goal of "openness to other parts of Germany" and replaced it with "realization of a united Europe." Years later, it was still far from clear what "a united Europe" would mean and what countries it would include and exclude in the future.

As we examine in the following chapters the Federal Republic's brand of democracy and German efforts to cope with momentous contemporary and likely future problems, we will recall the three peculiar German attributes we have described in this chapter, whenever one or the other touches upon politics and policymaking. The critical question is: to what extent do these extraordinary factors—unification, legacy of the Nazi past, geographic location—enhance or hinder the quest for a sensible balance between continuity and change?

2

Representative Democracy
Roots of the System

On October 16, 1994 Germans went to the polls to elect the thirteenth Federal Diet or *Bundestag* since the establishment of the Federal Republic. As far as the political parties, their leaders, and their slogans were concerned, the electorate was faced with a choice between continuity and change. In the weeks leading up to election day, the ruling CDU (Christian Democratic Union, its Bavarian sister party, the CSU (Christian Social Union) and the junior coalition partner, the FDP (Free Democratic Party) had campaigned with the perennial theme of governing coalitions in the Federal Republic: Make no experiments. Take no chances. Stick to what you know. Chancellor Helmut Kohl had condemned the recently formed SPD (Social Democratic Party)-led minority government in the eastern state of Saxony-Anhalt for depending on the support of the PDS (Party for Democratic Socialism), the successor organization to East Germany's communist party, SED (Sozialistiche Einheitspartei Deutschlands). Characterizing the PDS crowd as "red-painted fascists" and placing them close to the SPD, the Chancellor had warned of political extremism and shrewdly invoked the shadows of the Weimar and Nazi past. The SPD, the Alliance '90/Greens, and, most of all, the PDS had told voters with the same urgency that the country's problems cried out for constructive change.

When the election returns were tabulated in the early evening hours, a few changes were immediately obvious: the Greens had emerged as the third strongest party at the expense of the FDP, and the former communist party had run strongly in Eastern Germany. By returning the coalition parties to power, if only by a razor-thin margin, the electorate had once again upheld the tradition of not voting a ruling national government of the Federal Republic out of office.

While they stuck with continuity as far as the partisan make-up of the federal government was concerned, voters opted at the same time for change in many cities and counties in the state of North Rhine-Westphalia, where a multitude of CDU/FDP governments were voted out and replaced in many instances by coalitions of Social Democrats and Greens. Crucial here were the substantial gains by the Greens and the devastating losses by the FDP. Nobody suggested that these changes would threaten the political stability in those communities and beyond. After all, Germans had shown in the preceding years a tendency to remove governments at the local and state level and replace them with their opposition.

One of the localities where voters ousted their CDU/FDP city government and replaced it with a red-green coalition of Social Democrats and Greens was Bonn. This was perhaps still an expression of frustration on the part of residents who had fought the losing battle to keep the federal government from moving to Berlin. But a change of sites that was believed to upset the economic predicament of the city of Bonn and surrounding areas will have little or no effect on the fundamental structure of political life in the Federal Republic. The country's government and legislature are likely to operate in Berlin pretty much as they did in Bonn.

The Institutional Order Remains Unchanged

The institutional order established long before reunification remains the basic framework for German politics. Since formal-legal arrangements that provide carefully regulated ways for dealing with ordinary as well as extraordinary policy issues carry more weight in German than in American politics such institutional continuity matters. And because informal political arrangements are less common and more tenuous than in the United States it matters all the more. Such greater formalism stems from different customs and traditions and is reinforced in the German case by a deliberate reemphasis on politics under law after the traumatic era of totalitarian politics above the law under Hitler.

Nominally the Federal Republic does not have a constitution like the United States, although the so-called Basic Law serves as one. The Basic Law was created in 1949 by a "Parliamentary Council" rather than a constitutional convention of representatives of the preexisting states. The framers therefore declared it a provisional instrument for a temporary West German state pending the reestablishment of a unified Germany. The 1990 Treaty of Unification between East and West Germany called for a thorough reconsideration of the Law, if not an entirely new constitution. But little came of that. By and large the existing arrangements suited the ruling parties in the West whose representatives blocked all important reform proposals in an especially formed constitutional commission. This commission held extensive hearings and lengthy deliberations, but there was never any question of major changes. While this alienated political leaders in the East, the driving force behind the popular "revolution" against the Communist East German regime, most Germans were content to leave existing arrangements in place. The fundamental features of the provisional design of 1949 thus still form the constitutional framework for politics in the expanded Federal Republic.

In November 1992 a new national war memorial was dedicated in Berlin with the five leading public officials of the Federal Republic in attendance: the president, the chancellor, and the presiding officers of the Federal Diet, the Federal Council (of states), and the constitutional court. Each of them represented a major component of the constitutional system of checks and balances and none of them, in accordance with the Basic Law, held office by popular election.

The Basic Law is a much longer document than the American Constitution. The democratic order it sets out in considerable detail rests on a more elaborate system of reciprocal rights and obligations in what Germans call a *Rechtsstaat*, a state ensconced in law. According to its constitutional principles of responsible government all elected and appointed public officials must observe and uphold properly established rules concerning their selection and conduct and the scope of their authority. Under the constitutional principles of responsible citizenship the governed must obey the proper decisions of legitimate authorities. Should the governmental power be exercised illegally, however, one must not merely disobey the illegal exercise of governmental power but actually oppose it actively if necessary.

Hitler's rule was only three years past when anti-Nazi Germans undertook to design a new democratic order for West Germany with the advice and consent of the American, British, and French military governments. The framers of the Basic Law at that time found it easier to agree on what was necessary to protect democracy in the new state than on what it would take to promote it. Like generals preparing not to lose another war by learning from the errors that led to defeat in the last one, they concentrated more on avoiding the mistakes of a past they knew all too well than on constitutional engineering for an uncertain future. The Law was to provide ironclad safeguards designed to protect the new Bonn Republic from becoming yet another Weimar-type prelude to yet another totalitarian regime.

In order to prevent the concentration of power Hitler had acquired, the framers designed first of all a fairly complex and, in some ways, rather cumbersome system of checks and balances between executive, legislative, and judicial authorities at various levels of government. Convinced that the Weimar constitution had allowed misguided voters too much of a voice in public affairs, they provided for a more restrictive form of representative democracy. Unlike the United States, the only directly elected public officials in the Federal Republic are legislators—except for the mayors of some cities. Because the authors of the Basic Law thought the Weimar experience showed that nationwide plebiscites and referenda weakened rather than strengthened democracy, ordinary Germans had no opportunity to vote on such critical issues as their constitutional arrangements, German reunification, and European integration. The aforementioned constitutional reform commission would not go along with wide-spread demands for more direct democracy. What seemed valid reasons for rejecting it to the framers of 1949 were said to remain valid after reunification, more than forty years later.

Finally, the original authors of the Law felt that this time around the cause of political order was not well served if its enemies were permitted to use constitutional means for unconstitutional ends. A bill of inalienable rights was included offering individuals and minorities judicial protection against tyranny by majority rule. However, civil liberties that are in principle irrevocable, such as freedom of expression and association, are subject to proper restrictions in the "public interest" and in defense of the democratic order.

In two of its basic features—federalism and judicial review—the German constitutional order is more like that of the United States than that of any other country. However, it differs substantially with respect to the relationship between the executive and the legislature.

A Different System of Checks and Balances

American and German constitutional provisions for the relationship between executive and legislature reflect different conceptions of representative government. In the United States the federal and state governments consist of an executive and a legislative branch. In Germany the federal government does not include the Federal Diet or Bundestag and the state governments do not include their respective state legislatures. Under the American division of powers the voters' choice for chief executive shares a term-limited mandate to govern with the two chambers of a popularly elected legislature of which he is not a member. In Germany the head of the government is a member of the popularly elected parliament and owes his/her position to a majority in the chamber.

The president of the Federal Republic is its head of state, but not, like the American president, its chief executive as well. The occupant of the highest elective office in Germany can neither propose nor veto legislation and is more or less a political figurehead, barred from engaging in "partisan" activities and limited pretty much to playing a ceremonial role in public life. And all of the president's "public" acts, such as the annual New Year's address to the nation and meetings with foreign leaders, formally require the approval of the head of the government. The German head of state is thus essentially a republican version of the powerless constitutional monarchs in other democracies, except that he cannot stay on for more than two five-year terms and does not have political immunity. The holder of the office is a public official who can be impeached for exceeding his or her constitutional authority.

Here again the framers of the Basic Law were reacting to the Weimar experience, when a constitutionally powerful and popularly elected president played a key political role in undermining the democratic order and bringing Hitler to power legitimately. This time the chief of state was to be only indirectly elected by the people and have absolutely no constitutional powers for bypassing the legislature and making policy.

Under these conditions German presidents have to be far more circumspect than American ones in observing the constitutional limits on their authority. They may try to admonish or warn responsible policymakers in statements designed to express or mobilize public opinion and they may attempt to influence policy through informal consultations with prominent figures in public life. They have sometimes used the position for ostensibly nonpartisan observations on political developments at home, but normally they are kept busy with diplomatic functions that serve to promote their country's reputation abroad. So long as governmental leaders can count on solid legislative support they will not and need not accept presidential interference and advice.

The federal chancellor, Germany's chief executive, does not have the independent constitutional powers of an American president and Germany's legislature does not have those of the Congress. And while the American system of checks and balances was designed for a constant power struggle between the two branches of government, the German system provides for greater interdependence and closer cooperation between government and legislature. The authors of the Basic Law were far more explicit about the powers of the chancellor than the framers of the American constitution about those of the president. Above all, they made the head of the federal government in Germany more dependent on continuous majority support in the popularly elected legislature. But they also endowed the office with exclusive rights that may at times help a chancellor tilt the political balance of power in his favor.

A chancellor has only some of the constitutional prerogatives of an American chief executive. The scope of his authority to make top-level appointments outside the civil service is not as great, nor is his discretionary authority in the distribution of public funds. He is entitled to set general policy guidelines for his administration, to select and dismiss its top officials, and to establish as well as abolish cabinet departments and positions. Department heads are formally accountable only to the chancellor while he, in turn, is alone accountable to the Diet for the policies of his government and the conduct of its members. In contrast to the United States, the head of the federal government does not need the advice and consent of legislators for his cabinet and subcabinet appointments and can turn down each and all of their budgetary appropriations when these exceed his government's requests.

The full extent of a chancellor's overall authority over policymaking in his government has never been put to the test and remains a matter of dispute among interpreters of the constitution. The Basic Law gives cabinet officers a great deal of leeway in running their departments in accordance with the policy guidelines of the chancellor and that autonomy, in effect, diminishes his constitutional coordinating powers. The chancellor has the formal right of an American chief executive to overrule any members of his cabinet, but not the constitutional authority to bypass them entirely on major policy questions. The cabinet, not the chancellor, is the last resort for settling interdepartmental disputes. And the budget and all other measures requiring the approval of one or both houses of the federal legislature cannot be submitted without being first passed by the whole cabinet.

The elaborate provisions for the chancellor's prerogatives were in large part designed to prevent a repetition of the catastrophic consequences of governmental instability in Weimar times. A candidate for the chancellorship must first of all be nominated for the office by the federal president and then needs the support of at least half of the entire membership of the Federal Diet to win it. If that does not produce a chancellor, the deputies can nominate and elect someone else with a similar absolute majority vote. Should no one gain such support, a simple plurality will do for the third round. However, then—and only then—the Federal President can say no, dissolve the chamber, and put the matter to a popular vote in an election for a new Diet.

Once elected, the chief of the German government holds a more secure constitutional position than was the case under the Weimar regime. The president cannot remove an incumbent, and sitting legislators can normally only do so by electing someone else with an absolute majority. If there should neither be enough votes to support a chancellor nor enough to replace him, he need not necessarily at once resign. Under a thus far untested provision he can ask the president to let him have new Diet elections immediately, or to put them off for a while provided the Federal Council of the state governments will let him govern without the other chamber. The legislators, for their part, can put a stop to this if they manage to elect a new chancellor in time.

For most Germans the popularly elected lower house of the federal legislature is the most conspicuous arena of national policymaking. Important speeches and debates are televised and school children from all over the country are taken to watch "democracy at work" from the visitors' gallery of the chamber. But even with this, what ordinary citizens see and hear gives them a rather limited and not particularly impressive picture of the activities of the federal diet. Most of the Bundestag's work is done in committees and out of public view.

In Germany, as in the United States, the upper chamber of the national legislature stands primarily for the federal, the lower primarily for the democratic aspects of constitutional government. The Diet is supposed to be the principal lawmaking body for the entire country and the principal representative institution for controlling the Federal Government. On both counts its formal authority is far more limited than that of the House of Representatives and, unlike that body, the Diet is subject to premature out-of-term elections when it cannot come to terms with the executive branch. For example, if the chamber were to try to impose unwanted restrictions on the executive's conduct of foreign affairs, as the House has often done, it would risk dissolution.

Under the German form of checks and balances the Diet's independence in relations with the executive branch is more evident in its powers of control than in its legislative authority. Here the framers of the Basic Law did not follow the eighteenth-century separation-of-powers principles embodied in the American constitution but built on nineteenth-century parliamentary principles providing for more unified governmental authority. Accordingly, they gave the chamber exclusive control over the selection and removal of a chancellor and his government. They charged it with supervising the executive on behalf of the people through interrogations, investigations, and binding regulations. The Federal Diet's committees ordinarily do not have the formal investigatory powers of congressional committees. It takes, however, only one-fourth of its members to set up special committees of inquiry into government conduct. But while the representatives of the German people can summon executive officials to appear before them, they cannot, like members of the Congress, compel them to disclose information, reply to questions, or debate an issue. A chancellor may refuse to respond to charges from the opposition in the chamber and, unlike associates of U.S. presidents have done, his subordinates need not claim "executive privilege" to remain silent.

In Germany individual legislators are less important targets for pressure group politics than members of the U.S. Congress, largely because the constitution gives them much less lawmaking authority. At the federal as well as at the state level, the principles of majoritarian government put the initiation, formulation, and enactment of legislation directly in the hands of the executive branch. In contrast to the American separation of powers, nearly all federal laws originate with the executive branch, whose top officials are also leading members of the legislature. Divided government, as Americans know it, cannot exist under the majoritarian principles of the Basic Law and it is therefore not particularly important that close to half of the Diet's committees may be headed by members of the opposition. Government bills are shepherded through the chamber by members of the executive branch who may at any time interject themselves into the legislative process. The chancellor and his cabinet officers have not only the aforementioned right to silence, but also the right to voice their views in committee sessions and from the rostrum of the chamber whenever they wish.

The Distinct Style of German Federalism

The framers made federalism an unalterable part of the Basic Law not so much to safeguard the rights of the constituent states as to prevent another dictatorial concentration of power at the center. Like the American constitution, the Law provides for a geographic division of public authority between national and regional bodies but puts federal law above state law. Accordingly, the constitutions of the new East German states had to conform to the Basic Law's requirements for "republican, democratic, and social government based on the rule of law." State and local governments throughout the country must be based on majorities in legislative bodies "chosen in general, direct, free, equal, and secret elections" by the enfranchised population. The rights and freedoms guaranteed by the Basic Law apply to the sixteen states or *Länder* in the same way that the American Bill of Rights applies to the states. And since the Law prohibits capital punishment, it cannot be imposed by any German court.

But federalism in the Federal Republic is not the same as American federalism. Except in Bavaria, politics in the German *Länder* are not distinguished by the kind of regional traditions that color politics in American states. The jurisdictional division between national and subnational authorities is also less clear-cut than in the United States and federal-state intergovernmental relations are more closely intertwined.

Attacks on a supposedly bloated, meddling federal bureaucracy do not carry much weight in German politics. Unlike the U.S. system, the states are responsible for the implementation of most laws. Therefore, relatively few public officials work for the federal government in Germany. At the same time, the wide scope of federal legislation leaves little room for the variety in state and local regulations that one finds in the United States. For example, there is only a federal income tax, one nationwide value-added tax, and opening hours for retail stores are the same in all states and communities.

The sixteen Länder of the Federal Republic do not have the fiscal powers of the fifty American states and accordingly depend far more on nationwide revenue-sharing arrangements. How much they can spend and for what rests almost entirely with national measures that determine the allocation of public funds to federal, state, and local authorities. An equalization requirement, which provides for the redistribution of tax income from richer to poorer states and municipalities, has been a perennial source of conflict between the haves and the have-nots. The issue has loomed particularly large in the post-unification politics of fiscal austerity. Such arrangements give German regional and local authorities a much bigger stake in decisions on the size and shape of the federal budget and the nature of federal grants than their American counterparts.

Under a less decentralized and more consolidated form of federalism than in the United States, the far greater administrative responsibilities of the states at the subnational level are matched by their more far-reaching constitutional powers at the national level. The state legislatures control half of the votes in the election of a German president and the state governments half in the election of all federal judges. Most important of all, the Länder governments participate in national policymaking through the Federal Council (*Bundesrat*), the upper house of the German legislature. In this body the representatives of the states, unlike U.S. Senators, are not directly answerable to the people. The several votes allotted to each state are cast as a unit by state governments that are only indirectly accountable to the voters by the way of the state legislature. A chancellor who lacks support in this chamber of state governments can no more dissolve it and schedule new elections than can an American president in disagreement with the Congress. Because the Council's makeup depends on legislative elections in the states, state elections play a far more important role in national politics than in the United States.

In some respects the Federal Council is not, like the United States Senate, a coequal chamber of the national legislature. It can only delay, but not block legislation passed by the popularly elected Federal Diet when the bills in question do not directly affect the states, notably defense and foreign policy measures. However, most legislation—including all that involves European Union issues—must be approved by the Federal Council. Bills on revenue sharing, education, and law enforcement as well as all constitutional amendments require a two-thirds majority, permitting a minority coalition of state governments to block such measures.

In recent times German unification and European integration have both reinforced a tendency for state legislatures in the Federal Republic to be weaker and state governments to be stronger than their American counterparts. The always more limited legislative authority of the Länder has been further eroded by federal and European Union measures that have enhanced the executive authority of their top government officials. At the same time the power of German state governments to delay, if not block national legislation has increasingly allowed them to promote regional as well as party interests through constitutional processes unavailable to American state governments. Federal governments that lack the votes in the Council to have their way are impelled to accommodate recalcitrant state governments with concessions. And when the Council turns down government bills passed by the popularly elected chamber, constitutional arrangements for resolving differences between the two bodies favor compromise solutions acceptable to critical state governments.

German federalism involves mostly intergovernmental relations and interbureaucratic negotiations between federal and state agencies that attract little attention on the outside. But major policy disputes involving the respective rights or obligations of the federal and state governments, such as the proper allocation of revenues, are likely to be widely publicized when that serves the partisan interests of political rivals in the national arena of German politics.

In Germany, as in the United States, state governorships have increasingly become launching pads in campaigns for the highest national office. But German governors have comparatively greater opportunities for capturing national attention and boosting their rise to national eminence thanks to the institution of the Federal Council. If a governor chooses to do so, he himself can represent his state and play a prominent role in this chamber. Moreover, state governors have the right to address the popularly elected Federal Diet and may use it to promote their political fortunes with nationally televised speeches supporting or opposing the leaders and policies of the current federal government. It is as if in the American Congress the states would represented in the Senate by their governors who would also have the right to speak in the House of Representatives if they wished.

In the case of local government, German federalism makes for nationwide uniformity across state lines. For example, by a recent amendment to the Basic Law nationals of other European Union countries who live in Germany are entitled not only to vote but also to run for local offices—a privilege not granted to noncitizens in the United States. But since local governments in Germany have less responsibility and power than in the United States, granting such political rights to noncitizens is not terribly important or controversial. Self-governing communities in Germany enjoy far less autonomy than their American counterparts and counties are essentially administrative subdivisions of the states.

On the whole the towns and cities in the Federal Republic depend financially almost entirely on what the central and state governments agree to distribute among them for designated purposes. Federal regulations do not allow municipalities to impose sales taxes or to determine what they may raise in property and business taxes. Differences in salaries and working conditions for employees of communities of similar size are insignificant compared to the United States since all German municipalities must observe nationwide standards concerning the qualifications, pay, and fringe benefits of local officials. Within each of the Länder, the state governments run some key local services themselves, most notably the police and the schools, and they closely control other services that they delegate to municipal officials. Local governments and councils are left to deal on their own with what are usually rather mundane political matters, such as the maintenance of local roads, recreational facilities, and the operation of public transport, sanitation, and utility services.

Outside the Federal Republic the older and simpler American version of federalism is much better known and appreciated than the German one, inside federalism "made in Germany" has been considered not only the more appropriate version for the Federal Republic, but also for a decentralized European Union as well.

A Constitutional Court with Formidable Powers

The Basic Law leaves the uniform administration of justice throughout the Federal Republic almost entirely to its Länder. Courts are usually state courts, and the judges and prosecutors that serve in them are appointed by the state governments in accordance with state regulations. Germany has only six national courts: the Federal Court of Justice (*Bundesgerichtshof*), four other, more specialized federal courts of last appeal, and the Federal Constitutional Court (*Bundesverfassungsgericht*).

Anyone and any group in Germany is entitled to go to the Constitutional Court with complaints that their rights under the Basic Law have been violated by public authorities. The Constitutional Court may overrule any other court on those grounds. In one landmark case, for example, it agreed that a ban on the showing of a film by an anti-Semitic ex-Nazi was contrary to the freedom of expression. In another ruling the court turned down a complaint from the German Employers Association, an influential interest group, that a federal law violated the constitutional protection of private enterprise. The Court gets thousands of constitutional complaints about the actions of authorities every year, but it need not and usually does not take them under consideration.

On the other hand—and once again in the light of Weimar experiences—public authorities may get the Court to ban specific organizations and to restrict activities that they hold to be inconsistent with the constitutional order and the duties of responsible citizenship. It thus agreed with the Federal Government in the 1950s that both the Communist Party and a neo-Nazi party should be outlawed as "anti-democratic" organizations; and in the 1970s the Court ruled that the protection of German democracy permitted loyalty tests for public employees and surveillance procedures that violated the right to privacy of communications.

While in the United States the power of judicial review is only one of the functions of federal and state courts, in Germany this authority rests entirely and explicitly with the Federal Constitutional Court and, to a lesser extent, with the constitutional courts of the states.

Having justices empowered to render binding decisions on the constitutional legitimacy of governmental acts was the most innovative feature of the new system of checks and balances that the Basic Law introduced into German politics. By imposing unprecedented judicial constraints on both executive and legislative power and letting a few judges have the last word, the German framers sought to correct what they saw as another major shortcoming of Weimar constitution. The firm establishment of the present regime has meant that more and more political issues have been formalistically defined, considered, and disputed with reference to the Basic Law and have required authoritative interpretations of its intricate and complex provisions by the Court.

The Court has original jurisdiction in constitutional disputes between the Federal Government and the state governments, between the Federal executive and legislature, between the various states, and between courts. The justices are required to provide a ruling when it is requested by members of these other constitutional organs. Unlike their American counterparts, the justices are not allowed to refuse to deal with contentious issues on the grounds that these concern political, not constitutional questions.

All this gives members of the Court more constitutional responsibilities than those of the American Supreme Court and that is reflected in differences of organization and composition. The German Court consists of two entirely separate eight-member chambers, one primarily for constitutional rights questions and the other more for judicial review issues. The sixteen justices are not nominated by the chief executive and confirmed by one chamber of the legislature for lifetime appointments, as are federal judges in the United States. Half of them are chosen by a representative committee of the popularly elected Federal Diet and half by the Federal Council of state governments to serve a single twelve-year term, a provision that Germans say precludes the problems of senility posed by lifetime tenure.

Justices thus charged and chosen have responded to the pressure of increasing demands for judicial review by gradually transforming the Court into a more active and less reactive institution than was originally intended. And in the process Germans have learned, as Americans have long known, that the constitution is what the justices say it is. In Germany their decisions have on the whole been less attuned to current public opinion than in the United States and less concerned with the meaning attached to constitutional provisions by their original authors.

Since in Germany the basic rights and federal structure contained in constitutional law cannot be changed by legislative action—as they can in the United States—what the Constitutional Court says in these areas remains the last word, but only for as long as the Court holds to its position. In other areas the Court may use judicial review for reinterpretations of the Basic Law that amount to changes by judicial fiat. In 1983, for example, it turned down claims that the Basic Law did not allow a chancellor with a majority in the Federal Diet to have the chamber dissolved so he could have new elections. While the content of these so-called evolutionary amendments may be controversial, the process itself is not. Other than in the United States, lawyers and politicians are in general agreement that judicial interpretations of the constitution should evolve with changing times and changing justices regardless of the intentions of those who first drew it up.

In exercising progressively less judicial restraint and more judicial activism the Court has come under attack for having usurped law-making and control functions that critics say belong exclusively to the legislature. What they find particularly irksome is that a body that is neither elected by the people nor accountable to them has on numerous occasions not just overruled the representatives of the people on major political issues, but actually told them what they ought to have done. In some cases of judicial review the Court has coupled its rejection of a piece of legislation with prescriptions for a substitute that would pass muster, as with a campaign finance law in the 1960s, an abortion law in the 1970s, and a census law in 1980s. In others it has qualified its approval with precise requirements for a constitutionally proper implementation of the legislation, as it did on a 1975 agreement between the two Germanys before unification and in 1993 on a new abortion law following unification.

German legislators go to considerable lengths to fashion laws that will pass judicial review by a particular set of justices, just as as American legislators seek to safeguard their bills against judicial as well as executive vetoes. Nonetheless, there have been times when the Federal Government, Federal Diet, and Federal Council have labored mightily to achieve agreement on a piece of legislation, only to have it tossed out by a few justices on appeal from a state government or from some legislators who lost out in the bargain. But that need not be the end of it. The limited term of the eight justices in each of the Court's chambers can before long lead to the formation of a more favorable majority.

There are clearly significant differences in the constitutional frameworks in which German and American politics unfold. The Federal Republic's Basic Law shows in many ways that it was born in the shadow of Germany's exceptional Nazi past and meant to prevent another Weimar prelude. What the two frameworks have distinctively in common is, above all, that they were designed to prevent a concentration of political power through formal checks and balances and through mutual vetoes in a system of divided public authority. Both governmental systems put democratic accountability before governmental efficiency in policy making, both serve to promote extensive deliberation and bargaining among policymakers, and both risk undue delay, immobility, and deadlock in situations that call for quick, decisive, and authoritative actions.

Parties—the Life-Blood of the System

Probably the most striking difference between the German and American system concerns the roles of the two countries' respective political parties. Parties formed in the three West German zones of allied military occupation following the collapse of the Third Reich even before a new governmental system had been designed and the Federal Republic established in 1949. The Western occupation authorities licensed parties whose organizers had no ties to the dismantled Hitler regime and were committed to create and support a pluralist democracy with competitive political parties. While guided and prodded by the Western powers, leaders of these parties were the principal architects of West Germany's new political order. In the driver's seat at the creation, the Federal Republic's founders reserved the most encompassing roles in the new political system for political parties and leaders like themselves.

In this respect, the intentions of the West German framers and their constitutional framework differed fundamentally from the American founders and their governmental design. Political parties did not exist at the time of the Constitutional Convention in Philadelphia. Suspicious of the selfishness of factions, James Madison and his fellow-framers did not delegate any roles and prerogatives to political parties. The framers' skepticism became part of the American political culture in which better government has traditionally been associated with weak parties and nonpartisanship—and not only during the Progressive era.

Given their country's experience, the West German leaders who authored the Basic Law had far more immediate reasons to be wary of political parties than America's founding fathers. After all, during the Weimar Republic the party system had been weak and an easy prey for Hitler's power grab. But instead of excluding parties from the formal delegation of prerogatives or confining them to function merely as organizational vehicles that facilitate competitive elections, the architects of the new Germany favored strong, reliable, democratic parties as the best guardians of West Germany's new political order. Leaders in the formative years of the Federal Republic were in fact suspicious of nonpartisan (*überparteiliche*) institutions and players because these had been tied to anti-democratic, authoritarian tendencies in Germany's troubled past. With this in mind, they rejected the idea of a nonpartisan bureaucracy. This decision enhanced the influence of parties because it enabled their leaders to use the power of patronage appointments to politicize the public sector on all levels of government. The most influential positions in Germany's bureaucracy, educational system, and public broadcasting are reserved for members of the establishment parties.

The constitution envisions and installs parties first and foremost as linkages between the people and the state, between the governed and the governors. But the provisions of the Basic Law and a host of statutes and conventions—all adopted and developed under the tutelage of party leaders—were used to institutionalize an intricate political arrangement that allows parties to direct and permeate the country's key public institutions (i.e., governments, legislatures, bureaucracies, military, interest groups) This led one observer to conclude that one doesn't find important political decisions in the German democracy which have not been "brought to the parties, prepared by them and finally taken by them."[1]

Because the political parties are the life-blood of its political system, the Federal Republic is often called a "party state" or a "party democracy." Consequently, when the system functions well, party leaders take the credit; when the performance is unsatisfactory, they must take the blame. To this day, the major parties and their leaders are credited, for example, with performing extraordinary well in building a new democratic state with solid political and socioeconomic concepts in the first postwar decades. But they also bear the brunt of criticism when the country's problems mount, as has been the case in the post-unification years.

By the end of 1992 a leading German newspaper recognized the term *Politikverdrossenheit* (disgust with politics) as "the word of the year." Thereafter, this expression became more fashionable yet to describe a widespread public discontent with politics in East and West Germany alike. In fact, many Germans were not at all fed up with politics but rather with the way the major parties and politicians seemingly misused the public trust. On the heels of scandalous revelations about corrupt, greedy, high-living politicians and back-room deals within and among parties, an increasing number of Germans believed that the established parties were governing more for their own than for the common good. *Parteienverdrossenheit* (disgust with parties) spread like a virus. A small but increasing number of fed-up rank and file members and faithful voters turned their backs on the "in" parties and switched to already existing small parties (several of them of the far-right variety) or newly established organizations (most of them middle-of-the-road reform alternatives).

Although these were minor changes, they generated worries about the return of a Weimar-like party system with a multitude of small parties. Domestic and foreign observers wondered whether changes in the party line-up would endanger the Federal Republic's traditional consensus politics. It was up to "Super Election Year—1994" with altogether 19 popular elections (from the election of the European parliament to national, state, and local elections) and a few state and local elections the following year to answer important questions as to Germany's party landscape.

In the end, the old parties had prevailed and some of the new kids on the block had become stronger and others weaker. With the turn of the century close, the partisan line-up was the following:

The Union Parties: CDU/CSU

Conceived in 1945 by its founders as an anti-Nazi and anti-Communist party with Christian values, the CDU united all of the center-right factions that had been organized by several separate parties in pre-1933 era and positioned itself in the political middle, to the right of the Social Democrats. While drawing most of its support among Catholics in the rural regions of the Rhineland and Southern Germany, the party embraced an agenda designed to accommodate Catholics and Protestants, conservatives and reformers, rural and urban interests. By the mid-fifties the center-right union parties supported capitalism with a host of social features (*soziale Marktwirtschaft*) and Germany's integration into the western alliance. This was the right stuff for a catch-all party or *Volkspartei* and a far cry from the parochial parties typical of the Weimar era.

As in the past, the contemporary CDU operates as a national party with the exception of the predominantly Catholic state of Bavaria, where the ideological tenets and the leaders of its sister party CSU are appealing to a regional electorate that is distinctly more conservative than the rest of the country. When it comes to national politics, the two parties generally act as one, coordinating their national campaigns, agreeing on a candidate for chancellor. So far, the CSU has been part of all CDU-led government coalitions. In 1980 the CSU's long-time leader Franz Josef Strauss was the union parties' designated candidate for the chancellor's office—in a losing effort. However, the relationship between the CDU and CSU has periodically gone through stormy periods. In many respects, but especially in regard to social issues, the CSU resembles the conservative and significant parts of the CDU the moderate bloc of the Republican Party in the United States.

The CDU's expansion into the Eastern states was facilitated by the existence of a Christian Democratic party there which had been one of the GDR's so-called bloc-parties. While in reality extensions of the ruling

SED, these parties were supposed to convey the appearance of a multi-party state. By the mid-1990s the CDU was the second strongest party in the East in terms of membership.

The Social Democratic Party

During the Weimar Republic the SPD, one of the oldest parties in Europe, was the only party to vote against the Enabling Act of March 1933 that gave Hitler dictatorial power. During the Nazi era, the SPD maintained an executive committee in exile and a readiness to rebuild after the collapse of the Third Reich. Immediately after the war, Social Democrats began to reestablish a highly centralized and bureaucratized mass party organization.

After disappointing results in successive federal elections the SPD dropped the Marxist ideology that had appealed to segments of the working class but scared away potential middle-class voters. Adopted by its 1959 party congress in Bad Godesberg, the SPD's new platform or Godesberg program abandoned the idea of class struggle and declared its support for the social market economy. Political reality had won out over theoretical principles. The party supported West Germany's participation in the Western alliance without embracing it as emphatically as the union parties.

For the next twenty or so years the basic positions were more or less agreed upon inside the party. But the old conflict between the pragmatic middle-of-the-road Social Democrats and the ideological left intensified in the 1990s, when the two wings disagreed over the party's positions on an array of issues stretching from economic and social policy to immigration, environmental protection, and foreign policy. It was becoming increasingly difficult for the top party leaders to keep their flock together. If they embraced the political center, they blurred the distinction between SPD and CDU and alienated the ideologues; if they espoused more traditional positions they offended the pragmatists.

SPD leaders and rank-and-file members who had assumed that their party would thrive among East Germans were in for a rude awakening. Before the first all-German election in 1990, the SPD united with a small East German Social Democratic party that had been founded two days before the fall of the Berlin Wall. But the consolidated SPD won less than 20 percent of the Eastern vote. Contrary to expectations inside and outside the party, most former members and supporters of the GDR's ruling party did not cast their ballots for Social Democrats.

The Free Democrats

Founded three years after the end of World War II to carry on the tradition of Germany's liberal parties, the FDP eventually defined itself as an alternative to the union parties and the SPD by taking a position somewhere between them. While its program oscillated between center-right and center-left, the FDP was in the first place the party of the business sector—more than the CDU/CSU—and advocated a German version of supply-side policies with as pure a market economy as possible and tax cuts. In some areas such as economic and social policy the FDP has been closer to the union parties, in others such as protection of civil liberties closer to the Social Democrats and the Greens. Thus, the party was been well situated to build coalitions with either one of the large parties. Although a minor party in terms of electoral support, the FDP has had for many years a disproportionate influence in national, state, and local governments.

But when the 1994 elections came around, the fortune of the party seemed to change. Exposed to weak and feuding party leaders, many traditional FDP voters thought that the party had lost its identity. By the end of "Super Election Year—1994," the FDP seemed on its way out. Its candidates failed to win seats in most state legislatures, local communities, and in the European parliament. And the party's renewed representation in the federal parliament and government was won only on the coattails of the Christian Democrats who had openly urged their supporters to use a peculiarity of the German election law to return the FDP to Bonn and into the government coalition.

A revival of the FDP in the crowded political region between the right-of-center CDU and the left-of-center SPD and Greens seemed doubtful. This was obviously the reading of one party faction that tried to recast the FDP in a right-of-center nationalist mold. But when the FDP of old managed to win representation in the legislatures of three states (Rhineland-Palatinate, Baden-Württemberg, and Schleswig-Holstein) in early 1996 and got a larger share of the vote than in the previous elections in each of those Länder, critics that had predicted its imminent demise fell silent.

Alliance '90/Greens

Born in the late 1970s as an amalgam of environmentalists, pacifists, left-radicals, equal rights advocates, and other grassroots splinter groups, the

Green Party managed to bring alternative viewpoints to the political debate which up to then had been dominated by the mainstream parties. After its first electoral successes on local and state levels, the party made a startling national breakthrough in 1983, when it became the first new party in the Federal Diet since 1957, winning 27 seats with 5.6 percent of the popular vote. A number of the party's original policy initiatives, especially on environmental issues and the controversy surrounding the stationing of U.S. Pershing and cruise missiles in the early 1980s in Germany, were eventually embraced by one or more of the major parties.

Dropping to less than five percent of the vote, the West German Greens suffered a setback in the first all-German elections in 1990, when they failed to win any seats in the federal parliament. However, a coalition between the East German Greens and the so-called Alliance '90 did. The Alliance '90 was founded as a fusion of the New Forum and other East German groups, which had advocated a "third way" alternative system in the GDR after the fall of the Berlin Wall instead of a full-fledged reunification with West Germany.

Before the 1994 elections and after the pragmatist "Realos" of the Green party had won a bitter family feud with the dogmatic "Fundis," the Greens and Alliance '90 formally merged into one party. By the end of "Super Election year—1994" the Alliance '90/Greens party had replaced the FDP nation wide as third strongest party. The Greens had shed their image as unconventional activists, abandoned their strict term-limits for the deputies of their former anti-party, and become one of the established system parties. Environmental protection, equal rights for women, social justice, and the rejection of military force have continued to rank high on the agenda of the Alliance '90/Green party.

Party members, especially those rooted in the East German Alliance '90, rejected the idea of left of center coalitions; they were especially unwilling to cooperate with the PDS or, as one party leader put it, with "national Bolsheviks." When top party leaders flirted with the idea of cooperating with the PDS, several of its East German leaders turned their backs on the party and joined the CDU.

The Party for Democratic Socialism

The PDS's showing in the first all-German elections in the fall of 1990, just weeks after the formal unification, was discounted as a temporary phenomenon of a transitional period, in which East German voters had not yet adjusted to the rapid changes in their land. Winning more than 11 percent of the total vote in the East and 16 seats in the Federal Diet, some of the party's eloquent leaders had tried to establish themselves as the voice of conscience—for example, in social matters or policies concerning asylum seekers and immigrants. However, only in one instance did the PDS make a difference in the 12th Bundestag: In 1991 the PDS deputies cast the decisive votes in the legislature's difficult and narrow decision to move the German capital from Bonn to Berlin.

After capturing almost 18 percent of the East German vote in the federal election of 1994, the PDS became, with 36 percent of the popular vote, the strongest party in those parts of Berlin that had formerly belonged to communist East Germany. In some districts, the party captured well over 40 percent of the vote. East Berlin proved to be no exception. By 1995 PDS members had been elected mayors of 175 local governments in the East. In East Germany, commentators concluded that the only truly eastern party had become a "people's party." Many disillusioned and dislocated Easterners, especially the older generation, looked upon the PDS as a convenient vehicle for casting a protest vote. But the party increasingly attracted young members and young voters as well. Close to 40 percent of the 18 to 24 year old voters in East Berlin cast their votes for the PDS in the 1995 state election. While pragmatic reformers and Stalinists struggled for power inside the organization, the party seemed to move toward a position traditionally identified with left-leaning Social Democrats. In the East the PDS offered an alternative to the left of the SPD and the Greens. However, in West Germany it got next to no support.

It was an odd moment for West Germans, when the 13th Bundestag was opened in 1994 with the speech of a deputy who had run on the PDS ticket: Because writer Stefan Heym was the oldest deputy, this honor had automatically fallen to him. Less than two years later, Heym resigned from his seat in protest against what he called "parliamentary plunder" after the legislature had voted by a two-thirds majority for a scheme granting its members pay increases of about 50 percent over the next five years. Heym's stand was especially popular in his home district in Berlin, one of the poorest around, and elsewhere in eastern Germany.

In the first years after unification the party's membership and electoral support were disproportionately drawn from the older generation and from professionals (i.e., civil servants, teachers) who considered themselves the big losers of unification. But as younger members moved up the party ranks, young East Germans considered the PDS the only genuine and distinctive East German voice among the political parties and an attractive choice. Thus, it was far from clear that the PDS was merely a transitional party as refugee-parties had been temporary political organizations in West Germany's postwar era.

The Republikaner and Other Right-Wing Parties

Founded in the early 1980s by Franz Schönhuber, a former and unrepentant member of Hitler's ruthless Waffen SS, the right-wing Republikaner Partei made its first electoral waves in early 1989, when it won 7.5 percent of the popular vote in the West Berlin election. Shortly thereafter, it won 7.1 percent of West Germany's popular vote in the European Community election. Schönhuber took one of the party's six seats in the European Parliament. Capturing 6.2 percent of the vote, the Deutsche Volksunion (DVU) won seats in the city state of Bremen in 1991 and 6.3 percent in Schleswig-Holstein's state legislature a year later. With 10.9 percent of the vote the Republikaner in Baden-Württemberg became the third strongest party in the state legislature. Moreover, Republikaner and other right-wing party candidates were elected into many city and county assemblies. Like other right-wing parties such as the German People's Union (DVU), the Republicans exploited most of all the influx of asylum seekers and other foreigners to stir anti-foreigner, nationalistic, and anti-democratic sentiments.

As 1994 began, the right-wing parties were represented in three state legislatures and in the European parliament. The Republikaner even occupied a seat in the Bundestag, when one of the CDU's deputies became a member of the Party under the threat of being ejected from the CDU. But instead of strengthening their position, as some observers had predicted, the right-wing parties were the biggest losers in 1994 and in most elections thereafter. They were unable to enter or reenter any state legislature and the European parliament and failed to reenter many local councils. When they managed to do so as the DVU did in 1995 local election in the northern city of Bremerhaven and the Republikaner in the 1997 local elections in the state of Hesse, they received less support than in the years between 1989 and 1993. The Republicans and similar parties have simply not managed to become a factor in German politics.

Why did the political right-wing lose ground in Germany at a time when similar parties mustered significant electoral support in other European democracies? Why did German voters buck the trend when in neighboring Austria, for example, the right-wing Freiheitliche Partei Österreichs won a stunning 23 percent of the popular vote just one week before Germany's federal election? Perhaps the most plausible explanation points to the shift to the right on the part of the most conservative faction within the CDU. Together with the Bavarian CSU, these elements embraced the right-wingers' anti-foreigner and nationalist agenda. It had been the battle cry "Germany for Germans" that had swept Republikaner and other right extremists into electoral offices. Once the CDU/CSU and eventually also the opposition SPD played the xenophobia card and abandoned the constitutional guarantee of an unconditional right to political asylum in the Federal Republic, the right-wing parties had won a victory but were, as far as most of their voters were concerned, dispensable.

Alternative Parties

Like the original coalition that eventually organized the Greens, grassroots political action groups in the 1970s and 1980s were typically single-issue oriented and fueled mostly by New Left type activists. While some right and left fringe groups emerged, the alternative parties of the 1990s were more often than not founded, led, and supported by former members and supporters of the establishment parties who argued that the major parties abused their power, were undemocratic, and had lost touch with the people. These mostly middle-class parties or alliances used the same arguments and had the same appeal as the "United We Stand, America" movement that emerged during and survived Ross Perot's 1992 presidential campaign.

Seventy percent of the voters who cast their ballots for the first Instead Party in the city state of Hamburg in late 1993 had voted for the three major parties (30 percent for the CDU, 20 percent the SPD, 20 percent the FDP) in previous elections. The faction won enough seats to become the SPD's junior partner in Hamburg's coalition government. But eventually Hamburg's Instead Party crumbled in the face of internal power struggles. In 1995, another alternative party or voters' initiative, newly founded by moderate former Social Democrats, won 10.7 percent of the vote in the city-state of Bremen. While no factor nation-wide or in larger states, hundreds of such instead or alternative parties calling themselves The Neutrals, The Middle, David Against Goliath, The Independents,

List for Protest Voters, etc., sprang up in West and East German communities poised to challenge the "old" parties, their politicians, and their politics. These groups found their strongest electoral support among young voters who held established parties in low esteem, but expressed trust in citizens' or voters' initiatives.

Perhaps the most interesting of these alternative parties flourished in Bavaria, where the loosely organized Free Voters *Freie Wähler* captured a stunning 16 percent of the vote in the 1996 local elections and were thus encouraged to compete in the 1998 state-wide elections. The Free Voters rejected traditional partisan politics and ideologies advocating instead nonpartisan, common-sense solutions. Since a significant number of the supporters of the Free Voters were disillusioned former followers of the CSU (as well as the SPD), the CSU's thirty-five-year-long absolute majority in this Southern German state was at stake. By 1997 the political establishment in Bavaria was bracing for what some observers called a possible political earthquake in 1998, with aftershocks in national politics as well.

In late 1993, the first post-unification East German party, the Eastern Party German Unity (Ost-Partei Deutsche Einheit) was established in an effort, as the founders explained, to give East Germans a voice in solving their problems, which they perceived to be more profound than those of West Germans. According to the party's leaders, once the goal of "inner societal unification" was achieved, their organization would be dissolved. While nobody expected the East-West gap to disappear soon, the first post-unification eastern party failed to catch on. In the eyes of many East Germans the PDS remained the only viable truly East German party.

The End of the "Two-and-one-half" Party System

The Christian Democrats and the SPD have been the strongest parties in the postwar period. In the first postwar election campaign the two parties ran neck to neck with the Christian Democrats winning a plurality of the vote. Thereafter, the CDU/CSU took a commanding lead and in 1957 became the first party in German history to win an absolute majority of the popular vote. Neither the CDU/CSU nor any other party was able to repeat this performance in the following elections. While winning majorities and pluralities in numerous state and local elections, the Social Democrats remained the second strongest party on the national level until 1972, when they won a slim plurality of the vote, outscoring the

CDU/CSU by just over one percent. Four years later, the Union parties recaptured their number one position.

As Christian and Social Democrats dominated governments on all levels, West Germany seemed on the way to a two-party system. When the electoral support for the Free Democrats dwindled in the second half of the 1950s and 1960s, most experts predicted that the FDP would fade away. Instead, for most of its first 45 years the Federal Republic's national governance was in the hands of a "two-and-one-half" party system in which the CDU/CSU and the SPD were either the strongest government or opposition parties, with the small Free Democratic Party holding the balance of power most of the time.

While building a new and strong German democracy and solidifying their power in the process, the major parties protected their turf against new rivals. Constitutional and statutory provisions designed to avoid the mistakes of the Weimar period, such as allowing nondemocratic parties and a polarized multiparty system, were used to prevent a weakening of the system by right- or left-wing parties or a multitude of small splinter factions. According to the Basic Law, "Parties which, by reason of their aims or the behavior of their adherents, seek to impair or abolish the free democratic order or endanger the existence of the Federal Republic of Germany shall be unconstitutional. The Federal Constitutional Court shall decide on the question of unconstitutionality." On this basis, one neo-Nazi and one Communist party were outlawed in the 1950s as antidemocratic political organizations. In the 1990s several extreme right-wing groups were banned as unconstitutional during the time that violent attacks against foreigners were at their height. But such measures also served to protect the established parties from challenges by new competitors.

Another legal obstacle has been even more instrumental in preserving the status quo of the party system: the so-called "five percent clause," which was adopted to prevent a repetition of the fragmented party system of the Weimar era. According to the current election law only parties winning at least five percent of the total popular vote or at least three constituencies are represented in federal, state, or local legislatures. While not a problem for the two large parties, the five percent threshold has been particular troublesome for the FDP.

After winning seats in local and state legislatures the Greens managed to jump the hurdle in the 1983 federal elections to become the first new party in thirty years to enter the Bundestag. The party system expanded again, after the two Germanys united in 1990. The major West German parties wasted no time in aggressively moving into the East and, not surprisingly, dominated the first all-German election. But two eastern parties, the PDS and Alliance '90, won also seats in the Federal Diet under a special threshold arrangement valid only for the 1990 election. It allowed East German parties to satisfy the five percent clause in the East German states. In 1994, the PDS could not satisfy the five percent requirement nationwide. The party captured, however, four constituencies in East Germany and was awarded an additional 26 seats so that the total number reflected its share of the nationwide vote.

The Pros and Cons of the Hybrid Electoral System

The Federal Republic's relatively young postwar electoral system differs markedly from the American structure. First of all, in the German scheme of proportional representation the seats in legislatures are allocated according to the share of popular vote each of the competing parties receives. Often, the share of those parties seated in the legislature is more than proportional because they gain from the wasted vote of splinter parties unable to fulfill the minimum requirements. Secondly, unlike other countries with proportional representation, Germany gives voters an opportunity to elect legislators in constituencies. This hybrid system was specifically designed to avoid the disproportionality of "first past the post" elections as practiced in the United States, in which winning candidates "take all" while the votes cast for the losers are worthless—even if their combined shares add up to more than 50 percent. At the same time, the direct election of district representatives was thought to enhance the accountability and responsiveness of legislators to their home districts along the line of the American experience.

When Germans go to the polls, they cast two votes—one for a constituency candidate, the other for a party. In national elections, half of the members of the Federal Diet are directly elected in more than 300 districts. But it is the vote cast for a party that determines the proportional allocation of seats in the legislature. For example, if a party is entitled to a total of 300 seats, but its candidates have won in 100 districts only, 200 representatives are picked from lists that each state party draws up prior to elections.

The two-vote ballot facilitates ticket-splitting by letting voters give their first vote to the candidate of one party and their second vote to another party. While not common in the 1950s and 1960s, ticket-splitting has become increasingly popular in recent years—for obvious reasons: the "in" parties play down their ideological differences and each of the two major parties needs a coalition partner to form a government. Therefore supporters of small parties especially, whose candidates have no chance to win a constituency, often cast one ballot for the contender of a major party and their second for the party of their choice.

This is an attractive option, if small-party voters prefer a prospective coalition partner of one of the two major parties. Supporters of the Free Democrats, for example, have voted frequently for CDU district candidates, when the FDP was committed to join a coalition with the CDU/CSU, but for an SPD candidate, if an SPD/FDP coalition was in the cards. Followers of the Greens have voted for SPD district candidates involved in close contests with CDU rivals, if only to support the lesser of two evils. The decline of the two major parties and the proliferation of smaller parties have encouraged increased ticket-splitting in the 1990s. With the survival of their party at stake in the federal election of 1994, the FDP appealed to CDU voters for their second vote. Since this tactic was obviously condoned by CDU leaders, enough voters split their votes between CDU and FDP to assure the small party's return to the Bundestag and the governing coalition in Bonn.

In the past, political experts have periodically weighed proposals to abandon the proportional representation principle and switch to a pure single-district plurality mode that would do away with coalition governments and produce one governing and one opposition party. But even in the 1990s, when some observers in Germany and abroad imagined the ghost of Weimar hovering over the revived multiparty system, reform proposals that would have amounted to a lockout of all small parties—not just right- and left-wing extremists—were doomed to fail. Even a grand coalition of the two major parties on the national level would not enhance the likelihood of such reforms, because in the 1990s, more than ever, both CDU/CSU and SPD needed the cooperation of small parties to form governing coalitions in most federal states and in many municipalities.

Intended to combine the goal of equal representation with the accountability of the single-district "winner-takes-all" conception, the mixed German system still fails to provide an ideal solution. It falls especially short in its inability to establish the close links between individual legislators and their constituencies that exist in the United States, because

Germans, unlike Americans, have traditionally based their voting decisions overwhelmingly on their party preferences and far less on the qualities of individual candidates. This explains why between 1961 and 1990 only candidates of the CDU/CSU and SPD were directly elected to the Federal Diet. Germans used to joke that if nominated, even a head of cabbage would win the votes of party loyalists. In the first all-German election in 1990 the Free Democrats managed to win one constituency seat in the city of Halle in the new state of Saxony-Anhalt because the party had a very popular candidate: Halle's native son Hans-Dietrich Genscher. The long-time FDP chairman and Foreign Minister in successive Bonn governments, he had worked hard for Germany's reunification.

In the United States a candidate must finance, organize, and define his or her campaign. In Germany candidates do not depend on individual financial means, fundraising, or organizational skills: their respective parties shape, organize and finance election campaigns. That is the rationale behind a common internal party rule that requires elected officials to give a specified share of their salaries to their party. Candidates must be party members, be nominated by their party, and run on their party's platform. As a result, winners are far more indebted to their parties than to the voters who elect them.

American voters hold their own Representatives and Senators accountable for their performances in office. Individual legislators' votes, cast on the floor of the U.S. House of Representatives or Senate, for example, can determine whether constituents support or reject them when the next reelection comes around. German voters are much more inclined to reward or punish the performances of parties, not of individual politicians. Even if defeated in their own districts, candidates can still win seats in the legislature, if they rank high enough on their respective party's list. The relationship between representatives and constituents is hardly enhanced by legislators' being able effectively to run for cover and hide under their parties' umbrellas nor by the second-chance provision for candidates defeated in their own districts.

While an instrument of power in the hands of party insiders who control or at least influence the candidate rankings on party-lists, this system does offer parties the opportunity to shape parliamentary bodies so that they are more representative of their members and supporters. The representation of women is a case in point. Unlike the Greens who started out as an equal opportunity party for both genders and eventually adopted a statute guaranteeing women at least half of their candidacies, legislative seats, and party posts, the three "old" parties were from the outset citadels of male power, where women were mostly relegated to second-class roles. But as the postwar generation moved into party politics, a new breed of female activists challenged the traditional "Kinder, Küche, Kirche" (children, kitchen, church) stereotype of the German woman's role and pushed for an adequate share of party power and public offices.

In 1988, after a long and bitter debate within the SPD, the party came to terms with the gender issue and established a women's quota to remedy the underrepresentation of women in influential party and public offices for a 25-year period. Since 1994 at least forty percent of all offices within the SPD must be held by women; by 1998 this quota must be applied to Social Democratic candidate lists and parliamentary seats. In the fall of 1996 the CDU adopted a women's quota that promised to fill at least one-third of party offices and parliamentary seats with women during the following five years.

The number of women in federal, state, and local legislatures and governments increased significantly in the 1980s and 1990s. When the Greens entered the Federal Diet in 1983, the number of female deputies increased considerably but amounted still to less than ten percent of the total membership. Following the 1994 elections, women occupied better than one-quarter of all seats in the Bundestag thanks to their higher placement on party lists. In contrast, when the 105th Congress convened in early 1997, the combined female membership of the U.S. House of Representatives and the U.S. Senate was merely 11 percent. Unlike their German counterparts, party leaders in the United States do not have candidate rosters at their disposal that would allow them to decide the percentage of women or minorities among their parties' legislative delegations. Also, in the American setting female candidates tend to be at a disadvantage because most of them do not have the fundraising abilities of their male competitors, who can draw more financial and other support from entrenched "old boy" networks. Only more recently, when organizations like Emily's List intensified their efforts to provide female candidates with campaign funds and knowhow, did more women win elective offices. In Germany, where not individual candidates but the parties handle campaign financing and strategies, female candidates enjoy the same resources and support as their male colleagues.

The increased representation of women in the Federal Diet, in the Federal Cabinet and in partisan leadership positions does not mean that women have boosted their political influence at the same rate. Close to the dawn of a new millennium political power in Germany remains in the hands of men. So far the country hasn't had a female chancellor or president. None of the major parties has been led by a woman. And only after the resignation of the governor of Schleswig-Holstein, was a woman, Heide Simonis, installed as the first female head of a federal state in 1993 (We will provide a more extensive discussion of the role of women in German politics in chapter 4).

From Chancellor Democracy to Party State

When Konrad Adenauer became chancellor in 1949, the Federal Republic was a defeated and destroyed land. Fourteen years later, when the 87-year-old Adenauer left office, West Germany had experienced a miraculous economic recovery and was firmly embedded in the Western alliance through memberships in NATO and the EC. Just as important, democracy had begun to take roots during the Adenauer era—perhaps in spite of, or perhaps because of his authoritarian traits. Elected chancellor in the wake of a surprisingly strong showing by the CDU in the first postwar federal election, Adenauer assembled a multiparty coalition government. Even before the CDU's overwhelming victories in the 1953 and 1957 elections, Adenauer was in firm control of the government. Acting as both chancellor and foreign minister in the early 1950s and taking care of the emerging defense matters as well, Adenauer could assure foreign officials that he was 75 percent of his cabinet. Leaving economic matters to his Economics Minister Ludwig Erhard who became the architect of the Federal Republic's social market economy, Adenauer reaped a great deal of the credit for the country's "economic miracle."

Adenauer exercised his power boldly throughout most of his three and one-half terms. But his reign occurred during an extraordinary period when new political, economic, and social structures were replacing the discredited and dismantled system of the Nazi years. The "chancellor democracy" that emerged during the 1950s proved to be an exception. It worked for a while in a country whose citizens were learning or relearning how democracy works. Adenauer asserted strong leadership and occasionally stretched his powers beyond the legal limits just as several of America's greatest presidents have done under unusual circumstances, notably Abraham Lincoln during the Civil War and Franklin Roosevelt during the Great Depression and World War II. For Social Democrat

Willy Brandt, the Federal Republic's fourth chancellor, Adenauer, once his bitter political opponent who had slandered him viciously, was in retrospect "a democrat, even if his vision of democracy contained authoritarian features" and "an outstanding figure who performed a significant function in German . . . history."[2]

After twelve years of his "chancellor democracy," Adenauer's decisionmaking model broke down in 1961, when the Christian Democrats lost and Social and Free Democrats won seats in the federal diet. For the first time in a position to forge a coalition government with either one of the two large parties, the FDP now held the balance of parliamentary power and forced Adenauer to make concessions—most of all a promise to step down by 1963. Toward the end of his reign, the "old man" got a taste of the political restraints imposed by the less powerful leadership model that became the norm for his successors.

With the small FDP most of the time in the parliamentary position to make or break coalition governments, the three establishment parties were obliged to pursue centrist policies and settle into a consensual "party government" mode in the decades following the Adenauer era. The partisan lineup in both chambers of the federal parliament required leaders who were more pragmatic than dogmatic and politics that was more about cooperation and compromise than about conflict and confrontation. There were less opportunities for the headstrong, individualistic leadership that had been Adenauer's trademark during the 1950s. The years between 1966 and 1982, during which time CDU-Chancellor Kurt Kiesinger led a "grand coalition" between Christian and Social Democrats (1966–69), followed by coalitions between Social and Free Democrats led by Willy Brandt (1969–74) and Helmut Schmidt (1974–82), demonstrated that the once unthinkable alternatives to the original coalition between the union parties and the liberals could work.

Under control of CDU- and CSU-led state governments, the Federal Council first emerged as a potent check on the federal government and the Federal Diet during the Brandt and Schmidt years. Then the tables were turned in the post-unification years, when Chancellor Helmut Kohl's coalition of CDU/CSU and FDP was restrained by a Federal Council in which SPD-led state governments had a majority of the votes.

Yet, when policy differences arose, compromise solutions proved achievable as long as membership in the Federal Government, Diet, and Council was limited to the three establishment parties whose various coalition combinations on all levels of government attested to their abil-

ity and willingness to cooperate in times of expanding government programs. After the Greens won seats in the Bundestag and their first representation in the governing coalition of a federal state (Hesse), it remained
mostly up to the three establishment parties to iron out conflicts between
the various institutions and coalitions. The achievement of consensus
became harder when Chancellor Kohl promoted a softer version of President Reagan's and Prime Minister Thatcher's supply-side policies during
the 1980s. Still, the cooperative model remained in place because most
policy differences arose over more or less piecemeal and not drastic
changes.

In short, the "old" parties had a firm grip on the decisionmaking
process. Established party leaders controlled the federal government and
the bureaucracy, had the say in the Federal Diet, and shaped the positions
that state governments took in the Federal Council. They made and
unmade coalitions and policy. Beyond their differences and their tough
partisan rhetoric, the entrenched parties managed to get along and bolster their shared power arrangement—especially when their policymakers were led and prodded, rewarded and punished by politically astute
chancellors.

Growing Intra- and Inter-Party Divisions

On the face of it, nothing has changed in the 1990s. The established parties continue to dominate and coordinate the governmental process, but
the dynamics of internal and external party politics have undergone
transformations that threaten the tendency to compromise within and
between the governing and opposition parties. To be sure, the established
parties dealt in the past with internal policy disputes and power struggles
between different ideological factions and personalities. There were also
plenty of clashes within the governing coalitions and between government and opposition parties—many of them far more divisive in rhetoric
than in substance. But the post-reunification era has brought many conflicts and issues that transcend the usual disagreements, rivalries, and
rhetorical posturings.

First of all, financing the restructuring of East Germany and integrating 16 million East Germans into the Federal Republic's extensive socioeconomic system at a time when West Germany's industrial sector is beset
by serious problems has meant hard choices for policymakers and thus
for the major parties. Whether, to what extent, and for whom to raise

taxes and cut social programs has become a constant bone of contention. Under these circumstances it is more difficult to maintain the will to find common ground that characterized the old arrangement in the decades of economic growth, increased government spending, and expanding social programs.

Unification added another dimension to the divisions within and among the political parties: Western and Eastern leaders, rank-and-file members, and supporters of national parties often have different interests and policy preferences—and not only with respect to fiscal, social, and economic policies. The abortion issue has been a case in point: East German Christan Democrats insisted on legalized abortion as adopted in the GDR (along the line of Roe v. Wade in the United States) while their West German partisans opted for a much more restricted abortion law. When nowadays the divisions within one party are deep, party leaders show reluctance to invoke party discipline in the legislature. Intra-party East-West splits show up occasionally in debates and votes in the Federal Diet, but are more often dealt with in behind the scene clashes and transactions of parliamentary party caucuses, party leadership councils, and cabinet meetings.

Just as American parties have balanced their tickets in past presidential elections to appeal to voters in the North and the South, national parties in post-unification Germany try to find some kind of an East-West balance when nominating members for party and public offices. Still, more than half a decade after unification many East German party leaders have come to complain that they play second fiddle to West Germans who are not doing enough to overcome the "inner division" between East and West Germans. At the same time, observers have noted that eagerness to nominate East Germans can backfire and widen the gap. In 1994, for example, Chancellor Kohl's handpicked candidate for Federal President, an unknown and undistinguished minister in the Eastern state of Saxony, was forced to withdraw from consideration after he made politically insensitive statements. Even before, many influential Germans, even politicians in Kohl's own party, and a majority of the public had refused to support the Chancellor's choice.

In the Federal Council, too, East-West divisions cut increasingly across party lines. While Christian and Social Democratic national leaders have never been sure that state governments controlled by their own partisans will cast their votes along the lines of their respective central parties' positions, the potential for this sort of internal party opposition has notably increased because the old West German and the new East Germam states have frequently quite different interests.

In addition to this new East-West dimension in national politics, the reemergence of a multiparty system has added more players to lower level governments. Thus, state governments, in which one of the two large parties depends on the support of another party, may be reluctant to follow their national party leaders in the Federal Council. The dominance of and cooperation between the old, established parties seemed to suit the West German electorate in the past, when these organizations furthered the various societal interests and members and voters felt represented by the party of their choice. The political parties connected the citizenry with the state, the governed with the governors. While showing some cracks before unification, the mortar that had linked society to the political institutions has disintegrated further in the 1990s, when substantial parts of the electorate have questioned the dominant major parties and their key role in the governmental process. As a result, the political parties and the representative system have come under pressure to be more directly responsive and accountable to citizens and voters.

3

For Better or for Worse
More Participatory Democracy

June 13, 1993 was a memorable day in the annals of German politics. For the first time a major party in Germany, the SPD, had conducted nationwide caucuses in which all members were given an opportunity to vote for one of three candidates running for the chairmanship of their party. Previously, no more than ten percent of the members had been offered a say in the selection of candidates for party and public offices. This time, to everybody's surprise, more than half participated. Two weeks later, the delegates to a party congress elected as their chairman Rudolf Scharping, who had received a plurality of the membership's vote. No longer would a small group of party activists choose their party's leaders and candidates for office. In an effort to stem the alienation among members and voters of all parties, the SPD had opted for what some party leaders characterized as a first shot at American-style primaries.

Given the differences between parties and electoral systems in Germany and the United States such an analogy was misleading in many respects. Yet, it was germane nonetheless: In the United States primaries were established in response to demands for more participatory democracy and less decisionmaking by mighty party bosses—first in the Progressive era of the early 1900s and later in the Vietnam War period of the late 1960s. In post-unification Germany, the SPD caucuses of 1993 came in answer to calls for more influence and participation by rank-and-file party members and less power for party elites.

Well before the SPD became the first of the old parties to make such a change, similar reform measures had already been considered by CDU, SPD, and FDP leaders. To reform or not to reform was originally a question that elites discussed and wanted to decide. But once the SPD made the move, it was applauded as a smashing success inside and outside the party. The genie of reform was out of the bottle. Rank-and-file members considered their participation in the selection of the party chair a beginning, not a trial balloon that could be inflated or deflated at the whim of their leaders. Feeling newly empowered, they hailed the dawn of a new democratic era in their party and vowed to insist on more open decisionmaking processes.

Middle-of-the-road Social Democrats who had not attended party meetings for years returned to them. As university-educated, activist minorities with left-leaning and postmodern ideals moved into big-city politics in the 1970s and came to dominate many SPD precincts and districts, old-time members had increasingly shunned party activities because they were far less concerned with the postmaterial values of the activist cliques than with their own bread-and-butter concerns. "Caucus Sunday" convinced many that the "silent majority" still had muscle and could select candidates whose predominant concerns and values were those of most SPD members and voters. Some precincts even won new members drawn by a major party moving toward a new form of an internal democracy.

In this atmosphere, reform-minded leaders in the SPD as well as in the CDU and FDP pushed for the implementation of more and lasting changes. To this end, they revitalized proposals to expand their members' participatory role, accept provisional, non-dues-paying members, and place especially qualified nonmember candidates onto their party lists. It was also suggested that voters should elect their local officials directly and that ten percent of the electorate should have the power to initiate plebiscites on local issues. Still more progressive reformers called for national referenda on key issues, something not provided for under the principles of representative government embedded in Germany's constitution.

Whether debated by the old parties, alternative organizations, or pundits, all of these reform proposals—some more realistic than others—aimed at opening up the political process and connecting partisans with their parties, constituencies with their representatives, the governed with the governors. The entrenched establishment, although in no hurry to have its power diluted, found its hands forced by the waning popular trust in the party state and the proliferation of reform-oriented new parties. In 1994 some of the SPD's and CDU's constituency candidates for the federal diet were no longer chosen by a small clique of delegates but by rank-and-file members. The CDU's 1995 national party conference gave rank-and-file members a say in personnel decisions. In the northern city-state of Bremen, the CDU offered nonmembers the chance to participate in party deliberations for up to half a year without paying dues.

The reforms have not been limited to the selection of party leaders and candidates or to the direct election of public officials; they have extended to policy issues as well. While CDU delegates have turned down a proposal that would make the party's major policy decisions subject to a ratification vote by the membership, a trend in this direction is sought. Stung by being bolted out of thirteen state legislatures, the leaders of the Free Democratic Party were desperate for a panacea and polled party members on policy issues such as government eavesdropping in battling organized crime. Following a disappointing showing for their party in the 1995 election for the state legislature in Bremen, SPD deputies sought to please faithful supporters and win back others by surrendering to the party's rank-and-file members their right to choose coalition partners for a government.

Just as earlier reformers in the United States assumed that a more open political process would result in better government, many Germans have come to favor "bottom up" decisionmaking for the sake of more effective policies. The five eastern states and four of the eleven western *Länder* have laws for local plebiscites. While local governments in Germany have far less prerogatives than their counterparts in the United States, this is nevertheless yet another effort to get citizens more directly involved in the governmental process.

The Swelling of Non- and Swing-voters

Apart from these modest new forms of direct participation, voting has remained for most Germans the only way to make their wishes known. In the 1994 federal election about 79 percent of eligible voters cast their ballots. In the United States such a high turnout would be a stunning record since only about 50 percent of eligible voters cast their ballots in recent presidential elections and significantly fewer in off-year congressional, state, and local contests. In the past the cumbersome registration requirements in many states inhibited significant numbers of American voters from casting their ballots, but even easier registration processes have not resulted in dramatically higher turnout levels. German voters do not have to register at all to vote because every community has up-to-date residency rosters of eligible voters. Also, while many working Americans do not vote because elections are held on weekdays, Germans do not have such a problem since elections are on Sundays.

In the decades following the establishment of the Federal Republic Germans, eager to show that they were responsible citizens in their new democratic system, felt it was their duty to vote. During the 1980s the turnout began to decline in both federal and state elections. When it dropped below the 80 percent mark and to the level of the first postwar federal election in 1949 (78.5%), this was widely interpreted as an alarming manifestation of the electorate's growing dissatisfaction with the entrenched parties—most of all the CDU and SPD.

Earlier, when approximately 90 percent of the eligible voters turned out to cast their ballots, the small segment of nonvoters was seen as politically uninterested and uninformed. But when nonvoters came to constitute more than one-fifth of the electorate in federal elections and one-third in state elections in the 1990s, political observers spoke of the "party of nonvoters" that attracted well-educated, well-informed, and politically interested young and middle-aged Germans who expressed their dissatisfaction with the available choices.

Party loyalties that once tied the vast majority of the electorate to one or the other of the two principal parties has diminished steadily, a trend that parallels the increase in independent voters in the United States. Since the mid-1990s, about one out of two German voters is an independent swing-voter. Young voters, far more than the older generation, identify themselves as independents. Not surprisingly, East Germans, who have no direct experience with the western parties that have expanded into their territory, show a particular inclination for swing-voting.

In the 1990s, the vast majority of German voters characterize their political leaning as "middle-of-the-road" and support objectives that used to separate the two large parties. Most of these voters demand for example more law and order, something that was once identified mostly with the policies of the conservative CDU/CSU. But the same people also cherish the social welfare state, a position once most strongly identified with the SPD.

Just as presidential candidates of the two major parties cannot win elections without strong support from the large political middle in contemporary America, German Christian and Social Democrats are also increasingly forced to compete for support from one segment of the electorate with similar policy preferences. That is certainly one reason why the once-clear distinctions between the major parties in Germany have become fuzzy. And just as many American voters believe that it does not make much of a difference whether Democrats or Republicans capture the White House and congressional majorities, many Germans conclude that it does not matter whether Christian or Social Democrats are the major governing or opposition party. While fringe groups have looked more attractive than in previous decades, most of them are unlikely to overcome the five percent hurdle in national and state elections. At the local level, where small parties do have a better chance to win legislative seats, governments have far less authority to make a difference in constituents' lives than in the United States.

The Fading Societal Milieus

Declining party loyalty, party membership, and election turnout are at least in part the results of socioeconomic and societal changes. Over the last few decades the working class, once the backbone of the Social Democraty Party, has shrunk steadily while the middle class has grown in (West) Germany's postindustrial setting. At the same time, the number of devout Catholics, once the largest bloc among the supporters of the Christian Democrats, has decreased markedly—especially among younger and middle-aged voters who are more individualistic and less likely than the generation of their parents to join associations of any kind. The social environments surrounding labor unions and churches, which once tied most workers to the SPD and most Catholics to the CDU/CSU, have disintegrated.

Revolving around traditional associations such as community groups, adult education centers, sports clubs, and neighborhood choirs, the old milieus represented distinct interests and enabled political parties to attract members and voters with specific policies. Indeed, all of the large organized interests were closely linked to and represented by one of the established parties: the churches, their welfare organizations, and the business sector had close ties to the Christian Democrats; the labor unions and their societal-milieu organizations to the Social Democrats;

business in general but especially the medium-size, independently owned firms (the *Mittelstand*) to the Free Democrats.

In contemporary Germany the traditional parties can no longer depend as much on automatic support from the fading milieus and their institutions. While many old people maintain sentimental ties to the preferred organizations of their younger years and vote accordingly, fewer and fewer young Germans, often fiercely individualistic, get acquainted with what is left of the milieus of their parents and grandparents. Instead of joining a Catholic sports club or a labor union's youth group, today's young Germans rather buy a membership in a health club and drop into a local disco when it suits them.

In West Germany, workers are still more likely to vote for the SPD than the CDU and a majority of Catholics still votes for the CDU, while more Protestants cast their ballots for the SPD than for the CDU. East Germans do not vote along these lines. Their communist "one class society" lacked the West German types of milieus. Accordingly, voting in East Germany does not reflect the remnants of the milieu-based patterns of the West. In the 1990 and 1994 federal elections, the working class in the new federal states voted overwhelmingly for the Christian Democrats, while the Social Democratic Party drew more support from professional people. At the same time, the CDU was the predominant choice of both Catholics and Protestants in the East.

The CDU and the SPD, class or milieu parties in the past, are now catchall parties. In the mid-1990s only four out of a hundred German voters were party members. Membership in the CDU and the SPD began to erode in the 1980s and then declined much more rapidly. The CDU's Bavarian sister party CSU held on to its membership and the Greens even registered modest gains. The FDP was never a mass party and continues to enjoy the support of a relatively small circle of well-to-do members of the business community.

Membership dues help to finance the parties' organizational and promotional work, but this source of income is far less important today than it was in the past. The parties have long cooperated closely in adopting and amending laws that have assured them generous public funding for their electoral campaigns, educational activities, and administrative tasks. German taxpayers' support, for example, elaborate party foundations that sponsor research and political education at home and abroad, especially in developing countries. Following the collapse of communism, the foundations have also assisted democratic groups and parties in Eastern Europe. In the United States research foundations of various ideological and partisan leanings, such as the American Enterprise Institute or the Brookings Institution, depend instead on private-sector donations and endowments. As newcomers in the political arena, the anti-establishment Greens at first attacked the generous allocation of public funds to the CDU's Konrad-Adenauer-Stiftung, the CSU's Hanns-Seidel-Stiftung, the SPD's Friedrich-Ebert-Stiftung and FDP's Friedrich-Naumann-Stiftung. But once they also became an established party, they, too, accepted public money for their Rainbow Foundation (Stiftung Regenbogen).

Less Confidence in Politicians and Politicial Institutions

The generous disbursement of public funds to political parties is but one of the reasons for the growing public sentiment that those in charge of political institutions and organizations are more concerned with their own than with the common good. In the mid-1990s, confidence in the so-called political class was shaken, when the major parties agreed on substantial salary hikes for members of the federal Diet although the country was in a recession and faced major cuts in social programs. Here ordinary Germans seemed to be prompted by the mass media's extensive and critical reporting on the underhanded ways in which salary increases were decided.[1]

Citizens' alienation from and contempt for politicians and partisan politics was already notable in the 1970s and 1980s in the United States as well as Germany, but it has substantially increased during the 1990s. Texas billionaire Ross Perot's role during the 1992 presidential election campaign and his respectable showing at the polls reflected Americans' frustration with the political establishment. Trying to explain this degree of public discontent and even cynicism in the U.S., media critics and politicians have singled out the American mass media's propensity to dwell on public officials' and public institutions' shortcomings and failures. In the Federal Republic, where most of the political news coverage had been tame by American standards, public confidence in political institutions and public officials has decreased markedly in the 1990s in a period in which the mass media have undergone noticeable changes and moved in the direction of their American counterparts.

Germans, especially the younger generation, increasingly shy away from getting involved in political and civic activities. Major figures among Germany's political, business, educational, and media elites blame advances in communication technology and the advent of commercial television for less civic spirit and more emphasis on self-realization among Germans. Many, who for decades could only choose between the limited program offerings of two public television networks, have become "couch potatoes" since privately held TV, cable, and satellite channels offer a great variety of programs. These developments seem to follow the patterns observed in the United States earlier, when the communication revolution, with its explosion of television channels, call-in talk shows, and on-line services reduced people's need for direct personal interactions.[2]

In the last decade of the twentieth century Germans, like Americans, have the opportunity to receive far more information than ever before. But as the number of television and radio programs has multiplied— gradually in the United States and more rapidly in Germany—it has become increasingly unlikely that family members, friends, or colleagues will watch the same television program, listen to the same radio station, or participate in the same interactive communication schemes. That means less opportunity to talk about one's shared information and experience. Moreover, as more political and civic information is provided by the media and actual participation much more possible via talk television, talk radio, and computer links, citizens of the Federal Republic have less need to partake personally in the meetings and campaigns of political parties, labor unions, professional associations, churches, and hobby groups. Asked by pollsters before the 1994 federal election for the information sources that guided their voting decision, more than 80 percent of the German voters named the news media with some 50 percent singling out television.[3] Mass-mediated information and discourse have replaced first-hand information and opinion received through direct contacts with party and interest group officials or rank-and-file members.

Solid Support for Democracy

Though increasingly dissatisfied with politicians and politics, most Germans have nonetheless remained unwavering in their support of liberal democracy as the best form of government.[4] That holds true for West and East Germans.

In the early 1990s public opinion polls revealed that East Germans appreciated democratic principles far more than the people in the other formerly communist countries of central and eastern Europe. This was really not surprising in light of the official and private contacts between the two Germanys and the inability of East Germany's communist rulers to jam West German television and radio broadcasts. Many citizens of the communist German Democratic Republic had watched West German television regularly and become familiar with democracy in the West. Not to eat the forbidden fruit of Western television meant to be ignorant. East Germans secretly referred to an area along the Elbe River in the vicinity of Dresden, where Western broadcasts could not be received, as "the valley of the clueless."

After unification East Germans suddenly realized that in one respect they all had seen a make-believe world: Living in united Germany was different from what television images had led them to expect. They were faced with the discrepancy between their media perception of democracy and capitalism and the inability of political and private institutions to fulfill those high and unrealistic expectations. To be sure, dissatisfaction with the gap between democratic ideals and political reality is a common and inevitable dilemma in democracies. But whereas those who grow up in democratic settings come to understand this disparity over time, East Germans experienced the gap between the democratic ideal and reality virtually from one day to the next.

West Germans were polled frequently about their attitudes toward the democratic form of government since the fall of Nazi Germany. They were surveyed at first by American social scientists who questioned the German people's ability to become reliable democrats. According to these data West Germans became gradually more democratic in outlook during the first forty years of the Federal Republic. This change is apparent in every-day life. For West Germans who were born after the establishment of the Bonn Republic the traditional Prussian qualities of automatically deferring to anyone in authority, such as government officials, bureaucrats, teachers, or bosses, are vestiges of a past that will die with their parents' generation. The old, authoritarian traits were questioned and thrown overboard by the protest movements of the late 1960s. Like their counterparts in the United States, young West Germans, led by activist students, demonstrated against American foreign policy, mostly the Vietnam war, and for far-reaching social changes, for example, in the educational system. As a result, today's young and middle-aged Germans do not bow and scrape.

Given their country's long democratic tradition, Americans take for granted a deeply rooted societal agreement on their basic form of government. Among Germans less self-assured segments of the elite, especially intellectuals, continue to reexamine the legacy of Germany's political tradition and question the extent of Germans' devotion to democracy. This proclivity has become more prevalent since the country was reunited. Some salute this tendency to continuously scrutinize and doubt the democratic fabric as a sign of healthy vigilance against antidemocratic stirrings. Others say it arouses unnecessary anxieties, arguing along the lines of President Franklin Roosevelt's advice during the Great Depression that "the only thing we have to fear is fear itself."

In response to survey questions in the mid-1960s about their views on the health of their democratic system, West German leaders were on the whole optimistic but many qualified that the Federal Republic had not yet been confronted by a real test of its viability in the face of a crisis—most likely an economic one. Some three decades later, when united Germany experienced the most severe economic crisis since the establishment of the Federal Republic, half of its most influential leaders believed that their society had strengthened its capabilities for dealing successfully with critical problems. But this faith in the stability of the political system was still tempered by the fear that extreme parties might pose a threat to German democracy.

These kinds of fears and doubts resurfaced at a time, when the composition of West Germany's population had changed profoundly. Most West Germans living in the last decade of the century were born after the Federal Republic was established, and several millions were children when the Third Reich went down in defeat. Thus, at the end of the twentieth century most West Germans have grown up in a consciously democratic environment. But as noted earlier, some 16 million East Germans, or about one-fifth of the total population, had no personal experience with democracy when the Berlin Wall was dismantled. The same applied to several million ethnic Germans, who left the territories of the former Soviet Union, Poland, and other Eastern European countries and settled in the Federal Republic. To put this into an American perspective, one would have to imagine that one out of four U.S. citizens had no first-hand knowledge of democracy at work and that most of these Americans were residing in several economically deprived states exclusively populated by newcomers to democracy. Picturing, furthermore, that decision-makers in Washington had adopted policies whereby the rest of the nation had to make great sacrifices for the sake of the newcomers, one would certainly expect major political and socioeconomic problems and a great deal of tensions between the oldtimer "haves" and the newcomer "have-nots."

In the West's old Länder the support for democratic values has been weakest among Neo-Nazi extremists, while most of the center-left Greens and their sympathizers have endorsed the existing system and its fundamental values. In the East's new Länder the members and supporters of the Party of Democratic Socialism (PDS), the successor party of East Germany's ruling Socialist Unity Party (SED), have been less sympathetic toward liberal democracy than other East Germans. The idea of socialism has remained attractive to a majority of East Germany's population and a sizable minority among its young generation. East Germans' sympathies for the socialist ideal has remained significantly stronger in the years following unification than West Germans' sympathies for Nazism in the post-World War II era. However, most people in the East have rejected socialism as practiced in the GDR and other countries of the former Eastern bloc. There is a recognition that neither the right nor the left can offer viable alternatives to democracy and capitalism. But while supporting democracy in principle, most Eastern Germans have not been satisfied with the way democracy has worked in the Federal Republic. A solid majority of West Germans, on the other hand, continued to endorse the way democracy functioned in their country. This support weakened in the face of the lasting economic problems and the high unemployment rates of the late 1990s. By 1997 a nation-wide survey revealed, for example, that 50 percent of all Germans, 53 percent of East Germans, expressed dissatisfaction with their own democracy.

Candlelight Marches and Grassroots Power

No other age group has been as committed to democracy as Germans under thirty. According to opinion polls, young Germans feel responsible for what is happening with their country and express a willingness to support grassroots initiatives, demonstrate, and light candles in defense of democracy and democratic values.[5] When they endorse the idea of getting involved to stand up for democratic values and constitutional rights, Germans can refer to one shining example of grassroots action: Between early November 1992 and early January 1993 more than three million Germans, an average of 43,000 daily, demonstrated against xenophobia and right-wing extremist attacks on foreigners in their country. Nightly candlelight processions through the streets of dozens of large cities and small towns constituted the largest protest movement in the Federal Republic's history. In Hamburg and Munich, for example, nearly one-third of all residents heeded the appeals of a few individuals and formed "chains of light" to illuminate their fellow citizens and pressure their politicians to deal resolutely with the perpetrators of violence. The domestic mass media covered these peaceful demonstrations extensively.

The message of the silent marches was not lost on the public at large nor on the decisionmakers. Opinion polls revealed that sympathies for this sort of violence plunged precipitously once the marches began. And halfway through the wave of demonstrations the federal government abandoned its mostly passive posture and announced a "broad offensive" against political violence; several neo-Nazi groups were outlawed. When they finally acted, decisionmakers reacted to the leading German mass media, which expressed the same sentiments as the candlelight marchers, and to the international press, which paid a great deal of attention to the developments in Germany. But the marches themselves were widely recognized as the decisive factor in affecting the public and, more important, creating an overall climate of opinion that forced the government to do something.

Traditionally, apart from the act of voting, grassroots pressure in the Federal Republic has been effective only when brought into the formal political process by one of the entrenched political parties or influential factions therein. The environmental movement, for example, affected policies when the Green Party brought these issues into the formal political arena, and the large parties, first the SPD and later on the CDU as well, embraced many of its demands. In the past, simply winning the hearts and minds of the public and opinion polls did not work for grassroots activists. For many observers it is still a truism that decisionmakers in the Federal Republic are far less influenced by grassroots actions and public opinion than their counterparts in the United States—not because German politicians are more principled and guided by stronger personal convictions but because they operate in a system that ties individual politicians closely to their parties. This protects elected officials in Germany far more than their American counterparts from being personally singled out for punishment, when the next election comes around.

As an isolated case the candlelight marches could be understood as nothing more than a rare exception to Germany's representative democracy and its limited participatory features. But parallel and subsequent developments—especially the changes in party identification and voting behavior as well as the reforms in the major parties' decisionmaking processes—point not just to a desire for more openness and greater popular participation in the Federal Republic but also to more actions along those lines. These developments cannot be fully understood without considering the mass media's role in German politics.

The Mass Media and the Legacy of the Past

While the Federal Republic's constitution guarantees freedom of the press and freedom of expression, these liberties are not quite as unabridged as in the United States. In 1996, for example, a court in Hamburg sentenced the American neo-Nazi Gary Lauck to a four year prison term for smuggling neo-Nazi periodicals, such as *Nazi Battle Cry*, into Germany. In the United States the right to publish *Nazi Battle Cry* and the same type of hate literature is protected by the First Amendment. Ironically, by the time Lauck was sentenced, home pages on the Internet had become new international meeting places and resource centers for extremists. In early 1996, the managers of the T-Online service of Deutsche Telekom blocked access to the World Wide Web site of Toronto-based neo-Nazi Ernst Zündel when informed by German prosecutors that their service was being investigated for possibly assisting efforts to incite racial hatred. Though Telekom officials complained that it was impossible to check all internet pages for anti-Semitic content, they quickly moved nevertheless to prevent their more than one million German subscribers from accessing Zündel's material.

Widely reported in the United States and unimaginable in the American setting, the case did not cause a big controversy in the Federal Republic. For most Germans vigilance against extremists from the right or left of the political spectrum is part of protecting their constitutional democracy against ideas and actions that threaten the existing system of government. Thus, censorship is used to prevent the distribution of hate literature—especially if close to Hitler's infamous views. Since it is illegal to deny that the Holocaust occurred, Zündel's public claims that the genocide never took place are not protected by Germany's constitutionally guaranteed freedom of expression and freedom of the press. Leftist extremists are treated the same way. In reaction to a wave of terrorism by the Red Army Faction (RAF) and similar groups in the 1970s, West

Germany adopted federal legislation that makes the glorification of terrorist violence in the media a criminal offense.

The U.S. Congress cannot adopt laws that abridge the freedom of the press and other First Amendment rights, but German legislators can and do so in order to protect other legal rights and specific values enshrined in the German Constitution—above all the protection of the democratic order. That may be difficult to understand from the American perspective, but the Federal Republic's major parties and the majority of the populace have agreed for decades on such curbs.[6] In the past this was explained by two exceptional influences in German politics: the experience of the Weimar years, when the young democracy lacked protection against forces undermining the Republic, and West Germany's proximity to the communist bloc during the Cold War era. Both of these factors provided "a normative context for action that draws attention to internal subversion and encourages the sacrifices of some civil liberties to protect society from radical opposition."[7] With the Cold War and the Communist threat gone, the legacy of Weimar seems still strong enough to continue such curbs on democratic liberties.

Even though some of these kinds of restrictions on civil liberties clash with the global business community and especially with the nationless Internet, German authorities have tightened them, not loosened them. In the summer of 1997, after threatening several Internet access providers with legal action for not blocking access to the sites of right-wing and left-wing extremists abroad, federal officials prepared a new "multimedia" law that promised to clarify who is liable when "forbidden" material is accessible over the Internet.

The prosecutors in Bavaria did not wait for the new, tough law. They indicted the official in charge of Compuserve's German operations on charges of aiding the distribution of pornography and violent computer games by not blocking Germans from getting access to this sort of material that is illegal in the Federal Republic.

The German Mass Media

Because the print and broadcast media had been the central part of government propaganda in the Hitler era, the existing press system was dismantled when the war was over. But this did not mean that a free press could flourish. Rather, the first newspapers published in defeated Germany were licensed and censored by the victorious allies. In the western occupation zones the military governments of the United States, France, and Great Britain used censorship to assure that the press would play a vital role in reeducating Germans to become dependable democrats; in the East the Soviets presided over the birth of a press that would spread the Marxist-Leninist ideology. While the western allies discontinued their licensing requirements in 1949 and gave the green light to a free press in the Federal Republic of Germany, the German Democratic Republic's media organizations came under the control of the ruling party and organizations conforming to the ideas of the communist regime.

The Federal Republic's mass media consisted for several decades of a privately owned press (newspapers, magazines) and a public broadcasting system (radio and television). Today the press resembles in many respects the American print media. Like the U.S. the Federal Republic has a few national but mostly regional newspapers and has also experienced the "mergermania" in recent decades. Germany's radio and television system has moved more recently toward the American model, when a multitude of new private cable and satellite channels began to compete very successfully with the two public television networks.

Political parties, labor unions, churches, employers organizations, and other societal groups must by law be represented in the supervisory councils of the public broadcasting corporations. But it is the parties above all that critics such as Conrad Schnippen say control public broadcasting:

> Political parties have taken over control of state radio and TV stations in two ways. They have amended what originally were liberal broadcasting laws so often that their intervention is now the law of the land, and they have gradually transformed the representatives of the general public on broadcasting councils into party-political representatives even though they may not always have party cards in their briefcases or handbags. Legally, political parties are not allowed to nominate more than a third of the membership of broadcasting councils. In reality they usually appoint two out of three or, indeed, nearly all council members.[8]

Although privately owned channels can and do reflect partisan preferences in their programs, there is no doubt that the political parties' influence on television and radio is no longer what it was before the emergence of commercial TV and radio stations and networks. The large number of TV channels, the fierce competition between them, and possibly the diminishing influence of the political parties in broadcasting seem to be changing the role of the mass media in German politics and to be promoting the tendencies toward a more open democratic system.

Mass-Mediated Electoral Politics

Months before the Federal Assembly elected a new German president in 1994, several contenders suggested that all candidates should participate in a live television debate to demonstrate their qualifications for the nation's highest office. To American observers, accustomed to such debates during presidential, congressional, statewide, and even local campaigns, the idea seemed especially compelling at the height of an extraordinarily caustic controversy over the fitness of CDU Chancellor Kohl's handpicked choice and those of his opponents. Johannes Rau, the Social Democrats' nominee, rejected the suggestion "out of respect for the presidential office." The television discussion never materialized. But the mere suggestion that some quarters favored a face-to-face encounter before live microphones and cameras was a remarkable departure from the traditional practice of party- and elite-centered politics and a nod in the direction of mass-mediated politics as found in the United States. Given that pollsters found that a solid majority of the German populace preferred to elect their president directly instead of indirectly as the constitution prescribes, the public probably would have liked a more transparent selection process.

German elites have for quite some time commented on and complained about the country's "media democracy" (*Mediendemokratie*) or "television democracy" (*Fernsehdemokratie*). But compared to the United States, where candidates for political offices for decades have depended far more on public appeals and public approval than on their influence within their own parties, the mass media have been less crucial in affecting the fortunes of candidates in the Federal Republic. In the United States the decline of political parties and the democratization of the electoral process has elevated the media, especially television, into the role of a power-broker and middle-person between electorate and candidates. The German media have also become more important as a link between party leaders and voters in a time when party loyalty is fading, swing-voters are flourishing, and party reforms are being enacted to enhance democratic openness and participation.

Following the proliferation of the broadcast media, Germans began to enter cyberspace as well. By the mid-1990s, several on-line services were available in the Federal Republic that connected rapidly increasing numbers of Germans to the global Internet. But just as an abundance of information has not boosted political participation in the U.S. as some futurists predicted, it has not enhanced political participation and civic life in the Federal Republic. Rather, at the threshold of a new millennium, German citizens, who traditionally embrace political ideologies and joined political parties, labor unions, and other groups, have been more interested in what their country can do for them than what they can do for their country.

Accordingly, political campaigns have altered their traditional strategies and tactics. Parties and candidates in contemporary Germany can no longer aim simply at getting the party faithful to the polls but must try to win over the growing number of nonaffiliated swing voters. This cannot be accomplished by playing the party circuit but requires broader appeals through the mass media. Moreover, given the decline of the party presses in the last decades, even party members must be addressed increasingly through media outlets that claim to be nonpartisan.

The 1994 federal election campaign, more than previous contests, demonstrated the shift toward mass-mediated electoral politics in the Federal Republic. Expecting a tough competition against his Social Democratic opponent, Rudolf Scharping, Chancellor Kohl fired the opening shots of his campaign in appearances on both private and public television channels. When opinion polls signaled that the Christian Democrats' reign and Kohl's political future were in jeopardy, the champion of old-fashioned machine politics heeded his media-savvy advisers' pleas to abandon his reluctance to use the press to go public and utilize the electronic media to reach many of those voters who did not attend campaign rallies as their parents and grandparents had done.

While German voters still cast their ballots primarily for parties and not for individual candidates, they are increasingly inclined to evaluate and compare the personal attributes of top contenders. The major parties' candidates for the chancellor's office have always more or less affected the outcome of national elections, as Konrad Adenauer or Willy Brandt demonstrated. But the recent changes within the political parties and within the electorate have forced candidates, especially those on top of the ticket, more than ever to compete personally for votes. This development has been magnified by the proliferation of private cable and satellite television channels, because commercial television—far more than the nonprofit public channels that enjoyed long years of a virtual broadcast monopoly—tends to focus on entertainment and personalities rather than on issues. Also, the abundance and competition of channels and programs offer politicians unprecedented opportunities to appeal to large audiences. Not surprisingly, researchers found that voting decisions in the first all-German federal election of December 1990 were based far more on the perceived policy competence of the leading candidates, the CDU's incumbent Helmut Kohl and the SPD's challenger Oskar Lafontaine, than on the overall evaluation of parties and their programs.[9] This influence of the electronic media is likely to increase in the years to come.

Television debates between the top candidates in statewide elections have already become common events—although not very popular ones. During recent federal election campaigns the leaders of Germany's major parties have not followed the American practice of live television debates between the major presidential candidates. But it seems just a matter of time before the candidates tapped by their parties for the chancellor's office will do so—although German chancellors are elected by the federal diet and not directly by the voters. During the 1994 campaign, Chancellor Kohl and his chief challenger, Social Democrat Rudolf Scharping, appeared on many interview or town hall types of programs. Surprisingly, the Chancellor, a heavy-set man in his mid-sixties who had been uneasy in front of cameras and microphones for much of his political career, proved a far more effective communicator than Scharping, a trim man in his forties. Kohl appeared relaxed and delivered catchy soundbites, whereas Scharping seemed stiff and gave exhaustive explanations. To be sure, parties do not win or lose elections solely on the strength or weakness of their top-candidates' telegenic abilities; otherwise the Greens' Joschka Fischer or the PDS's Gregor Gysi, both far more gifted communicators than Kohl and Scharping, might have won the election. But this particular campaign revealed that substance and serious political discourse are losing ground to visual images and sound-bites.

In the United States the decline of the old political parties, the proliferation of binding primary contests, and the concurrent growth of television have shifted important political functions from the parties to the mass media, namely those of informing citizens about political matters and politicians about the electorate's attitudes. Far more than the traditional party power brokers, the media have become instrumental in the recruitment of candidates and the strategies and tactics used in campaigns. In the Federal Republic electoral politics have seemingly moved into a similar direction. While the traditional campaign tools such as posters and personal appearances in party meetings are still used, they are less important than in the past. Mass-mediated activities are moving center-stage in national and state-wide campaign strategies. Even mass-rallies and other personal encounters between candidates and voters are increasingly tailored to attract the greatest possible media attention.

This trend was evident in the 1993 campaign for the chairmanship of the SPD. The contest was especially important, because the winner would be best positioned to become the party's candidate for chancellor. The three contenders, Rudolf Scharping, Gerhard Schröder, and Heidemarie Wieczorek, held the traditional politicking in regional and local party meetings to a minimum and concentrated instead on television appearances. The highlight of this media campaign was a town hall-style meeting on "Caucus Sunday," televised live, in which party members had an opportunity to question the candidates—an event straight out of the textbook on American primaries or party caucuses.

Young and middle-aged politicians, who have grown up in the age of television, are comfortable with the electronic media and in many cases skillful in exploiting television and interactive communication technologies in ways that the party bosses of the past could not have imagined. Many, if not most former party leaders would not have made it to the top under these conditions. It is hard to say whether these technological changes hastened a massive generational change in the federal legislature in 1994, when close to one quarter of the deputies did not run for reelection. In any case, most of those who retired from the Bundestag had grown up without television and begun their political careers in the 1950s and 1960s. Most of these retirees, among them a number of former federal ministers in the cabinets of Christian Democratic and Social Democratic chancellors, gave way to babyboomers familiar with media-centered politics.

Over three decades just about every federal chancellor and his principal rivals for the office came from the statehouses of the Länder. They used their regional power bases to move into and eventually lead the central party hierarchy. Traditionally, the climb to the top took many years in the major parties—especially for those aspiring to head a state or the federal government. Since careers in elective and appointed public offices have been closely tied to a political party, only those who worked their way up through the party ranks were able to succeed. This may be one reason why Germany lacks the political family dynasties that are common in the United States. Members of a new generation of Roosevelts, Tafts, Rockefellers, Kennedys, Bushs, and others do not work for years inside their respective parties to earn nominations for offices. Like everybody else with adequate financial resources and backing, they simply establish their own campaign organization and compete in primaries. In Germany, they would have to go through what is commonly known as the *Ochsentour* and work hard for many years like an ox in their party to obtain the nomination for a public office.

However, since the parties began to provide for more female representation, women have been able to shorten and in some cases even circumvent the *Ochsentour*. So have East Germans who have moved exceptionally fast into leadership positions to give their region more representation in their party.

The road to political offices still goes through the political parties, but chances are that dwindling party membership, weakening party loyalty, increased swing voting, and the growing role of the media in election campaigns and in intraparty competitions will further diminish the need for enduring the *Ochsentour* and favor the swift rise of media-savvy newcomers who understand and exploit the shift from programmatic to personality-centered politics.

From a systematic content analysis of the 1994 federal election's campaign coverage in television news programs, daily newspapers, and weekly news magazines, one study concluded that the German media reported more extensively on the personality traits and political characteristics of the candidates than on their policy positions.[10] In this respect, campaign reporting in the Federal Republic has now much in common with the American news media's emphasis on personalities at the expense of important policy issues. The problem in both countries is not that candidates do not speak about their policy agenda but rather that the press, especially television, prefers human-interest stories and captivating visual images to complex policy discussions and "talking heads." The candidates who fail to deliver soundbites, preferably attacks on opponents, or do not play starring roles in carefully staged photo opportunities will lose ground to opponents who provide what television favors. While this tendency has not gone as far in the Federal Republic as it has in the United States, recent election campaigns have shown developments in this direction. News reporting during the 1994 federal campaign pointed to "an overall tendency of a majority of the news media to portray the two [major] candidates [Kohl and Scharping] with more negative than positive statements and evaluations."[11] Here, too, reporting in the German media was not very different from campaign coverage in the United States. One wonders whether these reporting patterns encourage certain personalities to enter the political arena and discourage others from doing so.

In the United States, paid media, especially in television and radio, make up the most costly and perhaps the most important aspect of major presidential candidates' campaigns. During the primaries and the general election campaign period from Labor Day to Election Day, television audiences are doused with short commercials and longer infomercials. In Germany television ads constitute but a tiny fraction of the massive campaign advertising in the U.S. During the Federal Republic's first national election after reunification in 1990, for example, sixty-seven campaign ads, each 2.5 minutes long, were broadcast by twenty-one parties with the CDU and SPD airing eight each.[12] Unlike in the United States, where each candidate's paid air time depends on the size of his or her campaign chest, German parties, not individual candidates, are allotted a modest amount of airtime according to their electoral strength in the previous election.

Since these campaign spots are considered a public service aimed at informing the citizenry, the two public television networks and their regional channels are required to provide legal political parties with free airtime. Only the city-states of Berlin and Bremen are without such requirements. Private channels, too, must set aside "appropriate broadcast time" for parties to air campaign ads before federal elections. Depending on its strength in the preceding election, a party receives three, six, or twelve minutes airtime on each of the nationwide private channels. The question of how much money parties must pay for the placement of their spots has been an issue for several years with the going rate about 50 percent of a channel's usual rates for commercials.

Both the limited television advertising in German campaigns and the plentiful campaign spots and infomercials in the United States have had one common trait: their negative bent. But unlike American attack ads that typically feature in more than three-fourths of all cases anonymous announcers, German candidates themselves go on the attack in about two-thirds of the campaign spots.[13]

Leading and Following Public Opinion

With the weakening of traditional party-centered power sources, public opinion has become more influential. Unlike modern U.S. presidents who have relied heavily on enlisting the American public's support in order to realize their political agenda, German chancellors have not spent a great deal of time and effort to lead and shape public opinion. While recent American presidents have not only utilized prime time TV addresses to the nation and press conferences but also electronic town hall meetings to directly ask the public to tell their senators and representatives to vote for important presidential programs, recent chancellors have continued to rely mostly on bargaining in their own party, in their cabinet, and with leaders of the opposition and major interest groups—just as earlier presidents used to strike their deals with the congressional leadership and other influentials in the Washington community. It is true that a contemporary U.S. president must also bargain with congressional leaders, but both presidents and legislators do so with their eyes on the latest public opinion polls.

So far, German leaders are not as obsessed with and dependent on opinion survey or focus group results as are American politicians. But as party membership and loyalty has declined and unity within and between parties has been harder to come by, leaders have looked increasingly to public opinion as a means to get their way with fellow partisans and political foes. Even an old-style party politician like Helmut Kohl, though not embracing opinion-leadership like Ronald Reagan and Bill Clinton, was eventually persuaded by his advisers to use a bimonthly question-and-answer session with friendly journalists on a private TV channel to "go public." By the time of the 1994 election year, Kohl had become a frequent and effective guest on all kinds of programs in both private and public television.

Some observers of the German political scene continue to deny that public opinion affects decisionmakers; they point to the differences between day-to-day public opinion polls and the climate of opinion arguing that the latter entails a much broader spectrum of views that includes elites in media, business, universities, and interest groups. If anything, they argue, the climate of opinion, not opinion polls, affects decisionmaking. But just as public opinion polls have mushroomed and become influential in American politics, there has been a comparable proliferation of survey organizations and greater attention to poll results in Germany as well. As in the United States, the leading newspapers, news magazines, and public and private television channels in the Federal Republic have formed partnerships with survey organizations.[14] Many of the polls are tailored to journalistic needs and preferences and may not always contribute to a better understanding of the underlying trends in public attitudes beyond the short-term ups and downs that make for interesting reporting. Moreover, the political parties themselves and/or their think-tanks also commission opinion polls.

If the developments described in this and the previous chapter continue, it seems simply a question of time until German leaders, especially chancellors, will increasingly follow the example of American leaders, especially presidents, in utilizing the electronic media to lead public opinion and enlist public support on a regular basis—especially in the face of pressing problems that call for decisive policy responses.

American politicians have come to appreciate media platforms. President Bill Clinton answers questions on the "Larry King Live" call-in television program; members of congress respond to their constituents on public access cable channels; and governors and mayors take part in radio call-in shows. In the Federal Republic, leading politicians as well as backbenchers also have come to recognize the value of direct communication with their constituents between as well as during election campaigns. In late 1993, for example, the federal Diet invited citizens for the first time to partake in several extended call-in sessions during which some forty members of the Bundestag answered questions over the telephone. The print media also organizes frequent "citizens ask—politicians answer" call-in programs. Invitations to such programs are issued to and eagerly accepted by politicians on all governmental levels as welcome opportunities to communicate with the citizenry.

In Germany, as in the United States, adversarial and symbiotic relationships between politicians and the press have long existed side by side. As television has expanded and the news media begun to compete with political parties as the major linkage between state and society, politicians have increasingly exploited this medium. But they have also come to resent what they perceive as superficial and one-sided news reporting that in their view damages the reputation and weakens the effectiveness of political leaders both in the domestic and international arena.

In Germany, conservatives resent the "liberal opinion makers in Hamburg," where the weeklies *Der Spiegel, Die Zeit,* and *Stern* are headquartered, just as their American counterparts criticize what they perceive as a liberal media elite located in the country's Northeast (head-quarters of the major television networks as well as *The New York Times*, and *The Washington Post*). And German liberals feel indignant about conservative publishers and editorial writers of publications such as the *Frankfurter Allgemeine Zeitung* and *Focus* just as American liberals dislike the influence of *The Wall Street Journal's* editorial writers and other conservative media voices. In comparison to the Weimar Republic era, when about half of the daily newspapers were openly partisan,[15] party presses are not important factors in contemporary Germany. Subscriptions for once viable and influential publications of political parties, labor unions, and churches, have greatly declined; many have been forced to fold. The leaders of the large parties, unions, and of the churches must therefore rely more on the mass media to communicate with their members. At the same time, the viability of pressure groups has been enhanced by the growth of special-interest publications, special-interest radio and television programs, and, more recently, special-interest Internet sites. Since these media tend to cater to rather narrow interests, they could increasingly hinder the major parties' ability to incorporate all relevant societal interests under their respective umbrellas.

The progressive concentration of ownership that began in West Germany's print media long before unification (five publishing houses account for more than 40 percent of the daily newspaper circulation, four corporations for two-thirds of the circulation of general-interest magazines) expanded rapidly to the broadcasting sector when private television and radio became major factors in the 1990s. In the United States, media experts have pointed critically to the actual and potential consequences of leaving the control over the mass media to a few mega corporations and their bosses. In Germany just a few media giants also control the lion's share of the market, especially television. Germany is the largest European media market and second only to the United States in terms of TV advertising revenues. Given the restricted advertising time on the two public television channels, ARD and ZDF, and their shrinking audiences, private television channels are the beneficiaries. The three leading private TV channels—RTL, Sat 1, and Pro 7—collect more than three-fourths of the total TV advertising revenue. And only a few groups dominate the television market; one is led by the Munich media tycoon Leo Kirch, who also owns more than a third of the Axel Springer Verlag, the country's largest publisher of newspapers and magazines; another is controlled by an alliance between the mighty Bertelsmann publishing empire and CLT, a Luxembourg broadcasting company. Through joint ventures large foreign media organizations such as France's pay-TV leader Canal Plus and Rupert Murdoch's Sky Broadcasting, headquartered in Britain, have gained access to the German market. The bottom line is that private television, even more than the print media, is dominated by a handful of media-giants that compete fiercely for market shares.

The unification of the two Germanys made the media monopolies even more powerful. In spite of Western promises to transform East Germany's once government-controlled press into a free marketplace of ideas with many independent owners, the West German media conglomerates quickly became the dominant players in the eastern part of the country, providing the bulk of the much needed capital for the modernization of antiquated press operations. East Germans resent these developments to this day.

Pointing out that media power means political power, the American media expert Benjamin Bagdikian has warned that most mega-corporations in control of large shares of the media market "assert that they would never use their power for selfish purposes. But no corporation, media and otherwise, will fail to use its power if it feels a threat to its future or to its profits."[16] Writing of similar developments in the Federal Republic, one German media expert has noted, "As soon as several newspapers are published by a single publishing house, there is a risk that they may one day be subject to a single will, that of the publisher."[17] With respect to television some media experts in the United States have suggested that more public TV is needed to counter the uniformity and excesses of commercial television and assure quality and diversity in programming. In the contemporary German setting this would mean that public television channels should offer quality programs and thereby influence the programming of commercial television for the better. In reality, however, Germany's public television seems more influenced by private channels than the other way around—if only to survive in the fierce competition for viewers and survival. While political news is still provided mostly by public television and broadcasting, these channels lose ground to privately owned competitors.

In the mid-1990s, when private television had become firmly established, the Christian Democrats and their leaders intensified their attacks on the ARD, the first public television network with autonomous stations in the various federal states. Depending on the makeup of the government in a given state, the board and top managers of the public broad-casting station in that state have been closer to one or the other of the two major political parties. Since many of the political programs origi-nate in states traditionally ruled by Social Democrats or coalitions led by the SPD (the WDR in North Rhine-Westphalia, the NDR in Hamburg), conservative forces have launched campaigns to curb the fiscal resources and thus the staffs and programming capabilities of the public stations. These threats to tighten the purse-strings are driven by similar motives as the threats by conservatives in the U.S. Congress to shrink federal appro-priations for public radio and public television because of their perceived liberal bias. In the Federal Republic, unlike the United States, the defend-ers of the state-based public broadcasting system possess a formidable weapon to counter such attacks in that the governments in the federal states can withdraw their support for the ZDF, the second public nation-wide television channel. Given the long periods of CDU/CSU/FDP gov-ernments on the national level, the ZDF's programming has traditionally been perceived as more in tune with the Christian parties' politics and policies. Since media matters are, however, the domain of the states, the fate of the two public television channels are closely tied together.

Apart from this ideological infighting, which indicates an understand-ing of the broadcast media's influence, critics of public television point to the high cost of financing the ten broadcasting stations of the ARD and the national ZDF. Even though Germans have always paid monthly fees for the right to receive over-the-air radio and television, several ARD sta-tions as well as the second public television channel have frequently spent more than their share of the monthly fee income.[18] Private television and radio, on the other hand, do not receive a share of the mandatory broad-cast fee but depend on advertising income for their increasingly prof-itable operations or, in the case of private pay-TV channels, on user fees as well.

Since the advent of television, radio has been the forgotten medium as far as the experts are concerned. Most German and American communi-cation researchers have consistently concentrated on television and the print press while ignoring radio. However, the older medium has retained significant and faithful audiences in both countries, and not only among commuters who listen to their car radios. In Germany, for example, *Radio NRW* in the most populated state of North Rhine-Westphalia (ca. 18 million inhabitants) reaches about one million listeners during any given hour. Since the prohibition against private broadcasting was repealed, a growing number of local radio stations have emerged—many of them with local governments as part-owners. These stations have increasingly provided the glue that ties citizens to their local communities and regions far more than to their country as a whole or to the European Union. In this respect, local radio has reinforced the subsidiary principle of the European Union which leaves many matters to localities and regions rather than to national governments.

The New Media: Problems and Opportunities

Led by Ross Perot, all candidates in the 1992 U.S. presidential election came to appreciate the so-called new media, the television and radio talk shows that allowed direct exchanges with studio or call-in audiences. This effectively bypassed political journalists as expert intermediaries or filters. A growing number of German politicians have also come to value appearances on talk shows that shelter them from probing and provoking questioning by political journalists and allow them to address audiences that they otherwise would not reach. Lashing out at what they label "talk show democracy," German critics blame the media for facilitating a new political arena that they expect will further deteriorate the level of political discourse and the quality of information the public receives. But the American experience in the 1992 campaign and the subsequent practices to utilize the new media for political discourse (i.e., Vice President Al Gore and Ross Perot in a call-in talk show debate about the complex North American Trade Agreement, President Clinton's repeated electronic town hall meetings to discuss his health care reform plan) have shown that these formats can be skillfully used to inform the public and involve citizens in policy debates. Germany's public television, which commands a significantly larger audiences than public television in the United States, seems especially suited for substantive mass-mediated debates.

So far the trend is in the other direction. Thus, the appetite of a growing number of talk show hosts to offer their audience infotainment with guests from all walks of life and the changing nature of party and electoral politics have induced leading politicians increasingly to present themselves more as entertaining personalities and likeable human beings than as astute politicians. But as one of the most promising and most popular German politicians of the 1990s learned the hard way, cultivating this sort of media image is not without risks. SPD-star Gerhard

Schröder, the head of government in the state of Lower Saxony and a man perceived widely as a future candidate for the chancellor's office, had successfully integrated his attractive wife into his election campaigns and his reign at home. While he was a firm advocate of pro-business policies, she was an articulate voice for the cause of environmental protection. Together the attractive couple played the television talk-show circuit like no other husband-wife team in German politics. When the seemingly happy twosome separated in early 1996 after he reportedly found another, considerably younger love interest, the solid wall that had long separated the German media's reporting on politicians' public and private lives, came tumbling down. In what was for Germany an unprecedented "feeding frenzy," the media reported this saga extensively and prominently—even getting husband and wife to tell their sides of the story for mass publication.[19]

In this particular case, the politician, who had regularly used the media and his private life to further his political ambitions, removed the traditional demarcation line between public and private sphere, when it helped his cause. This made it easy for the media to change their long-standing rules of the game. In the U.S., the feeding frenzy mentality of the mass media and the press's appetite for scandals and character issues in the political realm dates back to the post-Vietnam and Watergate era, when Americans felt betrayed by their political leaders and took greater interest than before in the personal attributes and flaws of public officials. In the Federal Republic, the hands-off stance of the media with respect to the private lives of politicians survived far longer. Just as members of the predominantly male Washington press corps at one time did not dream of reporting the private escapades of presidents and other leaders, the German press ignored or undercovered these sorts of happenings for a long time.

As German politicians emulate American politicians' eagerness to appear on all sorts of television shows, even at the expense of baring their private personas, the boundaries between public and private lives will fade for the general public as well as for the media. As a consequence, American-style sensationalism may become more familiar in the German setting and contribute to the public's cynical view of politics as it is believed to have in the United States.

In spite of remaining differences that characterize the political role of the mass media in Germany and in the United States, many of the changes and trends in the Federal Republic described in this chapter move in the direction of earlier developments in the U.S. As the American example demonstrates, a shift toward media-centered politics offers political elites and citizens ample opportunity to communicate with and sometimes even understand each other. But the mass media's reporting formats are more likely to trivialize politics and politicians and magnify the public's negative and cynical view of the governmental process and the political class.

In the American experience the moves toward greater mass participation, whether in the candidate-selection process through primaries or the use of referenda to settle policy issues, combined with a more prominent role of the media in politics, has not necessarily resulted in better candidates, better officeholders, or better policies. There is no reason to believe that these sorts of developments in Germany, if more than a passing fancy, will fare better than earlier developments and changes in the United States. Still, opening up the political process and involving more citizens promises, if nothing else, a healthy democratic relief for people who might otherwise look for more ominous alternatives to get rid of their frustrations. And this may enhance the legitimacy of political leaders, parties, and other institutions as they try to cope with Germany's formidable problems in the years to come.

PART TWO

Problems, Issues, and Prospects

4

The Impact of Societal Change

Most American visitors get their initial impression of Germany in Frankfurt-on-the-Main when coming into the city from its vast modern airport. Huge office towers line the horizon, high-rise hotels and sleek apartment houses abut on tree-lined avenues, and fancy shops, restaurants, and discos cater to expensively dressed customers. Farther out are plush suburbs where some of Germany's many millionaires have their villas and mansions, and pleasant residential communities where commuting office workers live in comfortable homes surrounded by carefully tended gardens.

Tourists who arrive by train get quite a different picture when they emerge from Frankfurt's ancient railroad station. Here the streets are lined with rather dreary-looking department stores and office buildings and jammed with cars and delivery trucks. In crowded fast-food eating establishments, coffee bars, and subway stations people speak German with an accent, or converse in another language entirely. The curious visitor will learn that four out of ten Frankfurters are not citizens of the Federal Republic, though they may have lived there all their lives. The people who reside in the city's more modest apartment houses and the children that go to its schools are largely foreigners, especially Turks.

Of course, such first impressions are bound to be superficial. They provide a glimpse of the social diversity of modern Germany, but give little or no idea of how much life in Frankfurt and the country beyond has changed since the early years of the Federal Republic.

Much of Frankfurt had been leveled by American bombs in the Second World War. The remnants of its residential areas were for the most part either barely habitable or taken over by the American occupation forces. Until mass transportation facilities were patched together again, tens of thousands of so-called expellees from lands that were no longer German spent long, weary hours bicycling between jobs in the city and "temporary" quarters with few amenities in surrounding towns and villages where they were not welcome. For more than a decade most people did not have the money to buy a car and the household appliances that were standard equipment in the homes of the American military stationed in the Frankfurt area. In the false hope that Frankfurt and not Bonn might become the capital of the new German Federal Republic, the city government for some time did little to advance reconstruction. Enterprising real estate speculators, however. bought up empty lots and burned-out ruins on the cheap, in the expectation of far-reaching socioeconomic changes in Frankfurt, as in the rest of German society.

After the end of the hierarchical Nazi system it seemed for a time that profound changes in Germany's political order might be accompanied by equally basic changes in its social order. A return to a pre-Nazi past of deep social and cultural cleavages and a ruling class of landed aristocrats and captains of industry was out of the question in both parts of the now divided country. The new rulers in the East held that their authoritarian political system would produce an egalitarian Communist society. Those in the West argued, more successfully, that the development of a modern capitalist market economy would bring Germans economic and social democracy along with political democracy. In the Federal Republic of the mid-1950s a leading sociologist saw "a far advanced breakdown of social distinctions." And three out of four people in a 1958 public opinion poll said that that a capable child of poor parents faced no serious obstacles to social advancement.

In those early years of the Federal Republic most of its citizens resided in small towns and rural areas. Only a third lived in cities with a population of more than 100,000—such as Frankfurt—where politics and lifestyle tended to be less conservative. Close to half of employed West Germans—mostly men—were blue-collar industrial workers who usually belonged to a labor union and voted for the Social Democrats. The Christian Democrats and smaller conservative parties got far more support among the 20 percent or so of the voters who were in white-collar occupations, especially from professional people and businessmen. And they got just about all of the votes of the some 10 percent who were self-employed farmers and fishermen and belonged to the exceptionally powerful and effective "Green Front" of German agricultural interest groups.

A university education was just about mandatory if one wanted to make a career in government and politics, but not many people had one. Compared to their contemporaries in the United States, most West Germans had relatively little schooling in basic academic subjects. Less than two out of ten (16%) had more than the traditional eight years of elementary education and and only a privileged few (4%)—almost all of them men—had secondary school degrees that allowed them to get a higher education.

There were, however, ever more obvious indications that West Germany was turning into a modern country quite unlike the old Germany. By the early 1960s Frankfurt had its first high-rise office tower for all sorts of new commercial establishments, its first traffic jams in streets cleared of wartime rubble, and its first Turkish "guest workers" in jobs and in debilitated housing that were no longer good enough for the locals. Here and elsewhere it was becoming evident that West German society was fast changing under the impact of dynamic technological and economic developments and transformative public policies.

A modernization process that had taken many decades in twentieth-Century America was compressed into a comparatively brief period. Rural communities were absorbed into metropolitan areas and transformed into suburban bedroom communities. Average levels of education and income went up and average working hours went down. People quit farming for better paying positions in the cities. Fewer young people took traditional blue-collar jobs in mining and heavy industry, and more went into white-collar office and professional work.

Within twenty years of the establishment of the Federal Republic the differences in the living standards of its citizens had become far less polarized than among Americans. Fewer people were wealthy enough to live in luxury and and practically no West German lived in abject poverty. In the new affluent mass-consumption society more ordinary people could buy goods and services at prices they could afford. One no longer had to be very rich to afford a car for pleasure driving and to vacation on sunny beaches in foreign lands. Occupational, residential, and income distinctions that colored politics in the early postwar years were no longer particularly important by the 1970s. Polls showed that eight out of ten voters considered themselves neither working class nor upper class but middle class in their lifestyle, and neither left nor right but centrist in their politics.

This leveling of social distinctions became clearer as the West German baby-boomer generation that is now preeminent in public affairs came of voting age.[1] In the 1970s and 1980s studies of this age group showed a diversity in life styles and political concerns that were both cause and consequence of the erosion of intimate social ties among West German family, work, and neighborhood groups. Thanks to reforms that provided young people in the new Federal Republic with more schooling under a more open system of free public education, these West German baby boomers have on the whole been far more evenly educated than were their elders.[2] They were spared both the socioeconomic and cultural segmentation of West German society that had existed before their time and the political stratification of East Germans society under of Communism.

In the years leading up to unification the Federal Republic's political life increasingly reflected these dynamics of social change. In West Germany the old ideological left-right distinctions between political parties became increasingly meaningless with the emergence of a socially less polarized electorate. The programs and policies of the major contenders for governmental power, the Christian and the Social Democrats, grew more alike as both parties reached for the vital center. The CDU relied less on the loyal support of conservative farmers, shopkeepers, and old-line civil servants and more on socially more progressive business managers and professional people. The SPD changed from a narrowly based blue-collar working-class party into a broadly based social-reform party that appealed especially to well-educated baby boomers in white-collar public service jobs, such as teachers and social workers. Traditional pressure groups of declining social groups like the Green Front of the farmers lost while modern social movements like the environmental Greens gained influence in electoral politics.

That was before unification. Social changes that came in its wake have not been as smoothly accommodated in politics. Previously established patterns of voting and governing were unsettled by the sudden expansion of German society from less than sixty to more than eighty million people and by the social impact of economic changes.

More than twenty percent of the eligible voters in the 1994 elections were newcomers to the Federal Republic, accustomed to the totalitarian politics of Communist societies and unfamiliar with West German ways.

Some of these new citizens were so-called *Aussiedler*, people of German ancestry from Russia and Eastern Europe, but most were East Germans. And about one in four voters in the new states supported the Party for Democratic Socialism (PDS), the post-unification version of their former ruling party.

As we noted earlier, unification caused severe socioeconomic dislocation in the new parts of the Federal Republic. It suddenly took East Germans out of a tightly organized and sharply segmented collectivist order and thrust them into a far less politicized and polarized open society. This produced new social divisions. On the one hand there were the East Germans who managed to improve or, at least maintain their social position under the new conditions, on the other there were those who found themselves diminished in status because they were unemployed, unemployable, or forced into premature retirement.

Under the Communist regime social position was determined by a job outside the home. Just about everybody who was not too young or too old to be gainfully employed had an occupation and people who did not were considered social outcasts. When unification cost particularly women and older people their jobs, it also deprived them of social status.

The once privileged few at the top of the steep Communist social pyramid fell the farthest. In the days of the German Democratic Republic the vast majority of East Germans were just rank-and-file members of its hierarchical organizations and no more than one out of ten belonged to the ruling establishment. After unification former senior government and party officials, high-ranking military and police officers, leading university professors, and industrial managers were reduced to living on modest incomes from pensions or private employment. Most of the top positions in the flattened-out social pyramid of postunification East Germany went to West Germans.

Unemployment has been higher and average income lower in East than in West Germany, but pronounced differences in the overall social structure of the new and the old parts of the Federal Republic have been waning. One notable exception is the rapid growth of a substantial propertied upper middle class in the West but not East. That social gap could turn out to be politically troublesome should it persist. After more than forty years of Communism relatively few East Germans own a business, a home, or similar capital assets. In contrast, West Germans are to an increasing extent private property owners with a stake in public policies that affect the value of their holdings.

A redistribution of wealth from the richer to the poorer held more attraction for West Germans when most had little or none of their own than when East Germans and foreigners wanted them to share what they had come to possess. In 1949, when the Federal Republic was born, its citizens had for the most part lost what property they had once owned when it was destroyed during the war, or left behind in flight from former German territory in Eastern Europe, or wiped out by a drastic postwar currency reform. Middle-class status and middle-class politics were consequently based not so much on what people owned but on what they earned.

Property ownership has came to count a good deal more as it proliferated among ordinary West Germans as never before. Rising earnings and lower living costs, along with government policies promoting savings and investments, enabled people in all walks of life to become members of a new propertied middle class in the pre-unification era. Unification created a new socioeconomic division between the many middle-class West Germans with capital assets and the many East Germans with none. Baby boomers in the West, but not in the East, have been enriched by savings accounts, homes, and other capital assets left to them by their elders in the largest and most widespread harvest of inherited wealth in German history. Middle-class West Germans have had the money that middle-class East Germans do not have to buy real estate properties and business establishments of the former Communist state at bargain rates.

Unification has in effect accelerated the pace of socioeconomic changes that were already under way in West Germany when East Germany came into the Federal Republic. Structural adjustments of the economy to global competition have provided properly trained and well-connected young Germans in particular with new opportunities for social advancement through careers in the private sector. But there were also many redundant managers and technicians who have found themselves downgraded, dismissed, and prematurely retired along with industrial and office workers whose skills were devalued by economic and technological developments. In this as in other respects, German society has gone through similar changes as American society—with uncertain political consequences.

Church, Faith, and Politics

Every Saturday evening, the state-owned radio and television stations in the Federal Republic provide Germans with a "Word for Sunday" by a

Protestant minister or Catholic priest. These mini-sermons come to them as a public service of the religious establishment. Traditionally, the Protestant Evangelical Church and the Roman Catholic Church are the only organizations in German society—aside from the small Jewish community—that are by law provided, free of charge, with "adequate" time and staff positions for regular broadcast productions of their own. And though the audience has been getting smaller these denominational programs have not, for they are sustained by institutional arrangements between church and state and not by popularity ratings.

In contemporary German politics religious beliefs play a much smaller role and religious institutions a much greater one than in American politics. Church and state are not strictly separated in the Federal Republic. Whereas the American Constitution forbids any law "respecting the establishment of religion," the German maintains a traditional *Staatskirchenrecht* that gives the Protestant and Roman Catholic Church exceptional legal privileges at every level of government. Under constitutional provisions taken word for word from the Weimar Constitution of 1919, they remain "corporate bodies under public law . . . as they have been heretofore." What that means, in effect, is that they are in general ways subject to the constitutional authority of the state—like other private social institutions—and in particular ways entitled to special support and protection from the state.[3]

Unlike America's numerous independent churches, Germany's two established churches have not been financially dependent on voluntary donations from private sources and need not compete for them. Government funding and a special church tax that the state levies on their members have made them the richest churches in the world. And in Germany religious instruction in the public schools is not unconstitutional, as in the United States. In most of the states (Länder) it constitutes a regular part of the curriculum for Protestant and Catholic children.

Whereas in the United States church membership is entirely a private matter, it is first and foremost a matter of public record in the Federal Republic. Germans do not just join their Protestant or Catholic Church, but are officially joined to it with an entry in the public register when they are born and baptized. Thereafter they remain members of record for the rest of their lives if they do not take the trouble to opt out as required by law.

By that count most everybody was officially a member of one of the two established Christian churches before Germany was divided and then in West Germany. In contemporary Germany the two churches take in about seven out of ten people. Close to half belong to the Roman Catholic Church—more than twice the proportion of Catholics among professed Christians in the United States—and the rest are practically all members of the Protestant Evangelical Church.

Between them the two churches constitute a vast religious establishment that pays no property taxes and employs far more persons than any other private employer in the Federal Republic. They alone are exempt from German labor laws. People who work for them are not, like other employees, entitled to organize, to strike, or to participate in decisions that affect their working lives.

Federal, state, and local government agencies are required by law to deal with established church authorities not only on strictly religious matters, but also on a wide range of public policy issues. On the national level the Federal Ministry for Family, Women, Youth, and Senior Citizens thus consults the religious establishment on all sorts of social legislation. In the Länder, state departments for education and culture work more or less closely with one or both churches in running Germany's public schools and broadcasting stations. And at the local level, governments that want to set up and operate new hospitals and other publicly funded social service facilities cannot proceed unless and until local church authorities have declined to do it.

The religious establishment, like the political and economic establishment, owes its prominence in public affairs more to its institutionalized position in the constitutional order than to the mass support of devoted followers. In the Federal Republic organized religion is far less highly esteemed than in the United States.[4]

Germany has become a pagan country with some Christian remnants, according to *Der Spiegel*, a leading news magazine.[5] Its people are certainly no longer as devout as they used to be and as Americans still are. Surveys show that over recent decades— especially since reunification brought in millions of irreligious East Germans—the number who take their religion seriously has drastically declined, particularly among members of the Protestant Church.[6] Compared to the United States, relatively few people now attend church services regularly.[7] Most do not go at all, or only occasionally at Christmas and Easter time and for baptisms, weddings, and funerals. And as it has become socially more acceptable and legally easier for nominal members to leave their church, more and more West Germans have disaffiliated and therefore, like the many East Germans who never joined, need not pay an additional 9 percent church tax on top of rising income taxes.[8]

Devotion to Christian principles used to matter a great deal more in German politics than is the case now. Politicized religious differences between Protestant and Catholics that went back to the wars of the Reformation in the sixteenth century still played a part in the destabilizing party conflicts that promoted the Nazi rise to power in Weimar days. These denominational differences all but vanished under the emphatically un-Christian and, in some ways, decidedly anti-Christian dictatorship of Adolf Hitler.

Hitler's anti-Semitic racial laws made a mockery of Christian baptism by including not only Jews, but also converts and Germans with Jewish ancestors. And his systematic extermination of "inferior" people began with the murder of Christian children in religious institutions for the mentally retarded. In contrast to the cowed leaders of their respective churches, some Protestant and Catholic clerics and laymen were moved by their religious convictions to speak out against the Nazi regime and then met like-minded Christians of the other faith in prisons and concentration camps. Others came together in the small interdenominational groups that conspired against Hitler to bring an end to a catastrophic war. Less active anti-Nazi Protestants and Catholics found common ground in shared Christian beliefs that enabled them to withstand the ideological appeals and pressures of the Nazi system.

Surviving members of these groups were encouraged by the American occupation authorities to take leading roles in the post-Nazi political reconstructions of West Germany. The Roman Catholic Konrad Adenauer thus became the first and long-time Chancellor of the Federal Republic and his Protestant Minister of Economics, Ludwig Erhard, gained fame as the principal architect of the West German "economic miracle" of the 1950s.

Adenauer, Erhard, and other influential members of the Roman Catholic and Protestant Churches were founders of the Christian Democratic Union and its Bavarian affiliate, the Christian Social Union. Both were to be something entirely new in German politics, an interconfessional "Christian" party that was not tied to a particular religious, social, or economic group but committed to adhere to ecumenical "Christian" principles. And that proved to be a very successful formula for holding a "Union" of disparate regional parties together and winning it votes in predominantly Catholic as well as Protestant areas. For about two or three decades what distinguished the CDU/CSU from more emphatically secular West German parties in the minds of its socially quite diverse supporters was its broad-gauged, but explicit commitment to interdenominational "Christian" values.

The so-called high C note on the political scale sounded by the Christian Democrats in those years fell upon the receptive ears of a German electorate that was then far more devout than the present one. Coming as it did just after the Nazi regime, the new emphasis on common Christian values evidently met a need among many West German voters for spiritual sustenance, as they struggled to rebuild their lives during the first decades of the postwar era. The Christian Democrats' most constant supporters at the time came from the same social groups as the West Germans who attended religious services most faithfully—notably Roman Catholics, women, and residents of small towns and rural areas. Particularly for these people the Christian values proclaimed by the Catholic and, to a lesser extent, the Protestant clergy implicitly, if not explicitly, favored a vote for the CDU/CSU.

These days the electoral appeals of the Christian Democrats no longer sound a high "C."[9] The encapsulated social setting of the small towns and villages in predominantly Roman Catholic regions that used to produce their most devoted supporters no longer exists. Contemporary German politicians are much less concerned with voters' religious convictions than are their American counterparts. True, a professed atheist is still no more likely to be elected to a high political position in Germany than in the United States; and in the old West German parts of the Federal Republic—especially in the heavily Roman Catholic regions of the Rhineland and Bavaria—candidates for public offices find it useful to be considered church members in good standing.[10] But in most places they are more likely to lose than to gain popular favor by quoting scripture, leading public prayers, and courting prominent members of the clergy. In contrast to the well organized and militant activists of the "Christian right" in American politics, devout German Protestants and Catholics are not given to engaging in collective political actions on behalf of conservative Christian social values.

On the whole the clergy have become far less outspoken on political issues than was the Catholic Church especially for decades in West Germany and the Protestant more briefly in East Germany as the center of popular opposition to a disintegrating Communist regime. And the religious establishment has been losing battles in the legislative arena as its ability to sway voters has waned. Strong opposition from Protestant and Catholic bishops in recent years could not prevent the enactment of new state laws that did away with their denominational schools as well as new federal laws that have made it easier to disaffiliate from their churches, to get a divorce, and to obtain an abortion.[11]

This loss of clerical clout was demonstrated not long ago in a fight over public holidays. Almost all public holidays in the Federal Republic come on religious holidays of the two established churches. Easter and Whitsun (Pentecost) Sunday as well as Monday are, along with Christmas, federal holidays. In the states more Protestant and Catholic holidays add to the number of such "legally protected days of rest from work and of spiritual edification," as the Weimar Constitution put it and the Basic Law kept it. That means that on such days—as on every Sunday—schools, offices, and factories must stay closed, commercial trucking must keep off the roads, and public services must operate on holiday schedules. People with jobs get a day off without loss of pay, but also without the benefits of American-style holiday sales and shopping since the stores are closed. And though about a third of the population are not even nominal Christians, the Protestant and Catholic clergy maintain that this public observance of their holidays is a sacrosanct German tradition.

That view was challenged in 1994 when a new federal law required the states to strip one church holiday of its legal status. One paid holiday less a year for their employees was to compensate employers for their contributory payments to new federally mandated nursing care insurance. That pleased business leaders who refused to shoulder the burden alone, labor leaders who objected to any reduction in paid vacation and sick days, and political leaders wanting to take credit for a popular new entitlement program.

Clerical leaders, however, were anything but pleased. They could not prevent this solution to a political deadlock to begin with and then were dismayed by the public spectacle of an unprecedented debate in the media on the comparative monetary cost of their holidays for the German economy. As one prominent Protestant clergyman had it, this slighted and degraded the true quality of public religious holidays that were a "precious cultural possession of the German people." And with "industrialists and other interests" opposing the legal sanctity of Sundays and other church holidays on economic grounds he feared that more would be sacrificed.[12] That may well be so. Powerful German business leaders hold indeed that the economy can no longer afford so many mandatory holidays in the name of religion, and the religious establishment does not appear to have the power to stop them.

The pressure for economic readjustments in a less religious society is pushing the clerical establishment into new fights against new adversaries on new battlegrounds. For much, perhaps even most, of the remaining political power of the churches comes from their key roles as surrogates of public authorities in the welfare state under attack from business leaders. A substantial part of the state's "Social Budget" that business leaders want to be cut drastically goes to Protestant and Catholic agencies for delegated welfare services that would otherwise be the direct responsibility of government agencies.

The continuing transfer of social welfare services from public to private church-run agencies explains how the religious establishment has become Germany's largest private employer. The Catholic Caritas employs over 400,000 people in more than 24,000 institutions and the Protestant Evangelical Diakonie well over 300,000 in close to 28,000 institutions. In many German towns the best and sometimes the only local hospitals, nursery schools, and old-age homes are under the aegis of the Protestant or Catholic Church. In the state of North Rhine-Westphalia, home for more than a fifth of Germany's population, 80 percent of all social service agencies are run by the churches. With the increasing support of public monies they operate about one-third of Germany's hospitals and three-fourths of the agencies providing child care and services for the elderly.

The churches have thus sought to sustain their exceptional legal privileges and benefits politically by replacing religious services that most Germans no longer want with nonreligious social services that they do want. "Who but the Church could do it all?" in the words of a trade union leader resigned to accepting the price of church exemption from German labor laws. But that all has become too much for business leaders who insist that the economy would gain if the churches got less. It is a growing dispute that affects particularly the Christian Democrats since they, more than other parties, attempt to reconcile the interests of the churches with those of the business community.

A Diminishing Gender Gap

In 1994 a series of events featured women in German politics in strikingly different ways. Early in the year some 15,000 of them came to the capital proclaiming that "Women Move the Country." As one of the organizers of that demonstration in Bonn had it, Germany had seen nothing like this since 1911, when women from all over the country had demonstrated in Berlin for women's suffrage. But it was a rather modest gathering compared to some of the mass demonstrations staged by American women in Washington and was largely ignored by the national media. A local paper described the event as a gathering of "veterans of the women's movement and women's organizations, a few men, and hardly any women under thirty" that heard declarations of female solidarity from prominent women politicians of the major parties.[13] The federal minister in charge of the postal service, a man and a Christian Democrat, took the occasion to issue a special stamp commemorating the establishment of Germany's first nation-wide women's organization a hundred years earlier. Nothing came of a call by radical feminists for a national women's strike for equal rights.

Some time later Jutta Limbach, a Social Democratic politician from Berlin, became the first woman to head Germany's Federal Constitutional Court—an event widely noted in the media. It was, she told reporters, an indication that women were to an increasing extent provided with more responsible positions in German society and she pledged to attend especially to the concerns of women. With five women among its sixteen judges, the Court was according to Limbach a gender model that other institutions in the Federal Republic should emulate.

Then, toward the end of the year, Chancellor Helmut Kohl chose Claudia Nolte, a twenty-eight-year-old East German Christian Democrat, to head up the Federal Ministry for Family, Women, Youth, and Senior Citizens in his new government. Her gender was of no interest to the media—this position customarily went to a woman. Instead the emphasis was on Nolte's youth: she was the youngest person in German history to hold such a high office.

What American women's organizations battling for the Equal Rights Amendment sought and failed to get in the 1970s—an explicit constitutional commitment to equality of the sexes under law—has existed in the Federal Republic since it was established in 1949. The sixty-one fathers and four mothers of its Basic Law stipulated specifically that "men and women shall have equal rights" and that "no one may be disadvantaged or favored on account of gender." That has provided the constitutional underpinnings for government measures, legislative actions, and court decisions that have both promoted and reflected changes in the status of German women.

Eight out of ten German women consider themselves in a better position to shape their lives than their mothers according to a recent study. And so they are. Women have come long way from the model of the homemaker whose life revolves around children, church, and kitchen. Nazi efforts to revive the traditional roles of full-time housewives and mothers in a paternalistic family came to naught in the Second World War when a shortage of manpower called for more and more women to work outside the home. Then came era of the so-called *Trümmerfrauen*, the women who in the late 1940s and early 1950s had the job of clearing away the physical and psychological rubble left by the war in home and family without the help of the millions of German men who had been killed, badly crippled, or kept as prisoners of war for many years. In the following decades what remained of traditional notions of the proper roles for women proved increasingly out of tune with socioeconomic and political changes in both parts of divided Germany.

In West Germany the situation of women has reflected the spread of affluence, the weakening of class distinctions, and the individualization of lifestyles. The spectacular rise in educational levels has been particularly pronounced among women.[14] Among the baby boomers and, even more, among their children, women have come to expect and men have come to accept increasing gender equality in social roles. The most educated of the women have also been the most insistent in seeking as much opportunity and scope as men to shape their lives and their relationships.

Changes in the lifestyles of West German women have been particularly evident in their family relationships. The baby-booming 1950s were the "Golden Age of the Normal Family," according German social scientists. Women married young and had children early. If they had jobs they would quit them to raise a family. Divorce was uncommon and relatively few children were born out of wedlock.[15] In opinion polls nine out of ten people held that marriage was an indispensable social institution and that a family should include two or more children.[16] Intimate ties between parents and their offspring—weakened by the Nazi regime and wartime and postwar social dislocation—appeared to flourish again. Closely knit "nuclear families" seemed the mainstays of social stability on a bumpy road to an uncertain future.

But this proved to be no more than a passing phase in the postwar transformation of West German society and the situation of its women. An increasing number did not quit their jobs when they got married and more mothers went back to work as soon as possible to have larger family incomes for better living in a flourishing economy.[17] As in the United States, women still did most of the housekeeping and parenting. But with better equipment these tasks became less burdensome and time-consuming. Above all, public policies gradually provided legal underpinnings for changes in the status of West German women both inside and outside their homes.

The Federal Republic inherited all sorts of old German laws and regulations that discriminated against women when it was established in 1949 and its new Basic Law stipulated that these were quickly to be brought into line with the constitutional guarantee of equal rights. But for close to a decade next to nothing was done.

In reaction to the invasive social policies of the Nazis and the East German Communists and in the absence of much political pressure for change, West German governments and legislatures were in no hurry to institute far-reaching reforms. Conservative leaders of the dominant Christian Democrats considered equal rights for women in society and, more particularly, in the home not a matter for intrusive government regulations. In their view, constitutional provisions that put marriage and the family under "the special protection of the state" ruled out any measure that promoted gender equality at the expense of family solidarity.

In time the men who governed in the Federal Republic came to realize that social modernization called for the emancipation of West German women from their inferior legal positions as wives and mothers. As in industrial design, new forms were adapted to new functions. Since the late 1950s marriage and family laws that went back to to the days of Imperial Germany have been gradually brought into line with changes in society.

Women are no longer required to have their husband's permission to hold a job and husbands no longer have sole control of the family's property. Under the legal provisions for a new partnership marriage, rights and duties are shared equitably and decisions regarding the family's income and offsprings made jointly. And in divorce settlements and social security payments, housekeeping and parenting chores are considered the equivalent of monetary earnings from a job.

Such measures and special laws for the protection and promotion of women as mothers (*Mutterschutzgesetze*) have evidently done little to stem the erosion of family ties. These days West Germans marry less, divorce more, and tend to have fewer children than their parents or, increasingly, to have none at all. Women with jobs are not as ready as their mothers to forego an independent income and lifestyle for marriage and children. Those who marry are now less likely than formerly to devote themselves exclusively to raising a family and more likely have full-time jobs as well—though still not to the same extent as married women in the United States.

Married or not, West German women find it more difficult than American women to combine a regular job with caring for their children at home. Day-care facilities for the very young remain inadequate despite so-called family-friendly legislation for their expansion, school-age children do not spend as much time away from home in curricular and extra-curricular activities as in the United States, and after-work shopping opportunities for working mothers are still far more limited than in the United States.

In these respects the social impact of unification has been marked by major differences in the outlook of women in the old and in the new parts of the Federal Republic. Among East German women, according to opinion polls, there has been far more widespread commitment to work outside the home than among West German women, a much greater reluctance to sacrifice a career to family obligations, and a good deal less concern that it might be better for the children if their mothers did not work. Such findings illuminate a special "wall in the head" that divides East from West German women in the wake of their very different social experiences over more than two generations.

East German women had much less freedom to shape their lives under Communist rule, but they had all along more public assistance for their family responsibilities and social equality with men. Nine out of ten had jobs—about twice as many as in West Germany—and working mothers had better free child-care facilities than in the Federal Republic. Before unification families with children got priority assignments for affordable housing in East Germany, but since then a tight housing market has favored childless households.

It has consequently been especially difficult for women in East Germany to fall in with West German ways. Theirs had been a society where women worked the same as men and only social misfits were unemployed for long. They had become accustomed to a secure job until retirement that was not just a source of income and welfare benefits, but a measure of their social worth. Unification suddenly and unexpectedly forced these women into unwanted domesticity for the first time in their lives.

In the economic restructuring of East Germany what jobs remain have gone mostly to men. Almost eight out of ten of the long-term unemployed registered in East Germany in the mid-1990s were women. Those in their forties and fifties have usually been too old to acquire new skills and become pensioners early by special arrangement. Younger women have learned that having small children is a handicap in finding employment and catching up with West German lifestyles and increasingly have none. Since unification the birthrate among East Germans has dropped even faster and further than the already sharply declining one among West Germans. In both parts of the country the growing number of childless Germans raises the possibility of new, class-transcending conflicts of interests among women as well as men over the costs and the benefits of large public expenditures for mothers and children.

The shift from public to private ownership in the new parts of the Federal Republic has brought home to women there the sort of sex discrimination in employment that West German women have contended with particularly in the private sector of the German economy. The fact that they have come to have as much education as men has not shown up in a corresponding decline of gender inequality in the labor market. Women are still greatly underrepresented in well-paid white-collar occupations and overrepresented in insecure low-skill jobs. As in the United States, industrialists and bankers are still mostly men while secretaries and bank tellers are mostly women. In the new as in the old Länder of the Federal Republic it is on the whole a lot harder for women than for men with university degrees to pursue careers suited to their professional qualifications. And women who seek top positions in the world of business have found it even more difficult than in the United States to break through corporate "glass ceilings" that lets them look, but not move upward into executive suites and board rooms.[18]

Federal anti-discrimination laws provide that women must get equal pay and fringe benefits for equal work and and all sorts of state laws are more or less designed to level the playing field for working women (*Frauenförderungsgesetze*). But unlike affirmative action laws in the United States, such measures do not require employers in the private sector to to give women equal opportunities—if not preferential treatment—in hiring and promotion. German government leaders, legislators, and judges have been unwilling to do much more than to ask private employers to comply voluntarily with guidelines for gender equality in their selective personnel policies (*Frauenförderungsrichtlinien*). In this respect the "family-supportive" laws that entitle working women to paid maternity leave and let them reclaim their jobs for three years after they give birth have been counterproductive. German firms tend to favor men who can be counted on to stay with their jobs over equally qualified women who have or might have children.

Women have done better in the public sector where standards for their employment are set and enforced more readily and effectively by federal, state, and local authorities. About one out of three public employees is female, mostly in relatively low positions. Mandatory guidelines for the promotion of women have enabled an increasing number to move more easily than in the past into the higher ranks of the career civil service and get prominent judicial appointments.[19]

Which parties are in power has made a difference here, particularly in those areas of public employment that are controlled by the state governments—notably primary and secondary education. Social Democrats and, especially, Greens have thus been more energetic than Christian Democrats in promoting equal opportunities, and even preferential quotas, for women in the public service of states and communities in which they form the government. For instance, a gender equalization law sponsored by a Social Democratic-Green coalition in the state of Hesse allows women to receive credit for appropriate accomplishments as mothers and homemakers in place of adequate work experiences for a job.

Women have always constituted a majority of the eligible voters in the Federal Republic. They not only have the same right to vote as men, but these days also exercise that right like men. A "gender gap" and a distinctive women's vote do not enter into electoral politics as they do in the United States.

It was different, however, in the early postwar years of social change. Though permanent registration made it just as easy for women as for men to get a ballot, they did not exercise their voting rights to the same extent. The women's vote, such as it was, went far more to the Christian Democrats than the Social Democrats. This gradually changed as the now dominant generation of West German baby boomers came of voting age. Its female members have participated in elections as much as its males and, like them, have been more independent and less consistent in their choice of party than their elders.[20] The parties, in turn, have adjusted more or less readily to a higher rate of participation by women in politics.

The most notable change in that respect has been the increased prominence of middle-class and middle-aged women in public life. Such
women are not involved in politics as much as in the United States, but
they certainly wield a great deal more influence than in the past. Like
their American counterparts, they tend to be exceptionally well-educated, to live in suburban communities, and those with regular jobs are
more likely to be public school teachers, journalists, social workers, doctors, or lawyers than owners or managers of business establishments.
Many are West German women who came to politics by way of the massive university student movement of the late 1960s and then continued
on to practice what in Germany remain more unconventional forms of
participation in grassroots politics than in the United States—such as
organizing petitions, boycotts, and demonstrations. And from there quite
a few chose to go further into politics along the customary career path
provided by the major parties from local to state and, more rarely,
national offices.

To make one's way in government and politics in Germany, you must
be a dues-paying party member in good standing, and women are now a
much larger presence in the parties than in the 1950s and 1960s. In the
CDU and SPD they make up about a quarter of the membership and
among the Greens and in the PDS as much as a half.[21] More insistent
demands from more female members for more gender equality in the parties and through the parties have led to more women in policymaking
positions.

In the world of contemporary German party politics the sort of gender discrimination that is still common in private business is unacceptable. Conservative Christian Democrats have been slower than Greens
and Social Democrats to honor the egalitarian principles of the constitution in their organizations.[22] But in all of the major parties some form of
affirmative action to boost the role of their women in politics is supported by most leaders and members as we have described in Chapter 2.

How far this will take women politicians remains to be seen.

There are now a lot more women in leading party and government
offices than in top management positions of German industry. Affirmative action seems to have helped especially women in the new states to
compete for political positions on an equal basis with male party members. But on the whole, women have as yet not managed to do as well in
electoral politics as in the United States. Comparatively few women head
municipal governments and only one of the sixteen state governors was

a woman in the mid-1990s. The likelihood of a woman at the head of the federal government seems at this point quite remote.

As with other issues, the extension of equal rights for women has depended more than in the United States on interest alignments within Germany's comparatively cohesive parties and much less on separate pressure groups lobbying legislators from the outside. Independent groups have never had as much clout as, for example, the National Organization for Women (NOW) in American politics.[23]

An "autonomous women's movement" of radical feminists has not gotten very far in its efforts to fight apart from the conventional political institutions for women's rights to "self-realization." Some twenty years ago its campaign for the abolition of all legal impediments to abortions put steam behind grassroots pressure for the liberalization of a highly restrictive law from the nineteenth century. And when the Constitutional Court threw out the rather moderate reform legislation produced by the ruling Social and Free Democrats—a measure that was a good deal less far-reaching than the unrestricted right to abortion granted American women by the U.S. Supreme Court at the same time—the autonomous women's movement staged mass protest demonstrations in all major cities. But it then went into decline. Abortion on demand remained its principal rallying cry, but that was not enough for a strong feminist pressure group with substantial grassroots support outside the major parties.

In West Germany radical feminism has lost the attraction it once had for women of the baby boomer generation and holds little appeal for younger women, while it has entirely failed to take root in East Germany since reunification.[24] Marginalized from the frontlines to the sidelines in German politics, the veterans of the autonomous women's movement could not again lead mass protest demonstrations when the Constitutional Court once more threw out abortion reform legislation in the mid-1990s. Militant feminists had become something of an oddity and their call in 1994 for a general strike by women to liberate them from their social fetters fell flat.

More conventional groups have had greater influence on public policy by working with and through the political parties for women's rights. The largest and most prominent of these *Frauenrechtler* pressure groups, the "Council of German Women—The Women's Lobby," is far from a single-minded grassroots movement. A heterogeneous umbrella organization much like the German Employers' and German Trade Union confederations, it takes in some eighty large and small national women's organizations with altogether about eleven mill members—among them the women's branches of the major parties, churches, and trade unions, as well as a wide range of professional and special-interest associations for women.

The Women's Lobby enjoys the privileged status of a super-organization that has come to be recognized by federal officials as the only proper body for the expression of nonpartisan and interdenominational concerns of Germany's women.[25] But what counts for more in the political arena is that it has brought together for joint actions leading women from parties and interest groups that differ on other issues.

Although the rules of the Lobby let any of its constituent organizations block a joint course, the alliance has on occasion succeeded rather well in overcoming disparate interests for a common objective. Not long ago, for example, it managed to obtain broad support across party lines for a federal law that lets women get old age pension credits for looking after dependent family members rather than earning such rights through a regular paid job. And it successfully pushed for legislation giving employed women more free day care for children and invalid relatives while they are at work.

On more basic and controversial issues, however, the Lobby has not done as well. When it sought changes in the Basic Law that would explicitly commit all public authorities in reunited Germany to see to the advancement—and not just the protection—of equal rights for women, it did not get as much as it asked for. Under strong counter-pressure from business leaders and conservative politicians, the ruling Christian Democrats would agree only to a constitutional amendment that called for the promotion of equal opportunities for women, but failed to require their preferential treatment by private employers.

Radical or moderate, women's politics remain pretty much a West German show even after unification. Apart from a few prominent women politicians and public officials, like the aforementioned Claudia Nolte, East German women have not participated and seem unlikely to do so in the foreseeable future. The "wall in the head" that divides West and East Germans in general has created new fault lines among women as a political force in particular. The sort of broad gender issues that especially engage West German women activists—more freedom and better treatment for their kind—do not arouse much interest among East German women concerned more with more mundane matters than self-realization and preferential quotas.

All told, gender politics are not now and never have been as significant in Germany as in the United States. Nor are they, by current indications, more likely to be so in the future. Ongoing developments suggest less politics for women and more politics by women. Gender aside, women voters, politicians, and public officials appear to have more in common with similarly situated men than with each other. And with the gender gap diminishing among Germans, the interests of women are fragmenting more along socioeconomic, cultural, and political lines that transcend common interests based on gender.

Demography is Destiny

"Germany needs more Germans," proclaimed Hitler when he came to power, and launched a massive program to reverse a long decline in the birthrate. But whatever gains he had managed to achieve before the war were wiped out by losses in the war. In the end there were fewer Germans when the Third Reich went down in flames than when it was established. The German birthrate has become one of the lowest and most rapidly declining in the entire world.[26] While demographers expect the natural growth of the American population to continue at the current rate or better, they predict that the German population will drop another eight percent over the next three decades.[27] By present indications, it seems to alarmed citizens of the Federal Republic that there may no longer be any Germans in Germany one of these days—at least not any "real" Germans.

The Germans may not be on the verge of dying out, but they are certainly a graying people whose average age is rising much faster than that of Americans. And with the proportion of German children and young people declining in the population, the presence of relatively more senior citizens who can vote and more noncitizens who cannot looms larger in the political arena than in the past.[28] In the future the far-reaching impact of these demographic developments may turn out to be the most enduring aspect of the politics of social change in the Federal Republic.

They pose sensitive, but unavoidable questions for its leaders concerning the rising cost old-age benefits, immigration policies, and the treatment of aliens—questions that are also pressing on American politicians.

In Germany *Seniorenpolitik*, policies regarding the particular concerns of senior citizens, is moving even more rapidly to the forefront of public affairs than in the United States. What had been the Federal Ministry for Family Affairs became some years ago the Ministry for Family and Seniors. The periodic *Altenplan* of the Federal Government, which concerns the growing number of old Germans, presents these days more problems for the policymakers than the *Jugendplan*, which deals with the diminishing number of young ones. And an official "Commission of Inquiry on Demographic Change" has pointed to all sorts of sensitive policy issues posed by the rapid growth of "The Republic of the Old."[29] What matters most for political developments is that senior citizens are of increasing importance as the producers of critical votes in Germany's "party state" and as the consumers of vast benefits in Germany's welfare state.

Germany's democratic system has not given seniors as wide a field for political action as the American one. They have no nationwide mass organizations of their own, like the powerful American Association of Retired Persons (AARP), to lobby policymakers. A League of Senior Organizations has wielded little or no clout in pressure group politics and the "Senior Councils" set up by some state and local governments have remained strictly advisory bodies. Political participation by senior citizens of the Federal Republic has on the whole gone no further than voting for one party or another in legislative elections.

Some years ago the leaders of a small but militant organization of German "Gray Panthers" offered senior voters an opportunity to support a new party of their own called The Grays and got nowhere. Senior voters have stuck with Germany's two major parties more than younger voters, and the women among them—a substantial majority—have voted mostly for the CDU. Both the Christian and the Social Democrats count among their members a large number of loyal, if largely inactive old-timers past sixty—about one in four in the early 1990s—and both parties have sought to bring even more senior citizens into their ranks. The Christian Democrats even have a special *Senioren Union* to attract elderly supporters but not, as with its youthful counterpart the *Junge Union*, new leaders.

Senior citizens have become rare among German party leaders. The times are past when unrivaled prominence allowed Konrad Adenauer to remain chairman of the CDU well into his eighties and Willy Brandt of the SDP until he died in his late seventies. These days German politicians are far less likely than American ones to soldier on to a ripe old age, leaving it to middle-aged policy makers to deal with *Seniorenpolitik*.

It is mostly as an involuntary consumer of public policies for the aged that the average senior citizen of the Federal Republic gets involved in politics. In Germany such policies are fashioned by party leaders in the federal and state governments and not, as in the United States, by legislative committees lobbied by private insurance companies, health care organizations, and professional groups that deal with the elderly. Politicians and bureaucrats instead get help and advice from the emissaries of Germany's unique old age establishment of quasi-public social service institutions.

Germany's senior citizens have on the whole been well served by policies for the aged. Entitlement programs that are mostly the products of West German politics in the affluent days of the old Bonn Republic provide tax-supported old-age income, health care, and social service benefits that are on the average far more generous than in the United States. The old-age benefits of East Germany have been raised to established West German levels since unification. And the old-age benefits of the growing number of West Germans who have become wealthy enough to live rent-free in their own homes and get retirement incomes from savings and investments have not been reduced.

But can that go on? That is the contentious question which demographic and economic trends have raised for German old-age politics on the road from the Bonn to the Berlin Republic. Critics of the current arrangements (for more details see chapter 6) warn that the established pattern of one-sided transfer payments cannot continue as if there were no tomorrow. Otherwise, they say, a growing leisure class of retired people will be entitled to increasingly costly benefits and a shrinking labor force of employed younger people will be taxed more and more to pay for them. "The entitlement claims of the old threaten to overwhelm the younger generation," as one self-appointed spokeswomen in the SPD has put it.[30] And that worrisome prospect has led some of the critics to conjure up the fearful specter of a looming intergenerational conflict in the political arena between Germany's senior citizens and their juniors.

The welfare state's pay-as-you-go arrangement for tax-supported old-age incomes has come in for a good deal more criticism than its programs for tax-supported old-age services. The generous pension payments provided under the so-called generational contract drawn up German policymakers in the mid-1950s were based on two miscalculations that have come to haunt their present-day successors. The contractual terms allowed neither for the sharp decline in the birthrate after the post-war baby boom nor for the more gradual shift from full employment in the fifties to massive unemployment in the nineties. Now that far fewer people are contributing and far more collecting than had been anticipated in those days, a redrawing of the generational contract of 1957 seems unavoidable, but problematic.

Senior citizens cannot be expected to accept reductions in their bene-fits readily and German democracy gives them the means to slow, if not prevent changes through the ballot box. The senior vote in the Federal Republic—already larger than in the United States—is rapidly increasing while the proportion of young voters with a stake in their own and their children's education is declining. Germans over 60 will constitute 36 per-cent of the eligible voters by 2000—about a third more than in 1990— and by current indications their numerical weight among actual voters is likely to be even greater. The turn-out of such senior citizens has consis-tently been higher than in American elections —not least because per-manent registration makes it easier—and substantially greater than among Germans under forty-five.

In light of this it seems to German observers that the outcome of crit-ical elections in their party state will depend more and more on who gets the support from older voters, and that party governments will accord-ingly find it more and more difficult to go against the collective interest of senior citizens in the preservation of exclusive old-age benefits. For some that prospect poses such a threat to the interest of the young who have no vote that they demand the disenfranchisement of very old peo-ple and the enfranchisement of supposedly politically more competent adolescents.

But the possibility that senior citizens can and will be united in defense of special old-age interests, as in the United States, appears rather unlikely. Thus far at least, they have shown no more disposition to coa-lesce into a single-issue voting bloc based on age than than women vot-ers have into one based on gender. It is, moreover, a political formula that slights the autonomy of major party leaders in making policy for the aged. As in other areas of government, the German form of representa-tive democracy insulates policymaking processes more from electoral politics than in the United States.

It now looks as if German policymakers will have to cut old age ben-efits drastically if they do not find more money to pay for them. Eco-nomic developments rule out a substantial increase in social security taxes, as we noted earlier. That leaves the possibility of getting more long-term contributors to the retirement and sickness insurance sys-tems—the younger and healthier the better. To get them, according to various politicians, professors, and journalists, the country must acquire "new Germans" through immigration and naturalization.

As various demographic projections have it, repopulation through immigration could halt, if not reverse, the graying of Germany well into the twenty-first century. It would have to be immigration on a large scale and millions of young people in poorer countries are evidently eager to come. But most Germans do not not want theirs to become a country of immigrants from all over the world, like the United States. As two exasperated analysts concluded not long ago from various opinion polls, the vast majority clings to the illusion that the population can somehow be rejuvenated with neither a substantial and sustained rise of the birthrate in Germany nor massive immigration to Germany.

The Basic Law allows the federal parliament to regulate immigration just like the American Congress. Germany, however, not only has no quota system like the United States, but also has no real immigration law. "The Federal Republic does not regard itself as an immigration country [sic]" according to its Interior Ministry.[31] Officially none of the foreign-born who have come to live there have been immigrants. Before unification that legal fiction took in several million German-speaking refugees from Communist Europe and "guest workers" and their families from non-Communist Europe and Turkey. And then, starting in the late 1980s, came a huge inflow that within a few years brought more newcomers to the Federal Republic than to any other Western country, including the United States. Almost 3.5 million ethnic Germans poured in from Eastern Europe and the former Soviet Union and close to two million more "non-immigrants" asked for asylum as political refugees.

The ethnic German "out-settlers" (*Aussiedler*) are ostensibly coming "home" from foreign lands where their German ancestors settled. Under current regulations the foreign-born descendants of Germans who emigrated long ago to Russia have the same constitutional right to "return" and automatically become citizens as the Basic Law gave in 1949 to refugees from Nazi and Communist rule who were born in Germany.[32] And as these foreign-born Germans have on the average been quite a bit younger on the average than the native-born, their coming has somewhat slowed the increase in senior citizens.[33]

Eight of ten people asking for political asylum in a European Union country went to to Germany in the early 1990s. Some were genuine refugees from the warfare in former Yugoslavia, others had fled civil conflicts and persecution in Africa and Asia. Most of them, however, were people looking for a better economic existence in the Federal Republic. Instead of slipping illegally into the country, they sought to take advantage of an exceptionally liberal provision in its constitution for taking in political refugees.[34]

The sudden flood of almost two million destitute aliens living at German taxpayers' expense caused widespread popular resentment.[35] Relatively few eventually got permission to remain—including several thousand Jews from the former Soviet Union—but under the prevailing rules applicants for political asylum might stay on for years until they were ultimately turned down. Local officials of cities and towns where federal authorities placed these unwelcome strangers in the meantime were applauded for calling it an excessive burden on their communities. Opinon polls showed massive agreement with politicians and journalists who proclaimed that the lifeboat for aliens provided by German generosity was full and overflowing.

The leaders of Germany's major parties got the message. After much partisan wrangling and over vehement opposition from liberals and more radical leftists, they amended the constitution in 1993 to let German authorities refuse asylum to aliens from countries where they were not considered subject to "political persecution." And as that took in all of Germany's neighbors, future applicants would have to fly in—if they could afford it.[36] The number of new arrivals has been greatly reduced and less than one in ten bids for asylum are granted these days. But the unwanted thousands remaining "temporarily" in the country until a way can be found to expel them properly have served to sustain strong resistance to letting aliens come in as regular immigrants who can become citizens, as in the United States.

Germany has never been and can never be a "country of immigration" like the United States, according to leading members of the conservative majority in the preeminent CDU/CSU. As they see it, the fact that so many aliens want to stay for good does not make their coming any more desirable. A country with ever fewer jobs for its own people has no need for immigrants seeking work. And letting them come in sufficient numbers to make up for an aging native population would literally "alienate" Germany as it would be impossible to assimilate millions steeped in strange alien customs to German ways.

Such arguments appeal particularly to those Germans, among them many senior citizens, who are discomfited by the "non-German" ways of millions of *Fremde*—that is, aliens—already living in their midst. "As in all countries with a high percentage of aliens, many people have reservations toward foreigners" as a 1993 report by the Federal Ministry of the Interior put it.[37]

By many accounts Germany is the only Western country with a shrinking native population and an expanding population of legal resident aliens. According to census figures, their number jumped from slightly over one percent of the population in 1961 to close to nine percent in 1994. That seems about the same proportion as in the United States, but only because in Germany children born to alien parents in the country are not automatically native-born citizens. They are aliens and remain aliens—at least until their late teens, when they may apply for citizenship through naturalization.

Noncitizens tend to have more children than citizens and in the mid-1990s six out of ten of their children were born in the Federal Republic.[38] And as the aliens are on the whole a good deal younger than the Germans they put much less of a burden on old age programs.[39] Experts on the subject consider them "a major pillar of stability" for these programs because they pay in a lot more in contributions than they take out in benefits.[40] Far fewer aliens than Germans receive social security pensions and what they get is on the average a good deal less since their benefits are more often derived from wages in relatively low-paid jobs, such as stuffing sausages or washing dishes or cars.[41]

None of this matters to right-wing demagogues who want to keep "Germany for the Germans" and to Neo-Nazi skinheads who scream for the expulsion of foreigners. But though most Germans dismiss such slogans as nonsense, they are usually ignorant of the large amount that their policy-makers extract from the pay envelopes of relatively young aliens for the benefits of senior citizens. Their leaders know it and like it, but rarely refer to it in the ongoing dispute between and within parties and interest groups over the integration of several million non-Germans into German society.

What could be and should be done in this respect was not much of a political issue as long as most of the non-Germans were much wanted "guest workers" from European Union countries—notably Italy, Spain, Portugal, and Greece—who were not expected to remain and usually did not. That changed as the character and demographic significance of the alien population changed. The proportion of migrants from other European Union countries dropped from six out of ten in 1960 to only two out of ten in 1993. In that time an ever-larger number of supposedly temporary guest workers and the family members that joined them came from countries with which Germans felt far less political, economic, and cultural affinity—most notably Turkey—and stayed for good.

By the mid-1990s some six million legal resident aliens in the Federal Republic had on average lived there more than two decades and over two-thirds of them had been raised, if not born there. One out three were registered as Turkish citizens and it was particularly these people who were indiscriminately caught up in the wave of anti-alien sentiments and violence brought on by the mass influx of asylum seekers in the early 1990s. In the city of Solingen five women and children in a Turkish family died when Neo-Nazi hooligans torched their home.

In light of these developments leading figures in public affairs have come to agree pretty much that the preservation of the so highly valued social harmony and political stability in their country requires that more be done to integrate non-Germans into German society. There is much less agreement on just what that involves. Conservative Christian Democrats insist on total cultural assimilation "to the values, norms, and ways of living prevailing here."[42] Others hold with Social Democrats and Greens that non-Germans need not become just like Germans to fit in.

Such differences concern above all the uneasy relationship between Germans and the many Turks who live and work among them, but remain culturally and socially apart. Berlin and most major West German cities, like Frankfurt, have large self-contained neighborhoods where just about everybody is either from some small town or village in Turkey or a German-born Turkish national. Here distinctive traditional ways of life persist far more than among Germans and family ties are much stronger and extensive. Men get together after work in Turkish mosques, Turkish café houses, Turkish social clubs, and Turkish soccer teams. Women stay at home to care for large families and shop at Turkish groceries. Children go to school with Germans but are unlikely to play with them on the outside and adults who work with Germans are unlikely to count many among their friends.

For their part, most Germans rarely seek closer social contacts. Some like to munch Baklava and sip Turkish coffee served by Turkish waiters to the sound of Turkish music in exotic Turkish night spots. Some find it annoying when Turks disturb their Sundays in the park with noisy fun and games and strange smelling cookouts, or fail to keep their backyards neat in the German manner. What the average citizen living in the suburbs knows about these strangers in the cities comes more from unfavorable hearsay and accounts in the media than from direct encounters. And sensational reports of Turkish domestic conflicts spilling over into Germany, of Turkish tourist offices, mosques, and cultural centers bombed by Kurdish terrorists, and of the spread of Muslim fundamentalism in Germany make the Turks seem all the more alien.

These sentiments affect particularly the two out of three Turkish nationals who have grown up in the Federal Republic. On the whole, these young people are more urbanized, better educated, and have a much higher standard of living than their parents had when they came to Germany. And they are not as thankful for what the country has to offer them and less reconciled to their inferior social and political status and disproportionately high employment in relatively poorly paid jobs. For Germans they are Turks in Germany, but in their ancestral villages they are considered German Turks. And indeed they are in language and habit more German than most of the ethnic Germans from Eastern Europe and the former Soviet Union who are instantly given the privileges of citizenship.

"All persons shall be equal before the law," commands the Basic Law, "no one shall be disadvantaged because of homeland or origin." But aliens, particularly if they are not citizens of another European Union country, are in fact disadvantaged by law. Nationals of countries outside the Union, like Turkey, are not eligible for relatively secure civil service jobs, such as teaching, and are not just as free as Germans to live and work where it suits them. Whether or not they were born in the Federal Republic, they need resident permits and employment permits. And no matter how long they have lived there, they "may be expelled if they cannot or do not secure their subsistence cost and that of their dependents without drawing social assistance."[43]

What matters most for German politics is that a substantial number of men and women cannot really participate because they are not citizens. Like legal resident aliens in the United States, most of the native-born aliens in Germany may neither vote nor run for public office and are not entitled to as much constitutional freedom of assembly and association as citizens.[44] They can to some extent join Germans in political actions by common interest groups, such as trade union demonstrations. But as aliens they are not permitted to form ethnic pressure groups of their own, like Cuban and Mexican immigrants in the United States.

What it takes to be a citizen has in recent years become a contentious political question arising out of the partisan differences over the immigration and integration of aliens from countries outside the European Union. Federal legislation makes it a lot more difficult to become a naturalized citizen than in the United States. But in Germany the implementation and interpretation of such national regulations rests with the states and allows them some leeway in particular cases.[45] When a Turk born in Berlin made headlines as a champion boxer for Germany in 1992, local authorities instantly made him a citizen well ahead of less prominent applicants. More generally, aliens have found it easier to become naturalized in states governed by Social Democrats and Greens than in Bavaria, where conservative Christian Socialists have alone had the say.

Conservatives hold fast to the cultural conception of Germaness that makes the acquisition of citizenship on the whole a lot easier for ethnic Germans from far away lands than for aliens born in Germany. In this view, naturalization requires that people who are not German by descent become entirely German by assimilation before they can become German by law.[46] Others argue that naturalization makes it easier for people to fit in by giving them the civic rights denied to aliens. They see the conservative position as closer to the totalitarian Nazi notion of an ethnically exclusive and culturally homogeneous "German Peoples' Community" (*Volksgemeinschaft*) than to the democratic principles of the present constitutional order.

A resolution of such differences is complicated by the issue of dual citizenship. With some exceptions by special treaty arrangements—with Spain, for instance—the present regulations do not allow it. And that is as it should be, according to leading members of the CDU and CSU. Dual citizenship, they say, leads to conflicting ethnic loyalties. You are either German or non-German—you cannot be both.[47] In public policy this view has prevailed over Social Democratic proposals to allow at least aliens born in the Federal Republic to hold dual citizenship. But most of these, especially among the large number of Turkish nationals, have not been all that ready to surrender the passport they have for the German passport they may want—because they are not prepared to renounce cherished ethnic bonds to their ancestral culture.[48] That suits German conservatives and confirms their belief that American-style multiethnic politics will not do for the Federal Republic.

Other Germans, including some prominent Christian Democrats, attach less importance to Germanization, and they are less concerned about the prospect of more multiethnic German politics. This is an inevitable development in the view of both German and foreign observers since the Federal Republic is bound to admit and naturalize more aliens. "Within a few years there may be millions more Germans," according to the British weekly *The Economist*. Liberal and left-wing German politicians and commentators see their country already well on the way to a more "multicultural" society in which the separate values of various ethnic minorities enter into the pluralism of party and interest group politics.[49] And that, in their view, is all to the good because it serves to uphold German democracy under changing conditions.

Conservative Christian Democrats do not see it this way. They blocked a constitutional amendment for the protection of "ethnic, cultural, and linguistic minorities" proposed by the Social Democrats and Greens in the mid-1990s because, as they said, it would promote so-called multiculturalism. That might do for an immigrant society along the American model, but in Germany it would hinder rather than help the assimilation of aliens like the Turks and it would further particularistic social and political fragmentation instead of desirable overarching solidarity and harmony.[50]

The Christian Democrats may eventually have to give way and let more aliens become citizens and, thus, voters. And these, by present indications, could very well introduce more ethnic division into German party and pressure group politics. Polls show that the ethnic *Aussiedler* tend to favor the Christian Democrats, but that most Turkish nationals would vote for the Social Democrats and the Greens if they could. Elections to advisory bodies representing the interests of the aliens in major cities (*Ausländervertretungen*) reflect further ethnic divisions between and within their organizations. About one in five of the Turks in Germany belongs to a Kurdish subculture with ethnic ties to a people fighting for independence from Turkey. But for all that, German politics are not likely to take on the distinctive ethnic coloring of American politics.

In some ways the arguments over immigration, citizenship, and multiculturalism in today's Germany are not all that different from those in current disputes on these issues in the United States. German liberals on these issues have found much to emulate in the American experience, while in the United States proponents of more restrictive immigration and naturalization policies and less multiculturalism sound at times like conservatives in Germany. In both countries the differences revolve largely around questions about the nature of national identity, on how to combine ethnic diversity with political unity in a democracy, and—above all—on how to provide for both continuity and change in state and society.

For all the sound and fury that these questions produce in American politics, they are likely to prove a lot more problematic and troublesome in German politics.

5

Capitalism with a Human Face

Spring 1996. Public service employees are up in arms over Chancellor Kohl's austerity program fashioned to cut in one bold stroke some $30 billion in government spending. They protest that they would be affected unfairly. As the public service union ÖTV stages the first of a series of short warning strikes and interrupts public transportation, garbage collection, mail delivery, and even police activities, union leaders predict a long, hot summer of workers' protests and paralyzing strikes. All over the country opponents of the proposed reforms accuse the government of plotting to scratch the "social" from Germany's sacrosanct social market economy. Angered because the Chancellor has sided with the employers' associations during a recent meeting, union leaders refuse to participate in Mr. Kohl's *Kanzlerrunden*, the Chancellor's round-table discussions, designed to get labor, business leaders, and the government to work out their differences.

Removed from the labor unrest in the larger cities, the Nettetal, a valley in North Rhine-Westphalia, provides a picturesque setting for a meeting of the governors of Germany's sixteen states. But the heads of the Länder are not in the mood to enjoy the beauty of the place. They, too, are unhappy with the governing coalition's (CDU, CSU and FDP) austerity plan. Saxony's Kurt Biedenkopf and other members of the CDU and CSU support slashing spending and taxes in order to stimulate economic growth, and even SPD governors agree that the Federal Republic is faced with its greatest economic crisis ever. But the sixteen governors are unanimous in their message to the Kohl government: We will not agree to a reform package that shifts fiscal burdens unfairly from the federal government to the states.

In fall 1996, there are more and more bitter clashes between workers and managers over the implementation of newly legislated cuts in workers' sick pay. Headlines at home and abroad proclaim "The end of Germany's economic model" or wonder, "Is the model broken?"

Contrary to the United States, where adversarial politics are perceived as normal, sharply confrontational politics tend to cause anxieties in Germany. The Bonn Republic's democratic house rested for more than forty years on two pillars of strength: (1) a broad consensus on its vital role within the West's anti-communist camp, and (2) a degree of economic affluence that assured virtually everybody a comfortable and risk-free standard of living. When the Cold War and the need for a unified internal and external stand against the communist threat evaporated, Germany was left with its reliance on a strong economic performance. As cracks appeared in the remaining foundation of Germany's democratic edifice, so did worries about the soundness of the democratic structure and the reliability of its inhabitants.

Cyclical downturns in the Federal Republic's first forty years were typically accompanied by fears that transcended the problems at hand and questioned the soundness of the country's democratic fabric. Americans do not experience these sorts of anxieties, not even in periods of severe economic difficulties. Thus, in the 1970s and 1980s, when the traditional manufacturing industries in the United States' underwent profound restructuring processes accompanied by a permanent shrinkage of the workforce, no one wondered whether the nation's democratic institutions and economic arrangements could weather the storm of inevitable structural changes and massive societal dislocations. But in Germany the old concerns resurfaced in the years following unification as unemployment numbers climbed to record levels and were compared to similar conditions during the Weimar period, regardless of the vast differences between Weimar Germany and the Federal Republic.

The Economic Miracle Revisited

One would be hard pressed to argue with the success of the distinct style of German capitalism in the four decades after the birth of the Federal

Republic and before unification. The speed and the way the economic sector rose from defeat and disgrace was impressive by any measure.

Following a period of high inflation in the wake of the 1948 currency reform and a short stretch of record unemployment in 1949/50, West Germany's productive engine steamed high speed toward a stunning economic recovery. In the 1950s the gross national product (GNP) rose an average of about 8 percent and wages 5 percent per year, while unemployment decreased from 11 percent to less than 4 percent. During this time the government reestablished step by step old age benefits (i.e., social security) and introduced new benefits (i.e., child allowance beginning with a family's third child).

Whereas the spectacular growth rates of the initial ten years slowed down in the following decades, the Federal Republic's metamorphosis from a country in shambles to an economic wonderland continued even as the engine of success encountered its share of difficulties and stalled a few times along the way.

When the Berlin Wall crumbled, West Germany was among the wealthiest countries in the world both in terms of per capita income and per capita millionaires. Typically, the combined rate of inflation and unemployment—known as "misery index" and many a government's worst nightmare—was lower in the Federal Republic than in any other country except Japan. Germans enjoyed a standard of living that was among the highest in the world. The country's physical and cultural infrastructure— from a perfectly maintained highway and railroad system to municipal and state theaters and opera houses—was second to none.

As the *Wirschaftswunder* unfolded and Germany's economy outperformed most first-world democracies, many observers abroad tended to attribute this accomplishment to national character traits. Germans won a world-wide reputation for being predisposed to hard work, discipline, punctuality, thoroughness, and the like. Although many people in the Federal Republic, especially the young generation, no longer displayed these characteristics, the stereotype survived well into the 1990s. During the 1994 World Cup tournament in the United States American sports reporters frequently described the performance of the German national soccer squad in terms of its discipline, efficiency, precision, and relentless work. In reality, even in Germany a growing number of people had come to believe that Germans have forgotten the meaning of hard work. Lamenting that Germans were losing their work ethic, Chancellor Kohl warned that the "high level of prosperity in Germany has given many people the illusion that material security is automatically guaranteed."[1]

While the determination to work hard and rebuild their country was invaluable in the years immediately following World War II, the often repeated larger-than-life myth of Germans as a work-obsessed people and of the amazing "women of the rubble," who rebuilt their houses stone by stone with their own hands, does not explain the bulk of the monumental accomplishments during the original reconstruction period. Just as the westward move of American frontiers in pursuit of the American dream was facilitated by the availability of vast areas of unsettled land, the German Economic Miracle could not have occurred as rapidly and as thoroughly as it did without several factors that had nothing to do with the work ethic of the German people.

To begin with, as the chill of the Cold War was increasingly felt in Paris, London, and Washington, the Western allies recognized the strategic importance of their three occupational zones in Germany. Instead of continuing a policy of revenge and punishment, they stopped dismantling what was left of the industrial plant and allowed, accommodated, and actively assisted in West Germany's economic reconstruction. A major factor was the generous aid provided by the Marshall Plan. Moreover, export markets opened up for German products, because the Federal Republic was included in the emerging Western European community at an early date (i.e., membership in the Organization for European Economic Cooperation in 1949 and the European Coal and Steel Community in 1951), and in multilateral organizations such as the International Monetary Fund (IMF).

All of this occurred at a time when the Western industrialized countries were rebuilding and readjusting their economies after years of pouring most resources into their war efforts. It was a market in which the demand for goods was greater than the supply and in which West German workers and union leaders showed great restraint in their demands for wage hikes and other benefits. By concentrating on the creation of jobs, labor allowed the private sector to rebuild and flourish.

The availability of a highly skilled labor force was helpful as well. Although many Germans, especially men, had died during the war, millions of refugees from the East flooded into the Federal Republic before the Berlin Wall was built in 1961. When this part of the Iron Curtain went up, the exodus from East Germany had already provided the industrial sector in the West with a reservoir of capable workers.

By the 1960s, when additional and especially unskilled workers were needed, Germany imported so-called guest workers from Turkey, Italy, Spain, and other European countries, many of whom were employed in the coal mines and steel works of the Ruhr district and in the lowest paying jobs in hotels and restaurants. Germans who now could afford a comfortable lifestyle thanks to the generous material rewards of the Economic Miracle were no longer willing to fill these sorts of jobs.

Perhaps most important, the Federal Republic's political institutions, which were established in 1949, conceived and developed decisionmaking processes and rules of the game that shaped its political economy and proved highly successful for capital and labor during a long period of largely favorable internal and external environments.

In the 1990s, with the same institutional and procedural elements in place, the country was forced to deal with the monumental difficulties involved (1) in rebuilding Eastern Germany's economy and integrating the region into the socioeconomic system of Western Germany and (2) in restructuring the old Federal Republic's economic makeup in response to a serious threat to its global competitiveness. In addition, between 1992 and 1994 Germany was experiencing a recession, a calamity that had hit the other leading industrialized countries earlier. While more severe than previous cyclical downturns, the recession of the early 1990s alone could not have tested Germany's economic arrangements as did the changes in the domestic and global conditions and their far reaching consequences for the economic sphere. The much admired "German model" was in trouble.

The German Economic Model

Before examining the country's economic problems and the opportunities and limits for solving them, one needs to consider the nature of German style capitalism and the system that has perpetuated it since the early years of the Federal Republic.

During the federal election campaign of 1976, the SPD coined the term *Modell Deutschland* (German model) to convince voters that the party had been instrumental in molding the country's successful economic arrangement and should continue to lead the Bonn government in order to protect and perfect the considerable accomplishments. At the time, several Western European countries were led by social democrats who cultivated one or the other form of a social market economy, what

Germans call *soziale Marktwirtschaft*. But it was specifically the German model that was hailed by many experts abroad, especially in the United States. The respect for the German way of handling their economic sphere did not completely fade, when the country's public and private elites struggled to adapt the widely respected model to the changes at home and abroad. In the 1990s, President Clinton and his labor secretary Robert Reich made no secret of their admiration for the German model and their determination to utilize parts of it in the United States—especially its job training system.

While the Social Democrats had a hand in shaping this model, the foundations for the particular style of German capitalism were in fact laid during the first fifteen or so years following the birth of the Federal Republic, when the government was led by Chancellor Konrad Adenauer and its economic policy shaped by economics minister Ludwig Erhard.

Determined not to repeat the mistakes of Weimar, the founders of the new German republic wanted cooperation instead of societal warfare. That meant most of all preventing the class conflict that had plagued the country in the 1920s. The inherent contradiction between capital and labor was to be overcome by forging formalized relations between employers and employees and balancing the drive for profit with the promise of fair wages and social security. This could only be achieved within an economic arrangement acceptable to everyone.

Strongly influenced by the Western allies, West Germany's post-World War II leaders emulated many characteristics of Anglo-American capitalism. But from the outset, decisionmakers in Bonn rejected American-style laissez-faire capitalism and opted for a market economy with strong social traits. The result was an alternative both to capitalism and communism: what might be called capitalism with a human face. While the concept enjoyed broad support throughout the Federal Republic's history, its implementation was not left to the private sector alone. The government put itself into a position of a major economic player. Thus, in the era of Adenauer and Erhard, the Bonn government stimulated economic growth and especially exports by providing, for example, investment credits for basic industries such as the coal and steel sector, tax incentives for private capital investment and reinvestment, and credits for export-oriented enterprises.

West Germany's economy was throughout that era, as it still is, a mixture of mostly privately owned companies and a substantial number of wholly or partially state-owned enterprises. Traditionally the federal government has owned, run, and often subsidized the nationwide railroad system and the postal and telecommunications services. But in the 1990s, pressed by fiscal problems and global competition, the federal government hastened the pace of privatization. Thus, the postal and telecommunications services were broken into three independent entities (postal service, postal bank, telecommunications) to position them for privatization and international competition. After reducing its ownership in Lufthansa, the German airline, to less than 51 percent, the government announced plans to sell all its remaining shares. Still, at least for the time being, the share of publicly owned enterprises remains significantly larger in the Federal Republic than in the United States.

Local governments and regional cooperative bodies run and coordinate most local and regional commuter services. Municipalities as well as the states own or have large stakes in public utilities' companies. States hold substantial assets in corporations such as Volkswagen. Unlike the case in the United States, municipalities run most savings banks and have interests in the official banks of the states they are situated in. These so-called state banks or *Landesbanken* are at home and abroad strong competitors of privately held commercial banks. Moreover, state banks and local savings and loans can be and are used to advance the regional and local policies of their respective governments. But just as municipal and state governments in the U.S. have turned increasingly to the private sector to take over such traditional public sector tasks as garbage disposal or transportation to and from schools, municipalities in Germany began to experiment with similar solutions to combat their fiscal woes in the 1990s.

The Players on the Economic Field

Traditionally, government intervention in the marketplace has been and remains significantly higher in the Federal Republic than in the United States but is far more restrained than in government-directed economies and less direct than in the Japanese form of capitalism. The German version of postwar capitalism, unlike the Anglo-American laissez-faire style, has aimed above all for predictability and for consensus among the various actors and interests.

What, then, are the major institutions that made the German economic model function so successfully in the past? And who are the institutional players that are now being challenged to adapt the German model to the changed conditions of the 1990s and beyond?

Political Parties and Government Leaders

From the start, the social market model has enjoyed broad support by the political parties that shared power in one or an other combination for over half a century. This is hardly surprising because the CDU/CSU, the SPD, and the FDP were involved in creating, adjusting, and protecting the German model. The differences were mostly in the degree to which the *free market* components on the one hand and the *social* features on the other were emphasized. The small liberal FDP, a perennial junior partner in the federal government and up to the mid-1990s in many state and local governments, pressed consistently for more free market practices and less governmental interference. Thus, it was hardly surprising that the federal economics minister Guenter Rexrodt, a member of the FDP, made the most passionate appeal for free competition and against continued regulatory restrictions during a 1994 parliamentary debate to repeal the 1933 Rebate Law which prohibits merchants from giving customers a discount of more than 3 percent on goods.[2]

The Christian Democrats have been more favorably inclined toward the business sector, while the Social Democrats are more sympathetic to the social component of the German model. But both parties have been more pragmatic in their economic approaches than the Free Democrats who have steered a steady free market course throughout. The two large parties have always been willing to use the policy instruments of the government to further their objectives.

Still, as far as the basic rationale of the social market economy was concerned, namely to create a striving economic system that would enhance and maintain social and political stability, none of the three parties that mattered during the Federal Republic's first half century questioned this premise. With the exception of their short-lived grand coalition, either the CDU or the SPD governed with the FDP as a junior partner in Bonn; this partisan lineup foreclosed serious challenges to the existing arrangements.

To be sure, each serious economic downturn of the past pushed Bonn's governing parties into trying something different—a swing toward more interventionist, demand-side fiscal policy during the CDU/SPD coalition period in the 1960s, a partial retreat from Keynesian measures by the SPD/FDP government in the 1970s, and a move toward supply-side policies by the CDU/FDP coalition in the 1980s. These swings on West Germany's pendulum of economic approaches were in terms of their respective direction, if not their depth, similar to those that occurred during roughly the same times in the United States—from the flirtation with Keynesian policies during the Kennedy years to Reaganomics in the 1980s. Without far-left or far-right parties playing meaningful roles, none of the changes touched upon the basic philosophical underpinnings and values of the social market arrangement.

In economic policymaking the most influential players are those who hold key offices in the federal government, namely the chancellor, the finance minister, and the economics minister. A German chancellor wields far more power in economic policy matters than American presidents, and German ministers of finance and economics have greater influence than the Secretary of the Treasury or other cabinet members in the United States.

To what extent a chancellor and his staff involve themselves in the details of economic policy problems and issues depends on each head-of-government's background and inclination. As Chancellor Helmut Schmidt was intimately involved in all aspects of economic decision-making—far more than his predecessor Willy Brandt and his successor Helmut Kohl. Schmidt, who was the economics as well as the finance minister before he moved on to the chancellery, moved some of the economic ministry's authority to the ministry of finance. Over the years some of the economic ministry's jurisdictions were also transferred to newly created departments (i.e., the ministry for research and technology, the department for [global] economic cooperation and development). Not the economics minister but the finance minister became the predominant governmental player in the economic realm.

Given their personal and institutional ties and influence in their own parties, chancellors and federal ministers have been formidable actors in economic policymaking. Unlike U.S. presidents, German chancellors do not worry much that the parliament increases spending in the government's budget proposals. Adding any kind of additional expenditures for special interests is far more difficult than in the U.S. as deputies cannot adopt such increases unless they explain in detail how additional revenues will be raised. This gives chancellors, finance ministers, and the ruling parties a great deal of control over the budget—a far cry from the state of affairs in the United States, where Congress has the power of the purse. While the 104th Congress passed a line-item veto bill in 1996, the new law qualifies the new presidential authority in fiscal matters.[3]

German chancellors, key ministers, and influential civil servants especially in the federal ministries of finance and economics must also contend with other actors—most of all the states—when it comes to economic policymaking. Revenue sharing disputes among national, state, and local governments in Germany have been even more divisive than in the United States, because local and state governments are not allowed to levy the all-important income or sales taxes. These are set and collected by the central government, which allocates a share of those funds to states and municipalities. Because of the limited authority of the lower level governments to assess taxes of their own, they fight frequently and fiercely for what they consider a more equitable revenue sharing scheme and more leeway in their own economic initiatives.

When the Federal Council is controlled by states in which the opposition party governs alone or with coalition partners, the chancellor and his cabinet are forced to fashion compromise solutions. Just as the American electorate has more often than not opted for divided government in the second half of the twentieth century, German voters, too, seem to prefer a federal government and a majority in the Federal Diet that is checked by a strong opposition in the Federal Council. Given the economic and fiscal difficulties in the 1990s and the new political and partisan realities in a unified Germany, the standing Reconciliation Committee or *Vermittlungsausschuss*, the German version of congressional conference committees that work out disagreements between House and Senate bills, emerged as a crucial decisionmaking body, especially in fiscal matters.

However, even the most important aspects of Germany's economic policies are not dictated by party influentials and government officials on various levels. Economic decisionmaking involves an elaborate power sharing arrangement in which public and parapublic agencies as well as private interest groups have considerable influence.

Respected and Feared: the Bundesbank

September 16, 1992 was a "Black Wednesday" for the member states of the European Monetary System (EMS). Within hours the Spanish peseta, the British pound and the Italian lira lost between 8 percent and 10 percent of their value vis-à-vis the German mark. Britain and Italy left the EMS. Their currencies as well as those of Spain and Portugal were devalued while the French managed barely to hang tough and defend their franc. The crisis was set off when speculators dumped billions of dollars worth of what they perceived as weaker European currencies, switching their funds instead to the stronger Deutschmark to benefit from high German interest rates. Abroad and at home Germany's central bank or *Bundesbank* was blamed severely for having caused the monetary crisis by stubbornly sticking to its tight-money policy. Moreover, the German central bankers' insistence on high interest rates even in the face of economic slumps in the Federal Republic and other leading industrial countries came under fire as the major obstacle to economic recovery. Others believed that the crisis was at best a setback on the track to monetary union and at worst a fatal derailment.

At the time, George Bush was in the midst of a tough reelection fight against challenger Bill Clinton. Bush and his advisers hoped desperately for an economic boost before election day. For that to happen they encouraged and pressed the Bundesbank to loosen its tight monetary grip and thereby allow the Federal Reserve to do the same. Under massive pressure from Washington, European neighbors, and their own government the central bankers finally made a meager rate cut that did not really change the basic course. The European currency crisis lingered for months. And the German economy fell into a deeper recession. In the German news media the Bundesbank was accused of waging an "interest war" against the government and sabotaging Bonn's economic policies. One astute foreign observer of Germany's economic scene characterized the central bank as having succeeded the German military as the most feared German institution.[4] This was a widely shared sentiment at the time of the monetary crisis in 1992, up to then the most turbulent year in the Bundesbank's history.

In many domestic and foreign observers' eyes Germany's central bank towers above all other actors on the country's economic playing field. Jacques Delors, the former president of the European Commission once concluded that Germans believe in God and in the Bundesbank. While weakening considerably in their devotion to God (see previous chapter), Germans have so far not wavered in their faith in and support of their central bank. Indeed, the deeply rooted public trust in the commitment and ability of the central bankers to fight inflation and thereby protect the stability of the German currency, not the legal standing and authority of the institution, is its most important base of power and influence.

The German central bank like the American Federal Reserve were designed to insulate them from politics in general and from decision makers in the executive and legislative branches in particular. In either country the creators understood the different objectives of central bankers and politicians. Not surprisingly, the anti-inflationary measures of the Bundesbank are just as often resented by German government officials as are those of the Federal Reserve among administration and congressional officials.

Before leaving office in early 1993, Treasury Secretary Nicholas Brady fired one last parting shot at the Fed when he questioned the wisdom of its monetary policies during President Bush's four years in the White House. At the same time, the Kohl government was just as unhappy with the Bundesbank's tight-fisted stance. But while politicians in either country clash frequently with their central bankers, these encounters are generally less public and more muted in Germany than in the U.S. Occasionally, however, high government officials and central bankers do engage in open feuds in the Federal Republic as well. The central bank's opposition to a rapid monetary union between West and East Germany resulted in bitter discord between Chancellor Kohl and Bundesbank President Karl Otto Poehl that spilled over into their unusually blunt public statements and was said to have influenced Poehl's decision to resign from his post several years before his term expired.

In the mid-1990s, the chairman of the U.S. House Banking Committee, Representative Henry Gonzales, introduced a bill designed to inhibit the independence of the Fed and bolster its accountability to the legislative and executive branch. Although some other lawmakers supported still another effort to tame the Fed, the proposal was doomed to fail from the outset. This initiative is mentioned here, because a move to inhibit the central bank's independence is simply inconceivable in the Federal Republic unless an elected official is out to commit political suicide.[5]

Many Americans believe also that their monetary policy is best left to the experts at the Fed than to politicians, but they hardly glorify the Federal Reserve and its role as inflation fighter. For Germans, however, the Bundesbank's status is a sacred and untouchable part in a system built by a generation that lost its savings twice—in the Great Depression and at the time of the postwar currency reform. Germany's anti-inflationary culture is a vivid reminder that in this respect, too, the legacy of the past is alive and well. Public and elite obsession with the Deutschmark's stability has cast the Bundesbank in the part of an almighty guardian of the German currency. This reputation transcends Germany's borders. The

Bundesbank is widely regarded as the most independent and most influential central bank in the world.

Although undoubtedly formidable, the de facto power and independence of the Bundesbank does not quite measure up to that reputation, and it is in many respects comparable in role and reach to the American Federal Reserve. Still, there are marked differences. While American presidents, treasury secretaries, lawmakers, and other decisionmakers must accept frustrating waiting periods before the Fed releases its secret Federal Open Market Committee's monetary policy deliberations, members of Germany's federal government are allowed by law to participate in the biweekly meetings of the Bundesbank's decisionmaking Central Bank Council where they cannot cast a vote but can plead their case.[6]

Even chancellors can, and sometimes do, attend the meetings of the Central Bank Council. The Bundesbank Act gives the federal government the right to delay a decision by the Central Bank Council for up to two weeks. No chancellor or finance minister has ever forced such a postponement, but they have occasionally persuaded the central bank to delay its decision for the two-week period they have the right to enforce. The direct contacts between central bankers and government officials work in the opposite direction as well. As mandated by law the federal government invites the president of the Bundesbank to cabinet and other government meetings which deal with monetary policy.

German central bankers testify as expert witnesses before parliamentary committees on legislative proposals, but unlike their American counterparts they are not accountable to the legislative branch and not subjected to the rhetorical batterings by legislators as the chairs of the Federal Reserve frequently are when they appear before congressional committees.

But regardless of the differences in the formal and informal relationships between central bankers and politicians in the two countries, neither institution is completely immune to political pressure. In the past, the Bundesbank has more than once dropped its rates in the face of massive domestic pressure.

When the Bundesbank lowered interest rates in the spring of 1994, some observers tied the timely change in monetary policies to a series of upcoming elections, especially the federal election in October. At the time, Chancellor Kohl and his party trailed challenger Scharping and the SPD in the polls. Obviously, many voters blamed Kohl and the governing coalition for the bitter consequences of a prolonged recession. The change of direction by the central bank occurred under the stewardship of Hans Tietmeyer, a former close aide to Kohl, who had become president in the fall of 1993. Some suspected a connection between the rate drops and Kohl's uphill campaign fight because the conditions in 1994 were similar to those in 1992, when the central bank had raised its interest rates. Others believed that the economic circumstances were more than ripe for cutting rates—regardless of the timing.

Those who insist that the central bank is independent of electoral pressures and considerations point to the fall of 1990 when, under the stewardship of Karl Otto Poehl, the bank raised interest rates just a few weeks before the first all-German federal elections. But scholars who examined the Bundesbank's monetary policy over four decades found that before almost all federal elections the central bank pumped money into the economy. What party controlled the appointments of the Central Bank Council's members was the decisive factor according to one study.[7] If the majority was appointed by the governing party in Bonn or its political allies in the states, the money supply grew in the months preceding federal elections—with only one exception.[8] Such a correlation between monetary policy and electoral cycles casts serious doubts on the proclaimed political independence of the Bundesbank and nonpartisan monetary decisionmaking.

Apart from this pre-election effect, one also finds evidence that central bank appointees have sometimes abandoned their previous monetary approaches and partisan loyalties in favor of the institution's inflation-fighting mission. When push comes to shove, the institutional interest has often proved stronger than central bankers' personal backgrounds, partisan ties, and relationships with political friends and mentors. Bundesbank presidents Kurt Blessing in the 1960s and Karl Otto Poehl in the early 1980s opted for higher interest rates and thereby contributed to the fall of Chancellors Ludwig Erhard and Helmut Schmidt, their respective onetime patrons.

Because monetary policy affects a country's overall economic activities as well as its fiscal and wage policy, the central bank has frequently angered governing Christian Democrats as well as Social Democrats—just as the Fed has infuriated Democrats and Republicans in the White House and Congress over the years.

After all, while politicians cannot stop central bankers from tightening money and inducing, deepening, or prolonging recessions, they are ultimately accountable to the electorate. Although the governing parties' policies are frequently impeded by the central bank, politicians cannot run for cover in times of economic doldrums and blame the independent central bank for the painful effects of its decisions. German voters simply do not accept such arguments. In the 1970s and early 1980s the central bank curbed the SPD-led government's expansionary fiscal policies in times of lagging economic growth and increasing unemployment. In the early 1990s, the Bundesbank kept the leash on the CDU-led government's deficit-spending to finance Eastern Germany's reconstruction. In these and similar instances the governments and their leaders, not the central bankers, took the heat for the unpopular decisions.

The Bundesbank always has the last word in disputes over the level of interest rates. And while the federal government has the final say in disagreements over the exchange rate of the Deutschmark and revaluations, central bankers often get their way in this policy area as well. In contrast to the American Federal Reserve Bank's formal supervisory authority over bank holding companies (and thus most big U.S. banks), the Bundesbank has no such formal power; that lies with the Federal Bank Supervisory office. But in actual practice the central bank acts as an equal, perhaps even dominant, partner in all important regulatory and supervisory activities.

All in all the Bundesbank is not as mighty as its reputation. Just as Bonn's political decisionmakers prevailed over the central bank in the disagreements over the terms and timing of the currency union with East Germany, the Schmidt and Kohl governments overrode it in moving toward a European monetary union, a common currency, and a joint central bank. This development was hardly in the interest of the Bundesbank and its emphasis on independence.

In 1994 the European Currency Institute, a precursor of the planned European Central Bank, opened its doors in Frankfurt, the seat of the Bundesbank. Frankfurt will also be the home of the planned Central Bank of the European Union. From the German perspective this geographic choice suggests that the European Bank is to be modeled after the German one and follow the same monetary policies. But that may not be enough to compensate for the profound trust Germans have come to place in their Central Bank as guardian of their currency's stability. For nearly five decades this belief system was of tremendous political importance and politically usefulness in the Federal Republic; the Bundesbank will be hard pressed to uphold its reputation, when the Euro replaces the Deutschmark and the European Central Bank cuts into German central bankers' influence.

To translate the scope of these changes into the American context, one would have to imagine the U.S. Federal Reserve Bank subordinate to a central bank of a North American Union and the U.S. Dollar replaced by a new, joint currency for the U.S., Canada, Mexico and perhaps some other countries.

As the turn of the century approached, German pollsters detected dwindling public support for a more influential European Union and enduring majorities rejecting the projected demise of the German currency.[9]

Before this background it was hardly surprising that in 1997 the Bundesbank resisted the scheme of Chancellor Helmut Kohl and Finance Minister Theo Waigel to cook the government's books in order to meet the fiscal criteria for joining the European currency union. To achieve this, Waigel asked the central bank to reevaluate its gold reserves and thus provide the federal government with a clever bookkeeping tool to cut the budget deficit. In the ensuing public skirmish the Bundesbankers criticized the plan as a troublesome departure from sound monetary practice. As support for the Bundesbank's position mounted in Germany and in Europe, Kohl and Waigel capitulated. The incident strengthened many Germans' belief in their central bank as the guardian of monetary and fiscal stability, but it also raised questions as to the wisdom of a government determined to proceed with the currency union in the face of the country's tremendous economic and fiscal problems.

The Constitutional Court's Policy Reach

As mentioned in chapter 2 the German central bank is not the only unelected body with a strong voice in controversial matters—fiscal and other economic policies among them. The Federal Constitutional Court (*Bundesverfassungsgericht*) has weighed in as well—often when fiscal and other economic policy issues arise. In this respect, the role of the Constitutional Court has been similar to that of the U.S. Supreme Court with its long history of decisions affecting economic policies and jurisdictions. Given its high esteem in elite and public opinion, the Federal Constitutional Court's rulings in this area are less likely to be openly attacked by opponents than are comparable Supreme Court decisions in the United States. To be sure, over the last several decades opinion polls have revealed that the U.S. Supreme Court, too, has been more highly rated than the other two political branches of government and other public and private institutions. But many of the Supreme Court's more prominent rulings have been in the past far more controversial and critically received in the U.S. than decisions of the Constitutional Court in the Federal Republic. Franklin D. Roosevelt's court packing effort in the 1930s remains the most often cited reaction to a series of Supreme Court rulings affecting the Federal Government's economic policy and jurisdictions. There have not been comparable clashes in the Federal Republic even though some of the more recent Court rulings have annoyed political leaders and segments of the public.[10]

In late 1994 the Court ruled unconstitutional the so-called coal-penny (*Kohlenpfennig*), an electricity consumption tax used to heavily subsidize the coal mining industry, and ordered that it be eliminated within one year. What West Germans paid since the beginning of 1975 amounted to far more than a penny—an 8.5 percent tax on their electricity bills. The Court found it unconstitutional to single out electricity users to bear the burden of this sort of surcharge that raised about $3.5 billion yearly.

More consequential for the federal government was a 1992 ruling of the Court declaring the country's income tax system unfair, unequal, and unconstitutional and ordering a major overhaul by January 1, 1996. One part of the ruling concerned the "working poor," who had been forced to pay taxes on their income, although it was actually below the poverty level. Many of these taxpayers had been forced to turn to public assistance. This, the Court ruled, violated the constitutional protection of human dignity.

Not only the Federal Constitutional Court but sometimes even the European Court of Justice can and does check German fiscal and other economic policy decisions. In the early 1990s, for example, the European Court invalidated German legislation that would have imposed a heavy vehicle tax on domestic and foreign road users. The law had been designed to make foreign *Autobahn* users foot a fair share of the German road bill. But because domestic haulers were to receive simultaneously a reduction in other fees, the Euro Court construed this as a violation of European Community law (as adopted in the Treaty of Rome) that prohibits any member country from enacting measures disadvantageous to foreign competitors.

The Lesser Known Watchdogs

While far less known to the general public than the Bundesbank and the Constitutional Court, the Cartel Office, the Council of Economic Experts, and several publicly funded economic think-tanks have also roles in economic politics.

The Cartel Office (*Bundeskartellamt*) was established in 1957 as the primary guardian against the reemergence of Germany's earlier corporate monopolies. But neither its establishment nor the merger law of 1973 prevented a multitude of major corporate mergers and acquisitions. This track record has rendered the Cartel Office impotent in the eyes of those who opposed this development. Critics tend to forget that the Cartel Office has not the same authority and independence in the antitrust area as the Bundesbank in monetary policy. Political decisionmakers in the federal government, not the Cartel office, have the final say in these matters, and the ministry of economics has repeatedly overruled the decisions of the antitrust agency.

When the prerogatives of the Cartel Office were debated in the 1950s, economics minister Ludwig Erhard recommended greater authority for the agency's antitrust experts. But Chancellor Konrad Adenauer, who had established close ties to corporate leaders, insisted on the supremacy of politicians in these cases. In designating the ministry of economics, not the justice department as in the United States, as the government's leading agency in antitrust matters, Adenauer assured that political and economic considerations would tend to outweigh legal ones in mergers and acquisitions. The rationale for allowing mega-corporations to exist received a further boost after unification, when the economic reconstruction of Eastern Germany depended on Western Germany's big business and on the willingness to acquire and modernize existing factories and other businesses in the East or to establish new ones.

The Council of Economic Experts (*Sachverständigenrat*) was established in 1963. The founding fathers, Adenauer and Erhard, may have hoped for a panel of experts that would put its stamp of approval on the federal government's economic course. It did not work out that way. The five-member panel, known as "The Wise," has complete access to the government's economic data and must release comprehensive yearly reports on the state of the economy. Unlike the U.S. Council of Economic Advisers, which serves the president and helps to formulate and even sell the administration's policy, the German Council of Economic Experts does not serve chancellors and their governments but is more often than not critical of their economic policy approaches. Instead of ignoring the panel's often unwelcome conclusions, the federal government is required by law to respond to and discuss each of the Council's reports in writing.

The Council of Economic Experts is prohibited from making explicit policy recommendations and the government is not at all required to follow the recommendations implicit in the Council's report. Nevertheless, the body's criticism of CDU- and SPD-led governments from Erhard to Kohl and from Brandt to Schmidt anticipated and probably affected eventual policy shifts. Thus, the members of the Council, who are generally drawn from the ranks of leading professors of economics, were early critics of the Keynesian policy approach of the SPD/FDP coalition government in the 1970s and were credited with paving the way for the shift to supply-side economics in the early 1980s.

In late 1995, as the date for the beginning of the European currency union approached, the Council suggested that this step should be postponed, since it was likely that only a few countries could meet the agreed upon criteria. This was in stark contrast to the official line of Chancellor Kohl and his governing coalition.

Finally, the Federal Republic early on created five economic institutes which are not under the control of the government but independently staffed and operated. East Germany too had several economic institutes but they were not independent of the powerholders and only one of them survived after unification. Although publicly funded, these think-tanks have been highly respected as independent and credible resources that have often contradicted the claims of governments, parties, and interest groups.

Of the quasi-public institutions and economic advisers and experts described here, none is as influential as the Bundesbank. When the Constitutional Court gets involved in the economic sphere, its influence is similar. But to one degree or another all of these institutions have influence on politicians, opinion makers, and other actors in the economic arena—among them the immediate players in the area of labor relations: the trade unions and employer associations.

Trade Unions and Employers' Associations

The German Federation of Trade Unions (*Deutscher Gewerkschaftsbund*, or DGB) and the Federation of German Industry (*Bundesverband der Deutschen Industrie* or BDI) are the preeminent umbrella associations of labor and business representing the overall policy interests of their members. As the official voices of labor and industry, the DGB and the BDI are consulted by the federal government with respect to new legislation and changes in existing economic policy. Leaders and policy experts of both organizations serve as advisers with considerable clout on interdepartmental working groups, testify before parliamentary committees, and confer with leaders and policy experts of the political parties. But neither of the organizations is the omnipotent representative of labor or business.

The labor movement that emerged in postwar West Germany was a sharp departure from that of the Weimar era, when unions were split into competing and bitterly feuding Socialist, Communist, Catholic, and liberal organizations. By rejecting close ties to political parties and churches, the labor movement was able to establish unitary, relatively centralized, noncompeting organizations (*Einheitsgewerkschaften*) that represented about four-fifths of all organized workers and united them under the DBG umbrella. White-collar employees, about half of them DGB members, and civil servants can join non-DGB unions (*Deutsche Angestellten Gewerkschaft*, or DAG; *Deutscher Beamtenbund*, or DBB).[11] As organized labor's chief spokesperson the DGB's national chairperson and the organization's lobbying apparatus have had more direct and formalized links to and input into governmental decisionmaking than the president of the AFL-CIO, labor's preeminent organization in the U.S. The DGB's bureaucracy, its own economic research institute, and diverse business interests depend solely on the resources and good will of its member unions. These autonomous unions, not the central DGB leadership and bureaucracy, have been labor's powerhouses.

The DGB as a whole does not get involved in the most important role of organized labor: collective bargaining. That is the sole privilege of the individual industrial-sector unions. In contrast to the mixture of industrial and craft unions that are united under the roof of the American AFL-CIO, all sixteen of the DGB's member unions are organized along functional, not occupational, lines.[12] The Metalworkers Union (IG Metall), for example, represents and negotiates contracts for all employees in the automobile and steel industry, the Chemical Workers Union for all workers in the chemical industry, the Media Union for all media workers—regardless of their specific jobs and skills: the machinist, the driver, and the electrician working in a newspaper publishing corporation are all represented by the Media Union, not by different craft unions. While each union has regional and local units and in this respect a degree of decentralization, all unions are top-to-bottom organizations, very different from the American model with strong union locals that call their own shots, for example, with respect to strikes.

Photographic Insert

(Facing page, top) 1945: The Reichstag building, past and future home of German legislatures, after the fall of Berlin in World War II.

German Information Center, New York

(Facing page, bottom) 1995: The Spectacular "wrapping" of the Reichstag by the famous artist couple Cristo and Jeanne-Claude symbolized Germany's political transition from the Bonn to the Berlin Republic.

German Information Center, New York

(Above) 1995: The Reichstag unwrapped and restored for parliamentary government.
German Information Center, New York

(Above) Lasting memorial: Here died a man shot by East German border guards while trying to escape the Communist state. *German Information Center, New York*

(Facing page, top) Bustling Berlin: Restoring the Potsdamer Platz to its central position in Germany's capital. *German Information Center, New York*

(Facing page, bottom) Before unification: East Germans demonstrating against their Communist dictatorship in 1989 and demanding free elections and a unified Germany. *German Information Center, New York*

Dawn of a new era: Border guards from East and West watching passively as East and West Germans take down the Berlin Wall.

German Information Center, New York

(Above) Together at last: East and West Germans celebrating the opening of the Berlin Wall.

German Information Center, New York

(Below) Sedate Bonn: West Germany's capital for nearly half a century.

German Information Center, New York

Regional Pride: Demonstrators in Leipzig demanding the reestablishment of their old state of Saxony in the federal system of reunited Germany.

Rebuilding East Germany: Street in Stralsund in 1990 and 1995.

German Information Center, New York

(Above) Post-unification disillusionment: East German demonstrators confronting West German officials with the slogan: "German unity, liberty, unemployment!?"   *German Information Center, New York*

(Below) Protest against violence: Young East Germans demonstrating against anti-foreign terrorism by neo-Nazi thugs.   *German Information Center, New York*

(Above) The impact of peaceful mass demonstrations: Candlelight marches against anti-foreign terrorism in the early 1990s swayed public sentiment toward more forceful governmental countermeasures.

German Information Center, New York

(Below) Issue for the 1990s: Deutschmark or the new European currency?

German Information Center, New York

(Above) Media-democracy: The chairpersons of the five political parties represented in the federal diet discussing the results of the 1994 federal election on
national television. *German Information Center, New York*

(Below) Gender equality: 1994 mass demonstaration in Bonn by women
demanding greater equality with men was the largest of this kind ever.
Deutscher Frauenrat e.V., Bonn

Other than the United States, Germany does not have "closed shops" or "union shops." Such an arrangement is prohibited by the Basic Law. Whatever a union negotiates in terms of wage increases and other gains benefits not only its members but nonmembers as well. In spite of this, union membership in the past has been and still was in the 1990s significantly higher in Germany (about one-third of the workforce) than in the U.S. (about 15 percent). But as layoffs and plant closings mounted in 1993 and 1994, the DGB's membership plunged sharply. In early 1995 the Hamburg local of the Public Servants Union (ÖTV) revealed plans to negotiate and sign contracts for its own members only in order remind "free-riders" that only union members have a legal right to the negotiated terms. This measure was meant to stop a further shrinkage of the union's membership. But neither the ÖTV's national leadership nor DGB officials supported their colleagues' plan. And the Confederation of German Employers' Associations announced that its members would continue to treat all employees equally. More important, the Hamburg local was reminded that the Federal Labor Court had ruled in 1967 that contracts negotiated between unions and employers' associations cannot dictate the exclusion of nonmembers.[13]

Unions in the Federal Republic, far more so than their counterparts in the United States, have always acted on behalf of both organized and unorganized workers and have been recognized by the political authorities in that capacity. This, besides their institutionalized, state-mandated role in labor relations and in the governmental process, has been a further reason for the trade unions' enduring political muscle—even in periods of dwindling membership.

In addition to participating in numerous governmental and quasigovernmental bodies and enjoying access to decisionmakers in federal, state, and local governments, organized labor is represented in and by segments of both major political parties. During the long periods of coalition governments between the CDU/CSU and FDP, the CDU's labor wing was generally able to serve at least as a brake on the scope of pro-business and anti-labor policies pushed by FDP, CSU, and elements in its own party. The continued existence of a labor wing in the CDU has lent credence to the DGB's claim of partisan independence, and this has facilitated union officials' communications and contacts with CDU chancellors and the coalition governments they have led.

Traditionally, the DGB's influence has been greatest within the SPD because of the two organizations' overlapping membership. At SPD conventions strong individual unions like the IG Metall or organized labor collectively have been able to control imposing blocs of delegates and therefore have had a say in the candidate-selection process and in the party's policy positions. Typically, a majority of SPD deputies in any given legislature consists of trade union members. However, the proportion of active functionaries, who manifestly represent the interests of organized labor in the Federal Diet and in parliamentary committees, has diminished in the last two decades. All in all, the ties between the DGB and the SPD have been in the past and remain closer than those between the AFL-CIO and the Democratic Party in the U.S.

Given labor's representation in the legislative delegations of both SPD and CDU, pro-union forces have occasionally crossed party lines to promote labor-friendly measures or to block pro-business legislation. In the past such aberrations from party discipline have been the exceptions, not the rule. Instead, the friends of organized labor have tried to further its cause in the privacy of intraparty councils and closed parliamentary committee sessions.

In the face of the vast economic problems of the 1990s, divisions within the labor movement and even within individual unions that had existed during the preceding decades became far more pronounced, as did differences among the members of the employers' organizations.

As the leading interest lobby for German industry and business the Federation of German Industry or BDI is comparable to, but politically far more influential than, the National Association of Manufacturers in the United States. The organization unites under its umbrella more than three dozen national trade associations of such sectors as the textile, automobile, and steel industry. But the BDI is not actively involved in negotiating wage and benefit contracts with labor unions. That is the realm of the Confederation of German Employers' Associations (*Bundesverband der Deutschen Arbeitgeberverbände*, BDA) and, even more so, of the BDA's member associations, which represent the shared interests of employers in literally all private-sector fields, such as banking, retailing, insurance, publishing, agriculture, and in the various regions of the country. While the BDI is primarily concerned with broader economic policy, the BDA concentrates on labor and social policy issues that are of special concern to employers. In these areas, the BDA lobbies and advises decisionmakers at all levels of government.

Finally, the German Industry and Trade Association (*Deutscher Industrie und Handelstag*, DIHT) and its regional chambers of commerce advance business interests in the broadest sense—for example, by taking positions on international trade issues or by promoting foreign investment or tourism in Germany. In this respect, the DIHT and its member chambers are comparable to the American Chambers of Commerce. But the German chambers are more inclusive in terms of membership, and they are more influential, in that they function as official links between the government and the private sector. Every firm in Germany is required by law to join one of the regional chambers of commerce as a dues paying member. In return, the organizations provide comprehensive services to all, but especially to small- and medium-size firms in form of information, advice, assistance in matters of trade, finances, training and retraining of employees, or even interaction with government agencies. While they are neither part of nor representatives of the government, German chambers of commerce are public law bodies with important and government-sanctioned responsibilities such as the function of granting licenses, direct involvement in the implementation of Germany's highly regarded vocational training programs, and participation in regional economic planning.

Facilitated by overlapping membership and a broad consensus on the political interests of business relative to other societal interests, the leaders of the three peak business associations frequently collaborate in national pressure group politics and those of BDI and BDA participate as observers in each other's board meetings. The closeness of the business associations was most obvious during a period in the 1970s, when Hanns Martin Schleyer was president of both the BDI and the BDA in an obvious but ultimately abandoned effort to unite the two organizations. BDI and BDA have jointly sponsored the Institute of German Industry, which conducts research on socioeconomic developments and organizes leadership conferences on business-related policy issues.

Far closer to the FDP and CDU/CSU than to the SPD, the Greens, and certainly the PDS, business has played a preeminent role in Germany's governmental process regardless of parliamentary politics. Besides their formalized contacts with the executive and legislative branch, officials of the peak and major sector associations as well as the top managers of leading corporations have access to chancellors, their advisers and ministers, and influential members in the federal bureaucracy. And especially in times of "divided government," when different parties enjoy majorities in the Federal Diet and the Federal Council, state governments become just as important targets of business, labor, and other interest group lobbies as the federal government.

U.S. presidents customarily reach out to the private sector to fill cabinet and other high-level administration posts—certainly a phenomenon that is helpful to business interests in general. But such a revolving door through which many members of corporate America enter public offices and through which they sooner or later return to the private sector has never been a factor in German politics. More recently, a few German leaders have suggested that some version of the American revolving door system would infuse new ideas, expertise, and energy into the governmental realm.

While representatives of large corporations and business associations do lobby individual lawmakers, especially members of key committees, access to and influence on individual legislators is far less important in the German than in the American system. Besides, like labor unions, business has also direct influence in federal, state, and local governments and legislatures through elected officials (mostly affiliated with the FDP and CDU/CSU), who hold or have previously held high positions in business associations or private firms. Indeed, especially large corporations encourage their employees to run for and hold public offices and accommodate such endeavors, for example, by granting them extra paid time off.

There are, to be sure, other influential private-sector interest groups, for example those representing farmers. Although one of the most densely populated major industrialized countries, the Federal Republic in the past has had an agricultural sector with formidable political strength comparable to the influence of farm lobbies in the U.S. Before unification, the mostly family-owned and small farms in Western Germany employed less than 5 percent of the country's labor force and contributed less than 2 percent to the country's GDP, whereas the large Eastern German farm cooperatives provided more than 10 percent of the German Democratic Republic's jobs and 7 percent of its GDP. Given the increase in farm land and agricultural employment, the peak agricultural associations gathered strength after unification. Membership in one of the local agricultural chambers which in function and legal standing are comparable to chambers of commerce, is mandatory for farm proprietors in most states. Most of the nearly 600,000 farmers are also voluntary members of the League of German Farmers (*Deutscher Bauernverband*, or DBV) and affiliated with an association of agricultural banks and cooperatives. While these three organizations have formally distinct functions, their overlapping membership, leadership, and interests unites them into a strong lobby that has been markedly successful in obtaining and retaining tax concessions, guaranteed price support, and generous agricultural subsidies.

For decades the farm lobby's political muscle was based on its ability to mobilize its loyal followers (farm families and perhaps even their employees) and deliver electoral support to the CDU and CSU (and in the past to the FDP as well) in rural areas. However, as the number of farms had decreased and employment in West Germany's agriculture declined from 25 percent of the total work force in the late 1940s to only 5 percent at the end of the 1980s, the *Bauernverband's* capacity to deliver a large bloc of votes has eroded. Just as crucial for the farm lobby's declining strength was a decisionmaking shift from Bonn to Brussels following the adoption of a common agricultural policy for the European Community.

Still, the agricultural lobby has retained influence within the parties it favors and is said to control blocs of delegates at party conventions, especially in the "C" parties CSU and CDU, just as the trade unions do within the SPD.[14] Accordingly, the *Bauernverband* has managed to prevent the elimination of farm subsidies and milk quotas, the more drastic shrinking of farm lands and other measures opposed by their clientele. But perhaps the most remarkable proof of the farm association's persistent political clout is that during the severe fiscal crisis of the mid-1990s, the government funded a newly created insurance plan that now provides old age pensions for farmers' wives.

The Stalling of an Economic Powerhouse

Germany's economy is by far the largest in Europe and the third largest in the world behind the United States and Japan and ahead of France and Great Britain. Already a powerhouse before 1990, the reunited Germany accumulated a gross domestic product (GDP) which was significantly greater than that of France and Great Britain, about half as large as Japan's, and nearly one quarter the size of the United States.' Even during the privatizing and rebuilding of Eastern Germany's economy, the five Eastern states began to add to the Federal Republic's economic output. In 1994 for example, the Eastern states' share of the Federal Republic's total GDP amounted to about 10 percent.

Industrial manufacturing has remained the centerpiece of the economy. Whereas the West German industrial sector's share of the GDP shrank from 49 percent in 1973 to 40 percent in 1990, East Germany still depended on industrial output for about two-thirds of its GDP. Western and Eastern Germany were, however, quite similar in that manufacturing and what was left of mining added up to the mainstay of their economic output and employment, followed by construction, trades and crafts, and the respective public sectors. In the old Federal Republic the combined public and private service sectors increased their share of the GDP from 48 percent in 1973 to 58 percent in 1990. This signaled that West Germany made efforts to move toward a post-industrial economy during a period when East Germany continued to concentrate on its heavy industries. In the mid-1990s, united Germany remained far behind the United States, Japan, and other leading first world countries in the development of a dominant private service sector.

Lacking adequate raw materials, natural oil and gas, or sufficient food supply and feed stuff, foreign trade has been and will continue to be imperative for Germany's economic well-being. Germany emerged as the world's leading exporter before World War I and continued this tradition after World War II. Before and after unification the United States and the Federal Republic ran neck and neck for the title of "the world's leading exporter" with each country winning in some years and finishing a close second in others. But trade has been far more existential for the German than for the American economy. Traditionally, Germany's export volume has represented about one third, imports more than one fifth of the gross domestic product while the United States' exports and imports have amounted typically less than 10 percent of their respective GDP totals. One of three jobs in Germany, but only one in ten in the United States have been directly export-related.

Germany is the world's third largest producer of motor vehicles behind Japan and the United States. Two of its automobile giants, Daimler-Benz AG and Volkswagen AG, top the list of the country's biggest industrial firms. But far more Germans are employed by the 4,000 or so engineering firms that manufacture a multitude of products from machine tools to industrial plant equipment. Germany also has a sizeable chemical, textile, and steel industry. The small and medium-size firms with up to 500 employees are in fact the backbone of the economy and constitute what Germans call the *Mittelstand*. To translate this term literally as "medium-size" or "middle class" firms does not capture its true meaning. *Mittelstand* refers to the amalgam of mostly family-founded and owner-run enterprises, typically with deep roots and long traditions in their communities, that employ four in five persons in Germany's workforce. It may well be that a corporate giant such as Mercedes-Benz is at any given time a reliable bellwether for the cyclical strength or weakness of the German economy (just as General Motors is said to be in the United States), but the *Mittelstand* reveals probably more about its long-term health outlook.

Exports are crucial for many *Mittelstand* firms and most, if not all, corporate giants. Germany's leading position in world trade has long been a cause for the country's economic strength and, more recently, for its considerable vulnerability. As a dominant player in international commerce and trade the Federal Republic has always been susceptible to external developments and conditions. This became painfully clear during the 1990s when the nation had to deal simultaneously with the high costs of unification and rapidly growing international competition on top of a severe global recession.

At the end of 1993, a grim recessionary year in the Federal Republic, nearly four million Germans were officially unemployed—more than 8 percent of the total workforce in Western, more than 13 percent in Eastern Germany. Because an additional two million persons were supported by publicly financed jobs and retraining programs, the real number of jobless men and women was closer to six million—by far the highest number since the dark days of the Weimar Republic. But it was far more symptomatic for the economic plight of the Federal Republic that the official and concealed unemployment did not diminish in the following years but reached new record levels.

The monumental task of remaking Eastern Germany's economy in the image of Western Germany's social market model fell on the shoulders of the public trustee agency *Treuhand*. Within four years more than 14,000 enterprises or parts thereof were sold or liquidated. An additional 20,000 small businesses such as restaurants, drugstores, and other retail stores were sold to private entrepreneurs as were more than 30,000 real estate properties. In the process of transforming Eastern Germany's inefficient and grossly overstaffed economic system, more than a third of a total of 9.9 million jobs were lost in the first three years after unification alone. It did not help the employment picture that the labor unions insisted on quickly bringing East German workers' wages up to Western Germans' levels in spite of a vast and persistent productivity gap in favor of the West.

Of the more than $200 billion that the Treuhand spent or committed during the first four post-unification years, less than one-fourth was recovered through the sale of assets. The high costs of unification (in addition to the debt accumulated by the Treuhand, some $100 billion per year were transferred from Western to Eastern Germany) and the severe global recession of the early 1990s pushed West Germany into a structural crisis that otherwise might have been delayed. As the country's traditionally exemplary public finances were put into the red, the public sector's ability to subsidize hard-hit sectors and thereby protect jobs in Western Germany was inhibited.

Experts had pointed to warning signals in the years before unification. One of their more troubling assertions was that each economic cycle left West Germany with a larger residue of unemployment which grew from 150,000 in 1970 to 900,000 in 1980 and to 1,7 million before the recession of 1993. This development was a symptom of Germany's waning competitiveness in the changing and highly interdependent global markets.

The United States, too, experienced recessionary jumps in unemployment during the 1980s and early 1990s, which diminished during subsequent recoveries. But unlike their counterparts in the Federal Republic, corporate America began to attack similar problems as early as the late 1970s and early 1980s. After losing jobs and corporate investments to low-wage countries in Latin America and the Far East, and losing ever more domestic market shares to cheaper and better Japanese products, the traditional industries in the U.S. (automobile, steel, textile, machine-building, rubber, etc.) underwent restructuring. As a result hundreds of thousands manufacturing jobs were eliminated. But systematic modernization and rationalization measures as well as lean labor contracts and wage/benefit roll-backs resulted in increased productivity and better products. At the same time, American high technology firms strengthened their competitive edge with respect to other advanced countries, especially Japan. Many well-paying manufacturing jobs were lost, but during the same period the U.S. service sector experienced a rapid expansion creating millions of low paying jobs.

In the Federal Republic's manufacturing sector the wind of change did not blow nearly as strong as in the U.S. As a result, its productivity gains, which had been the highest in the world in the 1970s, fell behind those achieved in the United States, Japan, and other industrialized countries in the 1980s. While labor costs dropped in the United States, they rose in West Germany. Well before the unification of 1990 and the following short-lived post-unification boom, *Standort Deutschland* moved rapidly toward pricing itself out of the global competition. Although still the leading or second exporter in the world, the Federal Republic began to lose a greater share of the global export market than any other country beginning in the second half of the 1980s. Even in their traditional stronghold, the export of machine tools, German companies' global market share began to decrease while Japan gained ground and became top exporter in the field.

West Germany's labor force earned higher hourly wages (i.e, in the mid-1990s on average $10 more than U.S. workers), worked shorter hours (1,650 yearly versus 1,900 in the U.S.), enjoyed significantly longer vacations (an average of five or six weeks a year versus two weeks in the U.S.), and collected more contractual perks (i.e., a thirteenth monthly payment for Christmas and "vacation money" for spending enjoyment during vacation) than their counterparts elsewhere in the world. Comparing labor productivity in nine leading manufacturing industries (autos, auto parts, consumer electronics, metal works, and steel) in Germany, the United States, and Japan, one study established that Japan led in five, the U.S. in four, and Germany in none of the industry categories. Just as troubling was the finding that Germany was a distant third in six out of the nine sectors examined.[15]

The Federal Republic's old manufacturing industries found themselves in a bind: they were squeezed by competitors in newly emerging markets as well as in highly industrialized countries. At the low end of the production ladder, Far Eastern and Latin American countries with significantly lower labor costs manufactured what used to be Germany's bread-and-butter products (cameras, watches, textiles, cars, motorcycles). But the production costs in the United States and other industrialized countries were also well below the German average as far as the traditional industries were concerned. Products "Made in Germany" used to command the highest prices in the world because of their superior quality and reliability, but this changed, when much cheaper cars, machine tools, and other products from competing countries achieved comparable standards of excellence.

Finally, Germany's eastern border became a similar economic demarcation line as the Rio Grande for the United States: Both of these industrial powerhouses had to face low-wage countries at the other side of their borders. Just as the U.S. felt the impact of cheap, unskilled labor in Mexico and other Central American countries, Germany did not compare well with production sites in the Czech Republic, Poland, and other formerly Communist countries, where wages were just fractions of what German workers earned. Moreover, unlike the regions South of the U.S. border, the "European Koreas" in Central and Eastern Europe offered a highly trained workforce. Explaining why his corporation had already moved a substantial part of its production eastward, one executive revealed that his firm's employees in Central Europe worked about 400 hours more a year than their colleagues in Germany and that the average hourly wage costs in Poland were only one tenth of those in Germany.[16]

Blaming the high labor costs in the Federal Republic for their industries' growing competitive woes, most business leaders failed to acknowledge that this was only one reason for their serious problems. During their many prosperous decades, corporate managers had failed to push ahead in their plants with rationalization and other lean production and management measures as had their foreign rivals. They also missed early opportunities to move into newly emerging markets, especially those in the Far East, as U.S. corporations did. Instead, before unification, West Germany's and later the reunited country's best customers were its fellow-members in the European Union. In the early 1990s, only about 7 percent of all exports went to countries of the Pacific Rim. Only belatedly, in the mid-1990s, did German industrial corporations and financial institutions move aggressively into the emerging markets.

In the most crucial manufacturing sectors (automobile, chemical, and machine industry) the Volkswagen AG was one of the exceptions to the latecomer syndrome. Well before other car-makers established production and assembly plants outside Germany and Europe, Volkswagen had a truly global production and distribution net in place—not only in the Americas but also in China and other emerging markets in Southeast Asia. Its global presence and outlook might well have encouraged Volkswagen to develop and decide to produce a modernized version of the once-popular VW Beetle, after an experimental and futuristic sort of "bug"—the "Concept 1" car—was shown and well received at the 1994 Detroit Auto Show.

But while Volkswagen and some other enterprises adapted in time to the new global realities, by and large the Federal Republic lagged badly behind the United States and Japan, especially in such technologies as computers and communications. Once a trailblazer in research and development, the Federal Republic was now spending less for research and development than the United States. As a consequence, between 1987 and 1992 the number of patents granted in Germany in the microelectronic field shrank significantly, while at the same time they were doubling in the United

States. The record was similarly troubling from the German perspective when it came to mainframe computers, office technology and lasers, energy technology, and the chip industry. Most of all, the chemical and pharmaceutical sector in Germany lagged badly in genetic engineering.

Many of the described problems have been caused and perpetuated by a multitude of statutory and regulatory prescriptions. The Federal Republic established early on and fine-tuned over the years an elaborate legal framework of rules, regulations, and processes within which the market forces operate and, just as important, cooperate with each other without constant meddling on the part of public officials. This dependence on law and order in the economic arena, what Germans call *Ordnungspolitik*, depends for most routine matters and conflict resolution on statutes, regulations, and standard operating procedures that leave very little to chance. For example, the whole area of labor relations is shaped by a complex system of legal precepts designed to foster cooperation between and among employers and employees and their respective top-level organizations. It is precisely this characteristic of the German economic model that made the Federal Republic for many years a most attractive site for industrial production or what Germans call *Standort*. But following the short-lived postunification boom of the early 1990s, Germans came to recognize that many aspects of *Ordnungspolitik* were either causing the economic difficulties that occurred or preventing early intervention to effectively solve them.

Change is especially difficult to achieve in a country with deep-seated preferences and aversions that are rooted in centuries-old traditions (therefore the reluctance to make needed changes in the education system and especially in the apprentice training) or in the lessons of the Weimar and Nazi past (therefore the adherence to regulations reflecting widely held anti-modernity sentiments and impeding technological progress, or a bias for security and against risk taking in business). In addition, the power of German decisionmakers over their own economic policy and sphere is impeded by the influence of global market forces and the European Union's supranational institutions and policies on domestic developments and decisions.

The Collective Bargaining System Under Pressure

The most crucial aspect of Germany's *Ordnungspolitik* concerns its intricate system of labor relations. Until recently the social contract that governed this area since the early years of the Federal Republic worked very well for both capital and labor: owners, managers and shareholders made excellent profits, while employees enjoyed high wages and exceptional benefits. For decades West Germans collectively experienced growing prosperity and one of the world's highest standards of living. Much of the credit for these accomplishments belongs to the multifaceted relationships between business and labor which were neither left to chance nor supervised directly by the government. Instead, both the dual system of codetermination (*Mitbestimmung*) and the collective bargaining scheme were shaped by codified legal prescriptions and overseen by labor courts with the supreme value of promoting cooperation and avoiding social conflict.

The system's emphasis on cooperation is reinforced by labor laws that do not encourage strikes but demand stringent conditions to be fulfilled before such actions are deemed legal. To begin with, strikes are forbidden as long as agreements are in force; if agreements run out, strikes during contract negotiations are legal only after all prescribed arbitration efforts have failed. Even then the DGB requires secret ballots in which at least 75 percent of a sector union's membership must support a strike before it can actually happen. The Federal Republic has experienced far fewer strikes than the United States or other comparable industrialized countries in the post Word War II era. Between 1979 to 1991, for example, the average annual number of strike days per 1,000 workers was 38 in West Germany compared to 216 in the United States.[17] Wildcat strikes have also been rare. These kinds of actions go against the grain of most Germans' preference for law and order. According to one foreign observer of the German scene, German employees believe deep down "that a strike is a sign of failure, an irritating symptom of disorder."[18]

Codetermination or joint decisionmaking by employers and employees (the two sides are called "social partners") refers to legally imposed collaboration arrangements both in the board rooms and on the factory or office floor. Labor representatives occupy either one-third (in companies with more than 500 employees) or one-half (in companies with more than 2,000 employees) of the seats on the supervisory boards of all limited and joint stock companies with the rest of the seats reserved for shareholders. In the coal and steel industry, where codetermination was introduced first in the early 1950s, deadlocks in the supervisory board or *Aufsichtsrat* are broken by a board-elected "neutral" chair. In large corporations outside the coal and steel sector with more than 2,000 employees, the boards are chaired by major shareholders who are typically the representatives of large stockholders such as banks or insurance companies. Moreover, the office of labor director in charge of human services must be allotted to a representative of labor who also becomes a member of the corporate management board (*Vorstand*). The latter is in charge of the detailed day-to-day running of the company, whereas the supervisory board sets the overall corporate policies. While the influence of labor on boards differs from case to case, representation at the top assures the employees' side, if nothing else, access to vital corporate information.

A comparable, legally prescribed codetermination feature does not exist in the United States. So far, even minimal labor representation in corporate board rooms is the exception not the rule in the American setting. Deviations from the norm have occurred only during severe corporate crises or massive restructuring efforts, when one or the other corporation allowed an industrial union to nominate a candidate for a seat on the board of directors in exchange for organized labor's moderation in contract negotiations. In the 1990s, for example, the steelworkers union has won one seat on the boards of a few "Big Steel" corporations.

While Germany's substantial labor representation on company boards has contributed over the years to maintaining the social peace that most Germans appreciate, it has also fostered cozy relationships between capital and labor at the top. Critics on both sides have lamented that the social partners have tended to coopt each other at the expense of either side's particular interests. When the full extent of the structural crisis was finally acknowledged in the hardest-hit industries, there was much blame to go around—most of all in the corporate board rooms, where the representatives of both capital and labor had avoided tough decisions and possible conflict in the name of cooperation and consensus. But the snug relationships that may have hampered change in the past have also helped to set new corporate policies in a period of unavoidable industrial transformations that almost always involved painful consequences—especially for employees.

On the second track of the dual codetermination system, firms with more than five employees must let their workforce elect works councils or personnel councils if the majority of their employees request it. Since German law does not permit closed union shops, members and non-members of sector unions are in fact elected to these councils. While often-times close to their sector unions, works councils are legally not under the jurisdiction of the unions. By law, company managers must regularly meet with their firms' councils, communicate with them in advance of all kinds of important decisions, and consult them on questions such as hiring, firing, promotion, work allocation, mass layoffs, plant closings, and other matters. While managers have the last word in most matters, they strive for consensus. If they fire employees over the protest of their works councils, they must be prepared for litigation. If mass layoffs cannot be avoided, managers are legally required to work with their personnel councils to jointly establish detailed plans to prevent or soften the shock of unemployment. Job reassignments within a company, severance packages, and retraining programs are common features of these "social programs," which typically involve financial and other forms of assistance by the public sector as well.

In the 1990s, four of five employees in Western Germany worked for firms with one or both modes of codetermination. This high level of codetermination has not been reached in the Eastern part of the country—at least not during the years of the massive restructuring phase.

While works councils can negotiate wages, benefits, and all sorts of conditions above and beyond the minimum standards of their industry's collective bargaining agreements, the negotiations of basic labor contracts are the domain of the labor unions. On a region-by-region basis each of the sector unions negotiates with its corresponding employers' association a one- or multi-year contract which becomes legally binding for all firms in the particular industry and the region of the country. Firms that are not members of an employers' association do have the option to negotiate their own wage and benefits packages with the appropriate union in their area.

In the past, when the Federal Republic's economy showed robust growth rates and the labor unions were strong, a company that chose to negotiate separately with its sector union was likely to pay higher wages and more generous benefits than the minimum levels contained in the regional contract agreements. But this was no longer a given in the 1990s as mass unemployment in Eastern and Western Germany weakened the unions' bargaining power. When employers convinced their employees that the survival of their plants and thus of jobs were at stake, even so seemingly natural allies as works councils and trade unions were no longer automatically in agreement on the best course of action. The elimination of 30,000 jobs at Volkswagen AG, one of Germany's largest employers, was avoided in 1993, when management and works councilors agreed to a four-day work week with partial wage cuts. In this case, the leadership of the largest unions, IG Metall, supported the compromise. In other instances, works councils and employees disagreed with the unions. While the job-saving compromise at Volkswagen enjoyed broad support at the outset, it was eventually questioned even by supervisors and workers who had championed the solution. But regardless of its merits and shortcomings, the Volkswagen compromise, like similar agreements in other firms, revealed that there is room to maneuver within the framework of labor relations under extraordinary circumstances.

And nowhere were the conditions more extraordinary than in Eastern Germany in the years following the fall of the communist regime. In the absence of West Germany's tradition of mostly friendly ties between works councils and labor unions, councilors in Eastern firms resented union pressures against compromise on negotiated wage and benefits agreements. When threatened by plant closings, East German workers, their councils, and union locals were willing to accept wage levels and other terms significantly less advantageous than prescribed in regional agreements. It was no coincidence that a labor contract in Eastern Germany's steel industry for the state of Saxony broke new ground by spelling out the conditions under which individual companies, members of an employers association, could make their own deals with the union.

The special provisions contained in the Saxony agreement were within the legal parameters of the collective bargaining scheme. This was not the case, when, for the first time in the Federal Republic's history, an employers' association unilaterally terminated an unexpired collective bargaining agreement that called for double-digit wage increases. Although occurring in one of the Eastern states, where the economic circumstances and the historic experiences were vastly different than in the old Federal Republic, this unprecedented break with the legally prescribed rules sent shock waves through Western Germany and raised fears as to the soundness of the German model.

A few years after unification it was clear that labor relations in Eastern Germany were not the same as in the Western part of the country even though West German labor unions and employers' associations had extended their operations to the Eastern states. The industrial unions of the discredited East German *Freier Deutscher Gewerkschaftsbund* were integrated into respective Western German sector unions while most managements joined the newly established Eastern affiliates of the Western employers' organizations. There was never any doubt that West Germany's social partners were determined to transfer their organizations and operational techniques to the East; they were equally resolute in claiming leadership roles in the Eastern states. To this end, both Western unions and employers' associations dispatched personnel and transferred funds to the East. Moreover, the regional reorganization was tilted strongly in favor of the West in that four of the five Eastern states were merged into existing Western regions with the sole exception of Saxony.[19] Since labor contracts are negotiated separately for each regional unit, this was a curious organizational solution in view of the drastically different economic conditions and needs in East and West Germany.

The initially fairly high membership in both labor unions and employers' associations in the Eastern states plummeted in the years that followed. Unparalleled mass lay-offs and plant closings caused a great deal of these declines, but these dwindling numbers reflected also the existence of some of the same tensions inside the labor unions and the employers associations in the old Federal Republic. Unification magnified these conflicts.

As for the labor union movement, the merger of the two German states has added an East-West dimension to the frictions between its liberal and conservative wings that had existed in West Germany before reunification. While the more conservative unions in the West (i.e., IG Chemie) have preferred traditional, distributive union goals with the preservation of jobs high up on their agenda, the more liberal elements (i.e., IG Medien) have championed objectives such as the shorter work week, environmental protection, workers' control over new technologies, and equal rights for women at the workplace. In the Eastern states, union members have rejected such "post-materialist" goals. Instead, they have embraced the protection of jobs as their overriding objective. While still playing a role in the Western part of the country, differences over "bread-and-butter" versus "quality-of-life" issues have found its strongest expression between East and West German unionists.

Small and medium-size employers in Western Germany resented the "fat" labor contracts negotiated by their associations and under the influence of the largest companies long before similar, but more divisive issues surfaced after unification in the Eastern part of the country. Although their demands for more flexibility within the existing format had gotten them nowhere, most firms in West Germany did not leave their associations and the collective bargaining groups. The prospects for less expensive separate deals with the then strong unions were simply too remote. Many East German employers, however, after initially joining their sector associations, gave up their membership and went it alone, when they realized that they could strike deals with the relatively weak unions in their areas that undercut the collective agreements. Emboldened by these practices in the East, small and medium-size employers in West Germany threatened to, and a number of them actually did, walk out of their associations.

The fact that opt-outs for troubled companies were agreed to by some sector unions was seen by many observers as a threat to the collective bargaining principle itself and its replacement by American-style firm-by-firm negotiations. But while some business circles may have aspirations to dismantle the collective bargaining system, most employers and employees believe that a breakdown would not be in the best interest of either side. After all, the institutionalized roles of organized capital and labor, which give both sides a great deal of leverage in the governmental process, are closely tied to the existing labor relations concept. Here the institutional interests of labor and capital converge.

In a period in which the German industry is adapting to the changing competitive realities in the global markets, the balance of power seems to tip in favor of the employers. In the 1990s German investment overseas has grown rapidly and outpaced foreign investment in Germany. German firms are building and acquiring manufacturing plants abroad. In view of these developments direct and indirect threats of plant relocations are powerful weapons in the hands of employers. When managements offer works councils, unions, and workers a choice between "give backs" and the loss of whole plants to France, Hungary, or elsewhere, the employers' side is likely to win.

In 1996 the fifteen DGB member unions went so far as to agree on flexible labor contracts that "should take into account the different requirements of employees and fit within the varying circumstances [of the economy] and companies."[20] And a year later IG Chemie, the union representing workers in the chemical industry, negotiated a contract that made official what had been taking place at the company level for some time: Companies that could demonstrate serious financial distress could ask their local unions for wage cuts up to 10 percent in exchange for job guarantees. Perhaps the most flexible among German unions, the IG Chemie had agreed several years earlier that companies could rehire long-term unemployed workers at reduced wages. While some critics warned that the far-reaching agreement between the chemical workers' union and the chemical industry could be the beginning of the end of the German collective bargaining model, others regarded it simply as one more step toward more flexibility in an otherwise sound arrangement.

Constant complaints about the Federal Republic's dwindling competitiveness are in the eyes of some observers part of corporate Germany's "strategic wailing" to justify overly drastic workforce reductions, wage and benefit cuts, tax relief, and other measures beneficial to the business sector. Indeed, although many corporations have improved their productivity and returned to profitability in the mid-1990s, they have continued their efforts to "hold the line" against union demands. Increasingly, corporate managers have attacked their own employers' associations for negotiating what they perceived as too generous contracts with the labor unions. Workers, on the other hand, have vented anger against their own unions for insisting on a shorter work week and rejecting flexible work hours.

The gradual move toward closer European integration does not necessarily help the cause of German labor either. In the mid-1990s, for example, German construction workers were appalled when crews from Italy, Great Britain, Spain, and other European Union member states displaced them at many construction sites in Germany. Technically employed and paid by sub-contractors in their home countries, these foreigners worked for far lower wages than Germans based upon their collective bargaining agreements. The Bonn government's efforts on behalf of EU measures that would have required equal pay for equal work for every employee at the same location were rebuffed in Brussels.[21]

According to a 1994 European Union decision, firms with more than 1,000 employees and offices or plants in at least two member states of the EU must establish supranational works councils before the turn of the century. The matter was debated for decades and met with vehement opposition from employers' organizations. But so far there is no evidence that supra-national works councils weaken the employers and strengthen the employees. A few dozen corporations, Volkswagen among them, have established European works councils voluntarily before Brussels acted. The members of these multinational bodies are involved in decisions affecting the employees in different countries. While conceived as an expansion of workers' codetermination rights, this new dimension in the codetermination scheme seems to offer corporate managements and boards excellent opportunities to pass the buck to their European works councils—for example, when the issue is the relocation of production from one country to another.

The Admired Educational and Vocational System

Many German business managers blame rigid regulations for the high level of unemployment and other economic woes. Until recently one heavily regulated area, the education and occupational training system, was exempt from criticism. One track of schooling is designed for high school students who are likely to attend universities (about 25 percent), the second for those who are likely to move directly into an occupation. For a young German the road to post-secondary education is not fundamentally different from the high school experience of an American student. With the exception of a few, fairly new apprenticeship programs in some regions of the U.S., especially where German companies established manufacturing plants, the Germany-style comprehensive occupational training is unknown in the U.S.

Germany's formal training, which generally lasts three years, is the precondition to work in carpentry, plumbing, printing, house painting, hairdressing, sales and hundreds of other occupations. The vocational training tradition goes back to the Middle Ages when the guilds of the leading trades licensed their master bakers, butchers, blacksmiths, etc., to take on apprentices.[22] During the industrial revolution the system was extended to industrial workers, and eventually to many white color workers as well. Typically entering the program at age 15 or 16, most apprentices spend four days a week in plants, offices, stores, and other worksites to learn a trade. At least one day a week they must attend a public vocational school for theoretical and practical training and reinforcement.[23] The government, trade associations, chambers of commerce, and labor unions work closely together in prescribing the required content of the work site training in each occupational specialty. At least nine of ten apprentices pass the mandatory certification exams at the end of their training period. And more than half of them are offered jobs by the companies they trained in.

In the United States, as in other highly industrialized countries unemployment among the under 25 year old population has been consistently and significantly higher than in the workforce as a whole. This has not been the case in Germany. Experts have credited the national apprenticeship program for this accomplishment. But as the German economy has begun its transition into the technologies and industries of the future, the traditional apprentice system has been slow in adjusting to the changed market conditions and demands. While training for a number of obsolete occupations is still offered and funded, it is not available for many new types of jobs with excellent prospects. Jobs in the new and rapidly changing technologies do not fit into the guidelines of the past which require many years of experience and certification on the part of experts in one specific field, before they can supervise the instruction of the young. And the long, comprehensive vocational education in one field does not prepare the workforce to shift from one career to another as it is increasingly necessary in post-industrial economies. Even the post-secondary education track has come under pressure to change—especially because most students do not enter the workforce before they are 30 years old. Another bone of contention is Germany's lack of American style elite universities. As a result, critics of the system argue, the nation does not produce a select group of highly qualified experts, innovators, and leaders who come up with new technological and managerial innovations and fresh public policy ideas.

The Consequences of Blue Laws and Other Regulations

In the early 1990s, when critics intensified their attacks on the encrusted regulatory peculiarities of Germany's web of regulations as inhibiting economic expansion and competition, they were, however, less concerned with the dual education system than with other, more pressing problem areas. The perhaps most striking example of legal handcuffs on business activities are federal "blue laws" which are for Americans in most places long forgotten remnants of the past. Used to shopping seven days a week till late at night, even 24-hour-around-the-clock supermarkets, diners, and other conveniences, most American visitors to Germany go through somewhat of a culture shock, when they encounter the restricted and inconvenient store hours of retail businesses.

One must have witnessed the Saturday morning rush of German shoppers in supermarkets, department and neighborhood to learn about the hardship that limited store hours impose on people who work during the week. For husbands and wives to shop leisurely after work for a new tv-set, a car, or for furniture was until recently simply impossible. The tribulation of dashing to and through crowded stores right after work or Sat-

insulin in 1988. Six years later governmental approval was still pending and the Hoechst plant in Frankfurt still empty. By that time, Hoechst's competitors in the United States had long gotten the approval of the U.S. Food and Drug Administration and were producing and selling genetically designed insulin. Given the cumbersome red tape at home, all major pharmaceutical companies have increasingly invested in American research centers and plants to conduct clinical trials and manufacture new products. It has not helped that the German taxation system has been less favorable toward research and development investments than comparable tax laws in the U.S. and other advanced societies.

Even after federal laws designed to speed up and simplify some of the described regulations were adopted in the 1990s, the affected businesses did not expect drastic relief because the obstacles on the road to new technologies and their applications mirrored the society's deep-seated skepticism and hostility toward technological progress and especially clinical tests involving humans. The idea of experimenting with genetic material did not appeal to a nation in which many were still mindful of the cold-blooded euthanasia and eugenics programs and experiments during the Nazi era. The reluctance to embrace technological advances has transcended genetic engineering and medical experiments encompassing many other areas such as nuclear power and computer technology. In this respect, German attitudes have differed a great deal from American public opinion. The flipside of this hostility toward technology has been a persistently strong sentiment in favor of environmental protection.

Another reason why Germany has been slow in embracing innovative technologies and new business opportunities and practices has been a strong societal preference for security and a similarly powerful aversion to risk-taking. The public and private sector's encouragement and support for entrepreneurial initiatives and ventures has been sparse in the Federal Republic as well as in in the state-run system of the German Democratic Republic,

It is no wonder that the numerous success stories in the United States—especially in computer, communication and bio-technology—have not been matched by the German experience. All too often first-rate research by German scientists and engineers were not turned into products by German companies. The fax technology, for example, was invented in Germany, but the Japanese were first to develop it into a marketable product.

For entrepreneurs venture capital, whether from banks, special risk capital firms, or private investors has been much harder to come by in

Germany than in the U.S. Rather than taking a risk for the chance to rake in windfall profits, Germans have preferred safe lending practices. This was a particular problem for East Germans who were eager to start their own businesses right after unification. Unable to satisfy the demand for collaterals most of them were unable to get start-up capital from a bank. Luckily, tens of thousands of East German entrepreneurs were able to tap into the same fund that had helped West Germans to rebuild their industries after World War II—the European Recovery Program or Marshall Plan provided by the United States in the 1940s and 50s. Because the original West German recipients of Marshall Plan money had not received outright grants but loans which they paid back with interest, the original $1.5 billion had grown to about four time the initial size in the 1990s. Five years after the fall of communist regime, nearly half of all small and medium-size businesses in East Germany had received seed money from the Marshall Plan. Once instrumental in the reconstruction of the Federal Republic, a new U.S. ally in the Cold War against the communist bloc, the Marshall Plan fund became the single most important booster of private business ventures in the former communist East Germany following reunification.

The tendency to avoid risk and cling to the status quo has not only impeded new business ventures but also progress and change in existing companies. Here the fiscal tradition of German firms and the interlocking relationships between the leading commercial banks, insurance companies, and large corporations have stood in the way of bold moves. Unlike in the United States where most companies are publicly traded and thus able to draw their capital from the stock markets, most German firms have been owned privately or by a handful of shareholders, often members of one family. When capital is needed, these firms borrow from their banks. But the financial institutions are more inclined to grant loans for seemingly safe business-as-usual projects than for trailblazing innovations and product developments. As the need to invest into the technologies of the future has become more urgent, firm managers have increasingly questioned a practice that gives bankers a veto over fateful decisions.

These traditional standards have hampered especially the expansion of upstart firms. For example, without a record of several profitable years behind them, small computer software firms with excellent business prospects and the need to expand, have been unable to secure bank loans or tap the financial markets by going public in the Federal Republic. By the mid-1990s, some of these firms looked directly to American stock markets to raise capital.

There was also the likelihood that many of the still privately held *Mittelstand* firms would eventually follow the Anglo-American model and raise equity by going public—in spite of their owners fears to lose more control to outside forces.

The Power of the Banks

Such fears are well founded because firms whose shares are publicly traded feel the influence of banks on a regular and direct basis. Unlike their American counterparts, German banks are allowed by law to own unlimited equity in other companies. As a result, banks, especially the "Big Three" (Deutsche Bank, Dresdner Bank, and Commerzbank) have traditionally owned big chunks of the nation's industrial sector, especially of the largest stock corporations. By the mid-1990s, Deutsche Bank, for example, owned 24 percent of Daimler-Benz, 26 percent of Phillipp Holzmann, and 32 percent of Kloeckner-Humbold-Deutz shares. More important, German investors tend to deposit their stock holdings with banks and unless otherwise instructed, the financial institutions can vote enormous blocs of proxies they hold as custodians as they please. It has been quite common that several banks combined control half or more of the shares voted at stockholder meetings.[25] In 1995 about 70 percent of the shares of the country's 400 largest firms were voted by banks. And as far as several of the largest corporations were concerned, the "Big Three" alone vote more than one third of the shares.[26] Since the law has allowed banks to transfer their voting rights to other financial institutions, this practice gives a firm's "house bank" enormous influence in corporate decision making.

Instead of competing with each other, as American banks do, German bankers are far more inclined to cooperate and respect each other's interest. And instead of shopping around for their loans, companies deal with their "house bank" only—usually a leading shareholder as well. This cooperative stance also prevails on supervisory boards, where bankers are represented in large numbers; bankers also chair the boards of several of the country's largest enterprises. Finally, leading bankers, the heads of insurance companies, and the top managers of large corporations are closely linked through a multitude of interlocking directorates. Thus, it is not unusual that the head of a leading bank serves on the board of a large corporation whose CEO is a director of a large insurance company whose boss is member of the bank's board. All of this can and has resulted in cozy relationships in which bankers have allowed corporate mismanagement while corporation managers failed to shop around for the best credit terms.

While they have been customarily major creditors and stockholders of the same corporations, bankers have been mostly concerned with safeguarding their outstanding loans—often at the expense of innovation and change. This conservative stance of the financial institutions and their contentment with modest returns on their equity investments have not always been in the best interest of a company's longterm health or other stockholders' returns. Managers of publicly traded companies in Germany, unlike their American counterparts, do not have to worry constantly about the next quarter's bottom line and the ups and downs of their firms' shares at the stock market. Usually the large German shareholders hold their stakes for many years and show little appetite for trades even in the face of poor corporate performances. In the past, many experts compared the German system favorably to the American arrangement with its fragmented ownership because they believed the German corporations' long-term outlook to be superior to the short-term considerations forced upon U.S. managers by stockholders out for a quick buck.

Only after the extent of corporate Germany's structural crisis became apparent in the 1990s did critics inside and outside the political arena begin to question the banks' powerful role, their built-in conflict of interest, and their intimate relationships with each other and corporate managers. Since the banks established and perpetuated their predominance in the nation's industry well within the boundaries of the statutory and regulatory framework, it has been up to the national government to decide whether or not adjustments are necessary.

In this area, as in those discussed above, the hands of public and private sector decision makers have been increasingly forced by the international environment and Germany's need to compete in the global markets. As the lack of available capital within their own country obliged German corporations to raise capital in foreign markets, the firms themselves, the major banks, and policy makers recognized that they had to adapt to the internationally accepted rules and practices of corporate governance. Thus, before Daimler-Benz became the first German company to list its shares on an American stock exchange in 1993, it had to switch to the more transparent accounting practices of U.S. corporations. Shortly thereafter, Deutsche Bank sold more than 3 percent of its Daimler-Benz shares and thereby reduced its holdings to just under the 25 percent threshold needed to veto any measure coming before the shareholders. The pressure to embrace internationally acceptable rules increased when state-owned companies such as the Deutsche Telekom were positioned for privatization. These transactions multiplied the need for foreign capital.

Aware of the growing concerns over the interlocking relationships between banks and stock companies, Deutsche Bank especially reduced its holdings in other firms besides Daimler-Benz. But increasingly critics inside and outside the country concluded that the modest voluntary changes undertaken by the banking sector would not be adequate. By the mid-1990s, even the German public was disturbed by what it perceived as the major banks' and their executives arrogance of power and wealth. When the CEO of Deutsche Bank characterized the $33 million owed to construction workers by one of his bank's bankrupt debtors as "peanuts," he enraged many of his fellow-Germans who felt the pain of mass unemployment and declining incomes. The major political parties, many experts, and public opinion agreed that reform was needed. The question was, how far governmental decision makers would and could curb the power of the banks—traditionally one of the most influential interests in the political process.

Government Subsidies and the Triumph of Politics

In some areas drastic departures from past policies seemed out of the question for the time being. Government subsidies fell into this category. Even chancellors and governing coalitions ideologically opposed to heavy and continued subsidies were not able to reduce or abolish them. Some of these sacred cows were older than the Federal Republic. Subsidies ballooned in the years following unification to around $100 billion a year. Surprisingly, only about one half of these funds went to Eastern Germany; the rest was pumped into Western Germany primarily to support the structural conservation of sectors such as coal mining, shipbuilding, railroads, and agriculture at the expense of new technology sectors, innovative projects, and entrepreneurial initiatives in the technologies of the future. Indeed, the share of government grants for research and development projects declined. Even when the structural dilemma of the industries of the nineteenth and twentieth century was perfectly clear, these old industries received more subsidies than the sectors most likely to determine economic strength and weakness in the twenty-first century. The dispersion of public funds remained a triumph of the entrenched interests over the new, not yet institutionally integrated interests. This explains that the agricultural sector continued to receive more in government subsidies than it contributed to the national product.

In Eastern Germany, too, political considerations are often more important than economic reasoning. This was behind the *Treuhand's* decision to form several management organizations for the purpose of saving outdated, unprofitable outfits for which private buyers could not be found. When the trust agency went out of business at the end of 1994, its successor agencies were left with some 150,000 employees working for these heavily subsidized firms. The numbers shrank as "negative value" companies were restructured with infusions of public funds and eventually sold to German or foreign interests, often with the promise for future subsidies in one form or the other.

The steel mill Eko (short for *Eisenhüttenkombinat* or ironworks collective) in the state of Brandenburg was a case in point. The plant's four blast furnaces and one cold-rolling mill had been constructed by workers' brigades in the early 1950s. In terms of technology, productivity, and product quality Eko was inferior to steelmakers outside the communist bloc. Given the highly competitive international steel market, Eko seemed destined to fail soon after the fall of the Berlin Wall and unification. But the plant's demise would have been the kiss of death for the community to which the mill had given its name—Eisenhüttenstadt (Ironworks City), a town of about 50,000 that had developed around the plant. By pumping more than $300 million into the outdated facilities, Treuhand kept Eko Steel alive at a time when modern steel mills in Western Germany could not utilize their production capacity due to soft demands on the steel market. When Treuhand finally found a taker for Eko Steel, it promised the Belgian corporation Cockerill Sambre more than $600 million in government subsidies in exchange for the promise to modernize Eko and protect 2,300 jobs. As one observer noted, "In total, that works out to about $500,000 for each job saved."[27] What did not make much sense economically, was in the eyes of political leaders a prudent decision in terms of the human aspect of German capitalism.

Outside Checks on Domestic Economic Policies

The Eko case demonstrated furthermore that German decisionmakers, just as the national governments in other EU countries, have lost sole control over what are seemingly questions of domestic economic policies. Because the EU has a policy of gradually shrinking the steel capacity of its member states, the takeover of Eko and especially the massive subsidy package needed the approval of all EU members. Several countries threatened to derail the deal, unless they were also granted exemptions from the EU's subsidy policies. Only when the complaining countries were allowed to subsidize plants or industries within their own borders could the Eko deal fly.

Also, the decisionmaking organs of the EU can and do bypass the federal government and deal directly with the governments of individual states and local communities (the latter often unite and form larger regions of shared interests) when it comes to allocating funds for regional economic development.

As EU policies and regulatory measures continue to escalate into most important areas, they constitute increasingly potent outside checks on the federal government's ability to affect the domestic economy even though representatives of the Federal Republic's national government do have, of course, influence within the organs of the EU.

The growing reach of the EU authorities into domestic matters occurs in addition to the effects of the global markets on national economies and decisionmaking. As other national governments, especially those in export-oriented countries, the Federal Republic, cannot ignore its own economy's role in and reliance on international markets. This is not limited to but most transparent in the financial markets.

Thus, after the German banking industry had come under fire because of several insider trading scandals, a new law went into effect in 1994 making insider trading a criminal offense and requiring safeguards against violations. Since German banks are the dominant players in stock transactions, they must now retain sharp demarcation lines between their corporate finance and trading departments. The newly established watchdog securities agency was patterned after the U.S. Security and Exchange Commission. In this instance, the German government reacted to mounting pressures, especially from abroad, to align the country's security industry with the regulatory standards in major overseas markets and thereby boost foreign investors' confidence in German securities.

Signs of Flexibility

To be sure, in the long list of complex policy problems caused by the shifts in the global competitive environment and the unification of the two Germanys, the government's response to insider trading constitutes no more than a footnote. Taken alone, these sorts of measures do not contradict the conventional wisdom that the German model with its emphasis on sociopolitical stability, predictability, cooperation, and consensus is ill equipped for more than the incremental changes that were made in the past. While this chapter has described in some detail the institutional and cultural obstacles to bold adjustments in the Federal Republic's economic policies, it has sketched a number of significant changes that would have been unthinkable a few years earlier, notably in the area of labor relations and especially collective bargaining. Moreover, taken together, the growing number of admittedly limited changes in the onetime static laws and regulations of *Ordnungspolitik* added up to a package of meaningful change.[28]

While nothing came easy, all actors showed signs of changing mindsets—perhaps most of all the general public. There was, for example, a growing public sentiment in favor of preserving jobs even at the expense of wage hikes, shorter work weeks, and the once-sacred workfree week-end. When the metal workers went on strike in early 1995, three of five Germans characterized their union's demand for a six percent wage increase as "too high." Union members were evenly divided on this issue. The majority of Germans rejected the union's demand for a 35-hour work week and supported the employers' insistence on week-end shifts to allow plants to extend the running times of their machine equipment.[29] On the other hand, expert observers and the public grew more critical of corporate mismanagement, the disparities between impressive corporate profits and drastic downsizing efforts, and the gap between the highest and lowest income levels.

At the end of the 1990s German business leaders increasingly blamed the checks on their country's parliamentary government for preventing reforms that were bold enough to reinvigorate the slumping economic engine and the attractiveness of Germany as a place to do business. Thus, when the SPD, the opposition party in the federal diet and the ruling party in the majority of states, rejected the Kohl government's comprehensive tax reform package in the summer of 1997, the business community was especially adamant about the flaws of a system that had effectively derailed what they had dramatized as the last best chance to reenergize the economy by lowering taxes. But the same critics who condemned the checks on their parliamentary government, when they did not like the results, attacked politicians at other times for consensus decisions, when they opposed the outcome.

Reaching the most fateful crossroads yet, the German model is being tested as never before. There are encouraging indications along with business-as-usual tendencies as to the outcome of this trial. New or more pronounced divisions within and between the major political parties, labor unions, and business groups interfere with the old consensus-oriented decisionmaking process and make for more adversarial relationships along the line of American capitalism. But the unchanged institutional arrangements, the formalized rules of the game, and the lingering legacy of the past continue to provide powerful impulses for continued cooperation and consensus-building. During the decades in which German decisionmakers had far more control over their country's economic destiny, the web of institutional ties and the unyielding framework of regulations stood in the way of major changes. Ironically, the same global market forces and supranational policies that impeded the power of national decisionmakers seem to become increasingly the catalysts for domestic change—in the realm of economic politics and in social policy as well.

6

Social Welfare State Under Pressure

Somewhere in the Federal Republic of Germany in 1995: A frail, old woman points agitatedly to a cushion that comforts her while she spends most of her days in a reclining chair. She is upset about already implemented cost-control measures in medical care. Instead of two pillows, as she had requested, her mandatory health insurance paid for one cushion only. "In the old days," she protests, "they approved everything I asked for." Her daughter and son-in-law are not sympathetic to her complaints, reminding her that the monthly insurance payments for her in-home care have just doubled thanks to the newly established mandatory nursing care insurance.

Somewhere in the United States in 1995: A frail, old woman hunches in a living room chair. Her face reflects sorrow as she overhears her alarmed daughter and son-in-law discuss proposed state cuts in the home nursing care she obviously needs, and the dire financial consequences for the whole family. Depicted in a powerful television commercial, the ad attacks one particular aspect of one governor's cost cutting contribution to the so-called Republican Revolution. Although dramatized to indict the inhuman nature of such social spending cuts, the scene looks awfully real to many TV-watchers—especially to ailing senior citizens without financial resources to pay for their care.

These episodes demonstrate that health care policies are causing complaints about perceived or real hardship in Germany and in the United States. But comparing mandated health care features in the two countries is like comparing apples and oranges. In the mid-1990s, when both countries grappled with mounting public indebtedness and the need to control government spending, Germany added nevertheless a mandatory nursing care feature to its state guaranteed health insurance system while the U.S. rejected the Clinton administration's health care reform plan that had compulsory insurance at its core. These differences show up not only in health care policies but generally in current approaches to social welfare programs in the U.S. and Germany.

Germans have not simply continued to expand their highly developed social welfare structure and bucked the growing problems and entrenchment trends observed in some other Western democracies. Just as the establishment of the new nursing care insurance was part of a broader health care reform initiative that included cost-control measures and higher payroll contributions, West Germany in the 1970s and 1980s and united Germany in the 1990s adopted a number of cost-control steps, albeit modest, to protect the solvency of the country's various social insurance funds.

At century's end, social assistance, what average Germans and Americans simply call "welfare," came under scrutiny in the Federal Republic. As fiscal problems worsened, home-grown "social cheaters," along with foreign asylum seekers who were caught collecting more than one welfare check, became the targets of elite and public outrage like "welfare queens" and illegal immigrants did in the United States. During a 1995 welfare reform debate in the U.S. House of Representatives, one member expressed the sentiments of many, when he held up a sign with the inscription, "Don't Feed the Alligators" arguing that "unnatural feeding and artificial care" create the same dependency among alligators as "welfare" does among the recipients of governmental handouts. Some German critics also identified certain features of their social assistance system as "rewarding laziness." But no official came remotely close to comparing the welfare clientele to alligators or to well-fed wolves as had elected officials in Washington. Such analogies would have been ill received in a society that was far more in agreement on the basic tenets of its comprehensive welfare state than Americans were on their substantially less generous social safety net.

When they encounter the term "social security," Americans think of the government's old-age pension insurance that was one of the programs adopted with the Social Security Act of 1935. For Germans, the quasi-public old-age pension insurance that was introduced in rudimentary form by Chancellor Otto von Bismarck in the late 1880s, is merely one element in the nationally mandated "social security" package encompassing a wide range of social insurance, social assistance and other benefits such as child allowance and education assistance. Even the labor relations model with the comprehensive workers' rights and benefits described in the previous chapter is considered an integral part of the country's commitment to ensure an adequate degree of "social security" for all. Most Germans take for granted comprehensive safeguards against the most common calamities of life and look upon the basic structure of their welfare state as the "social" ingredient in their "social market economy" arrangement and the fulfillment of the constitutional precept that the Federal Republic is a "social" state. It is no coincidence that for more than forty years a single executive department in the federal government, the Ministry of Labor and Social Affairs, oversaw an area divided between two departments (Department of Health and Human Services and Department of Labor) in Washington. In Germany, the federal Department of Health was created as late as 1991, when the CDU-led coalition government recognized the need for a separate ministry to tighten up its oversight and curb the costs of the health care sector through comprehensive reforms.

During the heated debate of the Clinton administration's proposed health insurance reform plan in 1994 opponents attacked the President's initiative frequently by citing the "l" and "s" words—the one for liberal and the other for leftist socialized medicine and socialism. As in so many policy debates and election campaigns before, these labels stuck. Once tainted as un-American and another addition to an already unruly American welfare state, the health care reform proposal lost elite and public support and was completely derailed. In Germany the debate surrounding the creation of a new long-term nursing care insurance centered around its funding methods and lacked the ideological demonizing and scare tactics used in the U.S.

In contrast to the United States, the basic premises and all features of the well-developed German welfare state have rested on a societal consensus spanning the ideological, partisan, and socioeconomic spectrum. There has been broad agreement on society's responsibility to provide a humane level of social security and on the individual's right to be protected by collective arrangements against the most common risks of life regardless of whether the economic hardship can be attributed to the individual or to circumstances beyond the individual's control. The policy debates of the 1980s and 1990s have centered around the recognition that Germany cannot sustain the largess of its social welfare programs forever under present conditions. While there has been considerable disagreement over the nature, scope, and direction of the changes needed, the debate over this lacked the stinging animosity of comparable debates in the United States.

Such profound dissimilarities are not surprising. The histories of welfare policies in Germany and in the United States reflect vast and persistent differences in what the political and business elites as well as the populace have understood in various periods as the legitimate responsibilities of the collectivity. Early beliefs in influential circles shaped the attitudes of following generations in both countries. In the face of the Industrial Revolution German socialists and Catholic reformers concluded that universal social policies could and should be used by "the state" to soften the harsh dislocations caused by the rapid industrialization on workers and their dependents. The idea was that individuals alone were unable to overcome the harsh predicaments of industrial capitalism regardless of where they lived and worked. Therefore, it fell on the national government to establish programs to provide a cushion against indigence.

Germany has always had some people whose poverty has had nothing to do with the uncontrollable adversities of life. Given the Germans' legendary work ethic, most citizens have looked down on such "asocial" element and many still do. Until the early 1900s, it was up to local government and private charity to provide for the poor. But by the 1920s the indigent in Germany had a right to public welfare according to a uniformed national standard of support. For most of this century the distinction between the "deserving" and "undeserving" poor has not played the prominent role in German attitudes toward the needy as it has in the U.S. In Germany the poor have traditionally constituted a significantly smaller segment of the population than in the United States, which has probably contributed to dissimilar views in the two societies. These attitudinal divergences continue to explain the two countries' different public policy approaches toward the destitute.

However, the first state initiatives in the area of social policy were certainly not driven by altruistic motives on the part of Bismarck and the authoritarian-constitutional monarchy but rather by the desire to ward off threatening demands by socialists and labor unions. Still, the social insurances introduced in the 1880s (health, workers compensation, and old age) were an official recognition that the nation bears a responsibility for the sustenance of its citizens. This was a clever top-to-bottom move to win workers' loyalty and tie the working masses to a state that offered protection against the normal risks of life, namely sickness, job-related disability, and old age. Because of their participation in administering the insurance funds and the 1890 repeal of a Socialist Law that had banned the Socialist Party and persecuted trade unions, workers embraced these social programs that would eventually serve as models for similar policies in other industrial countries.

Early on, the social insurance was designed with different contribution requirements and benefit provisions for salaried white-color workers, wage-earning blue-color workers, and civil servants in order to maintain and indeed accentuate the class distinctions between the different strata and thereby discourage all workers from uniting.[1] In 1927, during the waning years of the Weimar Republic, state-mandated unemployment insurance was added to the already existing social welfare programs. A few years later, during the Great Depression, the American version of the social welfare state was initiated. As in Germany half a century earlier, President Franklin D. Roosevelt's New Deal social programs were top-to-bottom responses that could also be interpreted as protecting the existing political and socioeconomic order against possible radical challenges. For many Americans the Great Depression contradicted the common view that poverty was simply the consequence of an individual's laziness or other moral shortcomings. People who lost their jobs and their savings also lost faith in the American promise that each individual had the ability to determine his or her own fortune. Moreover, given the severity of the crisis that affected people in all parts of the country, Americans no longer looked to their local communities or states for relief but rather to the national government.

The Federal Republic and the United States both expanded their welfare states in the post-World War II era of robust economic growth—the former significantly more than the latter. But while the results were supported by leaders and public consensus in the Federal Republic, large segments of American leaders and the public remained skeptical, if not hostile, toward rapidly expanding social programs, especially during the Johnson presidency.

In the early 1980s the electorate in both countries voted for leaders who promised socioeconomic changes in the 1980s—Americans for conservative Republican Ronald Reagan's "revolution," which included the promise of cutting social programs, West Germans for a similar *Wende* or turnaround as pledged by Christian Democrat Helmut Kohl. However, the sentiments on the two sides of the Atlantic Ocean were quite different: In America, many one-time enthusiastic supporters of President Lyndon Johnson's "Great Society" no longer believed in the ability of the "War on Poverty" policies to lift the poor "underclass." The programs designed for the benefit of the poor were first in line when Reagan's budget-cutters went to work. In the Federal Republic neither the effectiveness and necessity of social assistance nor other social welfare programs were at issue, but simply the recognition that a persistently declining economic growth rate demanded adjustments. It was not welfare programs for the poor but the far larger middle-class entitlement programs that were highest on the agenda when the Kohl government tried to lower social spending. Ultimately, in spite of political rhetoric and partisan infighting in both countries neither the Reagan revolution nor the Kohl's ostensible turnaround dismantled or significantly altered the entrenched welfare states.

But by the mid-1990s the socioeconomic situation had drastically changed in the Federal Republic. The high cost of rebuilding East Germany's economy and extending the benefits of the Federal Republic's welfare state to East Germans as well as economic and demographic disturbances forced Germans to seriously reexamine the long-term fiscal soundness of their social welfare edifice and consider significant changes. Some people questioned the desirability of a virtually risk-free society. But while concerns were voiced about the welfare state's tendency to curb individual initiative and encourage reliance on society, most of these arguments and proposals targeted the excesses, not the core, of the welfare state. In tone and substance nothing in these deliberations in the Federal Republic resembled the contentious words and initiatives of Republican congressional leaders and their supporters inside and outside of the Congress after their landslide victory in the 1994 congressional elections. Declaring many federal ("Big Government") programs and regulations bankrupt, especially those designed to assist the poor, they claimed a mandate for an assault on the welfare state and its alleged tendency to squash the traditional Christian values of the American family and community. Even earlier, during the 1992 presidential campaign, Democrat Bill Clinton had promised to "end welfare as we know it." As the presidential and congressional election of 1996 approached, congressional Republicans and Democrats adopted and President Clinton signed into law a welfare reform that effectively dismantled the Federal government's welfare responsibilities.

Not religious zealots, as in the U.S., but secular leaders with diverse ideological preferences shaped the "value" debate among German leaders that pointed to the need for more community spirit and less individual selfishness in the search for solutions to all kinds of social, political, and societal problems. But while appealing for more emphasis on the common and less on the individual good or pleading for greater involvement and self-help within families and communities, German advocates of a renewed community spirit did not suggest in the same breath to tear down major social programs for the benefit of the poor because, as one U.S. Representative put it during the 1995 welfare reform debate, poverty is not a material but a moral problem. Hillary Clinton, who reminded Americans that "it takes a village" to nurture children and led the campaign for a mandatory health insurance system, became one of the least popular first ladies ever.

The differences in elite attitudes, rhetoric, and social-policymaking that created welfare states of immensely different scopes in Germany and in the U.S. have reflected similar discrepancies in public attitudes toward social welfare in the two countries. The German public has, for the most part, been consistent in its overwhelming support for their country's expansive social safety net while the American populace has been less supportive of the government's comparatively modest or nonexistent role in this area. Germans have given their welfare state high grades; Americans have tended to dwell just as much, if not more, on the deficiencies of their system than on its accomplishments. Most of all, public sentiments in both countries have mirrored the profound differences in their publics' perception about the proper role of "the state" (the phrase pollsters use in Germany) or "the government" (in the U.S.) in the area of social policy, with Germans far more comfortable than Americans with comprehensive and centrally mandated social welfare programs. This discrepancy is consistent with comparisons of several industrialized democracies that found far higher degrees of public support for governmental welfare policies in countries with expansive social welfare systems than in less developed welfare states.[2]

Germans, who have long enjoyed "cradle-to-grave" social security, demand a great deal more of the welfare state than do Americans, who are used to limited social-welfare programs. While Germans overwhelmingly continue to expect the state to provide employment, shelter, and an adequate standard of living, most Americans adhere to the time-honored American ideal of individualism and prefer private initiative to government activism to address social needs. Accordingly, the two publics differ in their views on equal opportunity and people's control over their own destiny: The majority of Germans are convinced that one's socioeconomic predicament in life is predominantly determined by forces outside the individual's control; the majority of Americans reject this notion and maintain a strong belief in the each individual's ability to succeed and to make the American dream come true. Consequently, far more Germans than Americans think that the state or government must provide for those who are unable to care for themselves. This divergence accounts for other drastic differences in American and German public attitudes: About two-thirds of all Germans believe that the state should reduce income differences and dispense guaranteed minimum income; a firm majority of Americans oppose the government's hand in correcting income differences, limiting the yearly income each individual can earn, or providing everyone with a guaranteed minimum income. Statistical evidence shows that these attitudinal differences cannot be explained by the respective income and wealth distributions in the United States and the Federal Republic. While widening in the last two decades of the century, the income gap between top earners on the one hand and people with middle-level and low incomes is markedly smaller in Germany than in the United States. In terms of wealth distribution the Federal Republic does have a somewhat better record than the U.S. which is more unequal in this respect than any other comparable country.[3] But even in the mature German welfare state the distance between the super-rich and the rest of society is significant and growing larger.

Still, the actual quality of life for middle- and low-income people as well as for the poor in Germany is markedly better than in the United States. This is the result of far more generous divisible and indivisible social benefits in the Federal Republic—those which are explicitly part of the welfare state such as universal health care with its paid prevention and recuperation features (i.e., several weeks' stay and treatment in health spas) or other standard public policies such as equal educational access or well-maintained parks and playgrounds.

By the same token, perceived membership in a social class offers no way of directly comparing economic status in the two countries. Thus, when asked what social class they belong to, nearly two-thirds of West Germans and Americans identify themselves as members of the middle class. But this does not mean that the living standards of those considering themselves middle class is similar in the two nations. Interestingly, in assigning themselves to classes, West and East Germans differ a great deal in that only slightly more than one-third of East Germans identify themselves as belonging to the middle class while close to two-thirds consider themselves members of the working or underclass. This German difference has certainly something to do with lower income levels and nonexistent wealth and thus an objectively different standard of living in East Germany compared to the western part of the country. But East Germans' different frame of mind in this respect is also related to their past in the communist "workers' state," where working-class consciousness was cultivated.

Given their experiences in a state that provided them with their basic needs from, albeit often shabby, housing to jobs and child care, East Germans have continued to demand more of the welfare state than their Western counterparts. For example, although three in four West Germans believe that the state must guarantee everyone a job, nearly all Easterners (95%) insist on the right to work; and while three in five West Germans want the government to correct disparities in income distribution, better than four of five East Germans want this. In the post-unification Federal Republic, then, the support for the welfare state is even stronger than the already very firm backing it enjoyed in West Germany prior to the 1990 unification.

In Germany, there is no equivalent to the American distrust of the federal government and its potential for abuse of power at the expense of state rights and individual liberties. Nor do Germans share Americans' strong disdain for federal programs, rules, and regulations. Accordingly, well-orchestrated attacks on "Big Government's" incompetence and inefficiency by special-interest groups (such as the insurance industry's and other opponents' media campaigns against the Clinton plan during the 1994 health-care reform debate in the U.S.) would not be expected to sway the German public or governmental decisionmakers and therefore would not be mounted in the first place.

While less than in several other Western European countries, among them Denmark and Sweden, the individual and corporate tax burdens in Germany are significantly higher than in the United States.[4] Germans complain about their high taxes just as Americans do, and by the mid-

1990s a majority no longer considered tax evasion a crime but a clever move to beat the system—a signal that Germans might lose their reputation as the world's most honest taxpayers. Yet, in spite of the heavy taxation, the Federal Republic has not faced an American style tax revolt.[5] In early 1997, when Peter Graf, the father and business manager of tennis champion Steffi, was sentenced to a stiff prison term for tax evasion, the authorities sent a powerful signal to actual and would-be tax cheaters. Ultimately, most Germans prefer to pay rather than risk the guarantees that their comprehensive social security system affords them—from child allowance and free college education to health care, unemployment benefits, and old-age pension. Social assistance constitutes only a small part of total social outlays.

It has been estimated that about 80 percent of German families get benefits from at least one social program. It is probably for this reason that the welfare state has enjoyed overwhelming and unwavering public support in the Federal Republic. In the less generous United States, where about 50 percent of all households receive some form of social program benefit, public backing is less fervent.

According to opinion polls most Germans want the reassuring peace of mind that comes with knowing that the "state" will be there to help, when they need it most—even if the price is high. This emphasis on safeguards against the pitfalls of life does not only affect Germans' attitudes toward the collective risk-sharing in the welfare state but their private affairs as well. Germans save a greater share of their income and are more reluctant to live on credit or take chances in the stock market than Americans. Only about 5 percent of all Germans but 20 percent of the U.S. population own stocks. Whether acquiring a house, a car, or less expensive items, most Germans still act according to the old adage, "save first, spend later."

In view of such sentiments it is hardly surprising that most Germans are far more willing than Americans to put their money where their mouth is when it comes to supporting social programs. Indeed, when presented by pollsters with a choice between tax cuts or increased social spending, a majority of Germans tends to reject lower taxes and back additional funds for social welfare programs.

While policymaking in modern democracies is affected by both top-to-bottom and bottom-to-top sentiments, in the Federal Republic a solid public endorsement has strengthened the hands of those political leaders who back the established social welfare programs and are poised to introduce additional ones. For example, a vast majority of eligible voters supported the creation of the new nursing care insurance that was introduced in January 1995. In the United States, at about the same time, the Clinton administration lost its battle for elite and public opinion when it pushed for a universal public health insurance scheme that was very modest and very different than the comprehensive mandatory health insurance in Germany.

Even as the German system's present and future problems were increasingly debated in the 1990s, half of the population believed that they needed even greater social security in the future whereas a quarter were content with the protection of the existing safety net. Again, far more East Germans than West Germans looked for a further expansion of the welfare state.[6] Given this climate of opinion and the need to adjust the social system to the less favorable realities prevailing at the turn of the century and likely developments in the next century, German decisionmakers were in a quandary.

But in view of the Federal Republic's past politics, the country's governmental arrangement, the built-in preference for consensus, and, most of all, the deep-seated commitment to a "social" state and to "social peace" seemed likely to overcome party and interest-group disagreements and forge elite support for reforms in order to protect the soundness of the system. While nothing in a highly developed welfare state's politics of retrenchment comes easy, Germany's brand of politics and government seemed better suited than America's conflictual and fragmented political process to cope with a host of social policy problems.

Before analyzing the debate over the future of the German welfare state and the politics of social policymaking that were high on the agenda as the turn of the century approached, we review the central features of the country's major social programs as they were in place when the reform debate heated up in the second half of the 1990s.

Old-Age Pensions

Like the rest of Germany's social insurances, the old-age pension system was never a redistributive scheme. Instead, it adheres to the principles of the private insurance sector in that only an insured person is entitled to benefits which are calculated mostly on the basis of insured persons' contributions. People who were never covered or never paid minimum contributions for a limited time receive little or no benefits. Take the financial predicament of two old women in their eighties in a small town in northern Germany, life-long friends with similar backgrounds: Greta, a widow, collects part of her husband's substantial old-age insurance and in addition part of her own public pension, which she receives because she was employed for a number of years. In contrast, Erna, who never married, is not entitled to an old-age pension, because she was always self-employed and never contributed to the public pension insurance. While Greta lives rather comfortably, Erna, too proud to apply for social assistance, struggles to manage on her modest and rapidly shrinking savings.

What began in 1889 as a very modest statutory "invalidity and pension insurance," which protected a small number of workers with low incomes from complete poverty when they were disabled or too old to earn a living, grew over time into Germany's comprehensive pension system. Eventually, in the post-World War II era, most people in the Federal Republic did not have to make drastic changes in their life style when they retired—provided they had been employed for several decades. This was exactly the intent of the fundamental reforms enacted in the 1950s in response to statistical data and descriptive reports revealing considerable impoverishment among senior citizens who had no other financial resources besides their old-age pensions. The changes adopted in 1957 under the auspices of Chancellor Konrad Adenauer were explicitly designed to pay old-age benefits that allowed senior citizens and invalids not simply to subsist or substitute other financial resources but rather to live decently during their retirement years. This was to be achieved by tying pensions not simply to cost of living increases and thus inflation (as social security payments are in the United States) but to the development of wages and salaries and thus to productivity improvements. In linking pension benefits to inflation rates as well as productivity gains and adjusting them annually, the architects of the system made sure that senior citizens could partake in the postwar *Wirtschaftswunder* (economic miracle). At the same time, the old principle of "rehabilitation before pension" received statutory backing and was extended to measures preserving and improving insurants' health and thus their capability to remain in or return to the workplace.

With few exceptions salaried and wage-earning employees must be insured under the statutory pension insurance provisions just as their American counterparts are required to pay their social security taxes. In the Federal Republic, as in the United States, contributions are levied on earnings up to adjustable wage or salary limits (In the mid-1990s, for example, the monthly assessment level was 7,800 Deutschmarks). Since the early 1990s, mothers or fathers who take care of their children instead of holding down a job are credited with three years' worth of compulsory insurance contributions after the birth of each child. The introduction of this child-raising measure softened a traditional disadvantage of full-time parenting, namely reduced or no pension entitlements—in the eyes of critics a penalty that had especially hurt women in the past. Students, too, are credited with compulsory insurance contributions without actually paying social security taxes.

While some self-employed persons such as craftsmen, artists, and farmers are required to participate, most self-employed Germans are not obliged to do so—an opt-out provision that does not exist in the American social security scheme. Self-employed Germans can choose whether or not to remain in the system, and they may choose to reenter, it within five years of becoming self-employed. Many choose voluntary coverage. In most respects, the rights and obligations of compulsory and voluntary insurants are the same.

Pension entitlements depend on the length of an individual's contributory periods, past contributory earnings, and the current average earnings of all insurants. Because an individual's past earnings figure into the calculation of pension levels, these benefits mirror the considerable income differentials in the workplace. The side-by-side existence of separate pension funds with distinct contribution and entitlement provisions for different employment categories such as salaried employees, wage earners, farmers, miners, etc. contributes also to significant inequalities in pension amounts.

After several decades of employment in a well-paying job a German retiree receives a significantly higher old-age pension than a social security recipient in the United States who worked in a comparable job and for the same length of time. In the 1990s, the average pension stood at about 72 percent of the net income of average incomes earned by the workforce. But unlike social security benefits in the United States, German pensions are not significantly weighed in favor of beneficiaries with a history of low incomes; accordingly, the gap between low and high pensions is much larger in the Federal Republic than in the U.S.

Upon the death of an insured spouse, widows and widowers are entitled to 60 percent of the deceased insurant's pension provided the surviving spouse is at least 45 years of age, or raising children, or unable to work. While many senior citizens live rather well thanks to generous public pensions, those with less stellar employment records and their survivors just manage to get by. Still, nine of ten retirees, invalids, widows, and orphans in Germany live exclusively or mostly on the benefits they receive from the public pension insurance.

Men and women are entitled to their pensions at age 65. But since the flexible retirement age was introduced in the early 1970s, many insurants have begun to receive their pensions as early as age 60 (women) or 63 (men) without significant reductions, provided they fulfilled certain requirements with respect to contributory periods. Under certain conditions, unemployed men and women or those with occupational disabilities can claim their benefits before reaching the official pension age and without reductions. For decades, the average age of persons beginning to draw their public pensions stood at 60. By the mid-1990s, the average retirement age had edged downward. At the time, only one in three Germans over the age of 59 was still part of the workforce. Beginning in 2001 the early retirement options will be phased out gradually. The insured will still have the option to draw their pensions before their 65th birthday but their benefits will be substantially lower.

The pension funds try to restore an insured's physical or mental health rather than granting pension benefits prematurely provided the insured person satisfies contributory periods. The idea is, of course, that it is more cost-effective to rehabilitate people than to pay them pensions long before they reach retirement age. Thus, pension funds send their members to their own clinics or to private rehabilitation and convalescent homes typically situated in attractive spas far away from the major metropolitan areas. Qualifying members also receive vocational training or retraining.[7] In addition, the funds pay benefits to those who cannot work during both rehabilitation and training periods.

Unemployment Insurance

To lose one's job in Germany does not result in the financial hardship known to many of the unemployed in the United States. Germany's unemployment insurance, established during the Great Depression as the last of Germany's major social insurance programs, evolved into something far more than a collective funding mechanism for the purpose of providing cash benefits for the unemployed as we know it in the United States. Indeed, the German agency that administers the unemployment fund, has always been primarily concerned with the placement, training, and retraining of the unemployed. Appropriately named Federal Labor Office (*Bundesanstalt fur Arbeit*) and not Unemployment Office, this quasi-public agency with headquarters in Nuremberg, regional offices in each state, and local offices in cities and counties had until recently a monopoly in the area of job placement. In the mid-1990s, however, during a period of record unemployment, a law was adopted allowing private employment agencies to operate and compete with the public labor offices. If government officials expected newly established private employment offices to energize the job market, they were disappointed. Competition among employment agencies has neither miraculously created jobs nor prevented corporations from shrinking their workforces. Moreover, most unemployed Germans continue to depend on the nearest public labor office in their search for new jobs, if only to avoid paying placement fees. The public labor offices offer career counseling and placement assistance free of charge to anyone seeking these services regardless of whether or not a person has ever contributed to the unemployment insurance.

To be eligible for unemployment insurance benefits, which are not means tested, a person must have been employed and thus contributed to the unemployment insurance fund (via a payroll tax up to a regularly adjusted earnings ceiling) for a specified period of time prior to losing his or her job. In the mid-1990s for recipients with at least one child, unemployment payments amounted to slightly better than two-thirds of the salary or wages they had been earning, while for childless beneficiaries payments were slightly less than two-thirds of their previous earnings minus statutory reductions. How long unemployed Germans can collect insurance benefits depends on their age and the total length of their employment during the seven years prior to losing their jobs. The minimum entitlement period for unemployment insurance benefits (12 months) is considerably longer and the maximum period (32 months) strikingly longer than the uniform American standard of 32 weeks.[8] Persons who cannot meet the requirements for unemployment insurance benefits or have exhausted their eligibility can apply for means-tested unemployment assistance, which is about 10 percent lower than unemployment insurance benefits.

From refunding the costs for job applications or trips to prospective employers to granting wage subsidies to firms that hire otherwise not readily employable persons, the Federal labor office utilizes a variety of programs designed to keep people in the workforce and make it financially attractive for firms to hire people they would not employ otherwise. This is best illustrated by an example: Ralf, a West German, was in his late twenties when back problems forced him to give up the trade he learned and loved—carpentry. After collecting unemployment insurance for several months, the labor office placed him with a start-up firm specializing in computerized lithography. For one year, the labor office paid 50 percent of Ralf's salary in the expectation that he would carry his full weight after a 12-month training period.[9]

While such job creation schemes have not always succeeded, they often do work out, as in Ralf's case. He became a nonsubsidized employee after the first year on the job, and in addition his boss expanded his company primarily by hiring unemployed men and women under the work-creation program and keeping them on, once the wage subsidies were cut off.

From the outset, the idea of the job creation program (*Arbeitsbeschaffungsmassnahmen* or ABM in short) was that although the short-term costs of typical ABM positions might be higher than dispensing unemployment benefits, it was cheaper in the long run and far better in human terms to bring people back into the workforce.[10] For years ABM jobs helped to train or retrain otherwise unemployable persons and resulted in permanent jobs. In the past, the financing of such job creation measures was routinely covered by the annually designated ABM funds in the Federal Labor Office's budget. But after unification and the collapse of East Germany's economy, several hundred thousand ABM jobs, many of them fully funded by the labor office, were hastily created in the Eastern states in order to counter mass unemployment.[11] To be sure, a number of East Germans acquired new and marketable job-skills, especially in the construction and computer industry, but the vast majority of these jobs did not lead to permanent, nonsubsidized positions in viable fields and companies. Although the government did not inject additional funds into the ABM programs, the aggressive expansion of the ABM measures in East Germany exhausted the labor office's resources and forced cutbacks in ABM-initiatives with far brighter prospects in Western Germany.

Statutory Health Insurance

While we use the terms health insurance and sickness insurance interchangeably in this chapter, we are well aware that Americans use exclusively the former and Germans the latter wording. Regardless of terminology, however, the two systems are quite different. Most Germans are required by law to join one of the quasi-public, nonprofit sickness funds, whereas most Americans are voluntarily insured by private firms. The per capita spending for health care in Germany as well as the share of the Gross Domestic Product (GDP) has been significantly lower than in the United States.[12] In the mid-1990s almost all Germans were covered by a sickness insurance, but more than 40 million Americans did not have health coverage at all. While the mandatory sickness insurance scheme guaranteed quality health care to practically every German, the United States offered perhaps the best medical treatment in the world to those who were able to afford it either through health insurance or personal checkbooks. In short, the comprehensive and all around fine health care in the Federal Republic was more equally spread than the first-rate medical care in the U.S.

Contrary to critical arguments made during the American health care reform debate of the 1990s, Germany did not have in the past and does not have today a government-run national health service along the lines of the British model. The German government has never run hospitals and clinics or employed physicians and nurses. Members of the statutory funds are free to choose their own physicians for ambulatory care but referrals are required for nonemergency hospital treatment. Germans who are covered by a statutory sickness fund do get the same medical attention and care as Americans who are insured by private insurers. In fact, many general practitioners and even specialists in the Federal Republic still make house calls. However, the more than 1,300 statutory sickness funds are closely monitored and regulated by the federal government with respect to cost control. Yet, German physicians, including general practitioners, are still among the highest earners in the Federal Republic.

Typically nine of ten Germans are by law required to be enrolled in one of the statutory sickness funds which operate regionally and cover specific occupational groups or large companies. The mandatory insurance covers virtually all employed Germans with earnings below a statutory threshold as well as their nonworking spouses and children. The cost of sickness insurance in form of a payroll tax has steadily gone up, and has reached double-digit contributions in the 1990s.[13] These contributions are split between employees and employers. Recipients of unemployment benefits continue to be covered by the funds they had been enrolled in before losing their jobs. The statutory insurance is also held by law to provide health care for the unemployed, the recipients of old-age pensions, and welfare clients as well.[14] Persons above the regularly adjusted income threshold or the self-employed have the option of remaining in their respective fund or joining one in the first place. Many choose the statutory funds, while others enroll in private companies. Of the 10 percent of all Germans who are not insured by one of the statutory sickness funds, about 5 percent are privately insured. Most of the remaining 5 percent are public-sector employees who are covered by their respective government employer. Less than one percent of the population is not insured.

Germans who are members of a statutory sickness fund do not get a physician's or hospital's bill and enjoy virtually universal medical care. By the mid-1990s the most important in a long list of health care entitlements were the following:

- Unlimited visits at physicians' offices (or house calls) for preventive checkups and treatment without out-of-pocket expenses. Psychiatric care was covered as well.
- Unlimited hospital care, if required. Patients contributed about $7.00 a day for the first two weeks; thereafter no copayment was required.
- Prescription drugs with the exception of a small copayment (about $1.50 to $3.40) for each prescription.
- Dental preventive care and treatment and orthodontal services up to age 18. Basic dentures, when needed, but not the more expensive dentures. If patients had failed to undergo their regular (and paid for) dental examinations in order to preserve their teeth, they were eventually penalized in form of higher deductibles, when they need dental protheses.
- Hearing and vision exams, hearing aids, eyeglasses, wheelchairs and other equipment.
- Sickness allowance after patients' employers had paid wages or salaries for the required six weeks. 80 percent of a sick person's lost wages or salaries were paid for up to 78 weeks within a three-year period. Parents who cared for a sick child under 8 years of age received up to 5 days of full pay a year, single parents up to 20 days. A comparison of leading industrial countries established that the German labor force was best insured against illness. In sharp contrast, the United States was identified as the country with the lowest level of sickness benefits.[15]
- Funeral allowance to help cover the cost of burials.

Traditionally, the sickness funds have also granted monthly home care allowances for the chronically ill. However, the financial assistance provided for home care was in many instances insufficient and not at all available for institutional nursing care. Since 1995 these cases have been covered by a newly established mandatory nursing care insurance or equivalent private insurance.

Since 1995 all Germans must carry nursing-care insurance. Mandatory members of sickness funds are automatically enrolled in a newly established social nursing care insurance, while the privately insured must be covered by private carriers in a comparable fashion. The financing of the new social insurance is a departure from the traditional 50–50 split between employers and employees. Employers still pay half of the premium but are reimbursed by one additional work day per year.[16] Thus, nursing-care insurance is the only one among Germany's social insurances solely financed by employees.

Depending on the degree of a person's disability, the insurance furnishes different monthly cash payments for providers of both home and institutional nursing care, and it also provides medical equipment and material. The benefits for the most severely handicapped are quite substantial. Moreover, the nursing-care insurance pays old-age insurance premiums for family members who care for disabled loved ones without compensation—a newly introduced feature that benefits mostly women who are most likely to care for disabled parents or children.

Under the Accident Insurance Act of 1884 and following up-dates, only workers in the more hazardous industrial sectors were covered. But since the early 1940s, all employees and employers have been insured against accidents at their workplace and on their way from and to work. What began as a limited workmen's compensation type model has expanded into a universal insurance that covers the overwhelming majority of Germans—even children who attend day-care centers or schools and college students. In a departure from the funding modus of all other social insurances, only employers contribute to accident insurance.

Child Allowance and Educational Assistance

Besides getting a break in the form of tax writeoffs for dependent children, as Americans do, German parents also collect a monthly child allowance from the government for children under age 16. If children continue their education or vocational training, child allowances can be extended up to age 27 under certain conditions. In addition, a nonworking parent bringing up his or her child alone is entitled to a child-raising benefit until the offspring is two years of age.

Unlike their American counterparts, German parents need have no financial worries about their children's education. Since the 1960s Germany's public universities (and with few exceptions all universities are public) have not charged tuition. Even paying for room and board is not quite as difficult for Germans as for Americans with limited financial resources. Depending on their parents' and their own financial resources, college students are entitled to different amounts of educational assistance, half of which is typically given as a grant and the rest as an interest-free loan with very generous repayment conditions. In the mid-1990s, some politicians and educators suggested the introduction of a modest tuition in order to motivate students to complete their studies on time, but these proposals were condemned widely as attempts to revive the old principle of elite universities for the offspring of the wealthy.

Social Assistance: A Right, Not Charity

When visiting New York German tourists almost always ask to see parts of Harlem, the South Bronx, or Bedford-Stuyvesant as examples of grim urban poverty areas that they do not see in their own cities; nor are these visitors used to seeing people in the better parts of town searching with obvious embarrassment through curbside garbage cans for edibles. The welfare state prevents this kind of extreme poverty. In the 1990s German social scientists and media critics complained about the growing number of impoverished people in the Federal Republic and the fact that the number of welfare recipients had doubled within a decade.[17] But what passes as poverty in Germany constitutes a far better predicament than the plight of America's poor underclass.

In Germany, as in the U.S., a stigma has long been attached to collecting welfare benefits. Therefore, not all Germans who would easily qualify have applied for public assistance. This has been especially true for the elderly. But while toughening their stand against welfare cheaters in the 1990s, government officials go out of their way to educate the public about the availability of social assistance for those in need. A typical government booklet that was distributed in the 1990s bore the title "Social Assistance Your Good Right." Readers were assured that applying for and receiving welfare benefits "is not a shame." Another informative government booklet explained,

> Social assistance is intended to help people in need to live a life of human dignity. It is not a charitable contribution. Recipients are legally entitled to its help in situations which they cannot cope with alone. . . . Social assistance is available to anyone who is in need or in danger of becoming destitute and unable to overcome their difficulties either alone or with the help of family and friends. Whether you are to blame for the situation is irrelevant. You have a legal right to almost all forms of social assistance.

This is a far cry from the way American politicians speak of social assistance in the 1990s. Even supporters do not dare to characterize welfare benefits as a right of the poor. Thus, when Richard Gephardt met with reporters at the heights of the 1995 welfare reform debate in the House of Representatives, the minority leader criticized the radical reform proposals of the Republican majority but refused steadfastly to endorse the notion that the needy are entitled to welfare benefits. When reporters asked pointedly whether he wanted to protect welfare as an entitlement, he answered, "I don't know what you call it. You can't get hung up on that word. We are not trying to get people entitled. We are trying to get people to work."

Inside Germany, the basic cash payments received by German welfare recipients in order to provide for the necessities of life (food, hygiene) have been criticized as paltry given the comfortable standard of living in the Federal Republic. But contrary to the United States, where the major welfare program has traditionally targeted families with dependent children, Germany's social assistance programs benefit everyone. Unwed mothers, at the center of the welfare debate in the United States, are not an issue in the Federal Republic where mothers with dependent children are only one of many groups entitled to social assistance. Also, while welfare benefits in the United States are vastly different from state to state, all German recipients get, if they qualify, the federally established benefits regardless of where they live. Furthermore, in addition to the subsistence cash benefits many German welfare clients qualify for housing, child, and clothing allowance as well as Christmas money. The welfare offices also pay their clients' contributions to old-age pension insurance and sickness funds.

Clouds Over the German Welfare State

We have described the major components of the Federal Republic's welfare state in considerable detail as they were in place in the mid-1990s in order to give readers an idea of the magnitude of the German social security system and how it compares to the American model. The vast majority of the Germans have consistently favored the risk-free society as it evolved over more than a century and especially after World War II. But at the turn of the century, the German welfare state began to grapple with major problems shared by the United States.

The mandatory insurance, the main support of Germany's social safety net, is based on the principle that the healthy, employed, and working-age segments of society support those who are sick, unemployed, and retired. As long as a balance existed between contributions and benefits, the system functioned as intended. For many years, periodic contribution hikes and occasional slowdowns in the increases of benefits assured the soundness of the social insurance scheme. But as the turn of the century approached, the number of beneficiaries had risen disproportionately in comparison to contributors.

While the United States experienced parallel asymmetries in its social insurance systems (social security, medicare) for similar reasons—namely changes in its economic and demographic makeup, Germany has, in addition, faced some unique problems related to the country's reunification and the disintegration of the Communist bloc. Three developments in particular force the Federal Republic to consider and debate the future of its comprehensive social security design:

(1) The economic conditions that allowed the creation of the modern welfare state in the 1950s and 1960s changed in the 1970s and 1980s. Rapid economic growth and full employment, the two crucial features of the "economic miracle" era, gave way to modest expansion rates and a significant segment of unemployed in the work-force. Further, while changes in the global competition forced major industries in the United States (i.e., automobile, steel) in the 1970s and 1980s to modernize their production processes at the expense of jobs, West Germany's export-oriented industrial complex delayed drastic restructuring measures for well over a decade in spite of mounting global challenges. The collapse of the Soviet empire and the rapid emergence of former communist countries in East and Middle Europe as low-wage "European Koreas," forced the hands of industrial managers in the Federal Republic following a short

boom in the immediate aftermath of the country's reunification (see chapter 5). The net result was that many large and medium-size enterprises shrank their workforces dramatically and permanently. Fewer people paid into the social insurance but the number of men and women in their fifties and early sixties, who were forced into early retirement and began to draw their old-age pensions prematurely, grew dramatically.

(2) The dismal state of East Germany's socioeconomic system and its subsequent reconstruction in the post-unification years incurred massive social costs that were borne to a large extent by unemployment and old-age pension funds. Because of East Germany's high unemployment and large number of redundant workers forced into early retirement, many billions of Deutschmarks had to be transferred indefinitely from West to East Germany. While social expenditures in the western part of Germany constituted slightly less than one-third of the Gross Domestic Product (GDP) in the mid-1990s, they amounted to more than two-thirds of East Germany's GDP. The decision to bring social benefits in East Germany fairly quickly up to West German levels magnified the tremendous strain on the major insurance funds.

Moreover, large numbers of foreign asylum seekers and refugees as well as ethnic Germans made their way into the Federal Republic following the fall of the Iron Curtain. These newcomers added to the social costs by qualifying instantly for benefits such as health care, social assistance, or benefits for their children. Especially before 1993, when a constitutional change curtailed the influx of asylum-seekers significantly, some Germans found in asylum-seekers and foreigners in general convenient scapegoats for individual and societal difficulties just as some Americans have long resented illegal immigrants and even legal aliens as freeloaders.

(3) Finally, the aging of the population proceeded much more rapidly in the Federal Republic than in the United States or in any other industrial society. While we describe this societal phenomenon in some detail in chapter 4, here we consider those aspects of the lopsided demographics that affected the pivotal insurance principle of the welfare state. The rapidly increasing life expectancy that Germans share with the populations of the United States and other industrialized countries, as well as the German affinity for voluntary and, of late, increasingly forced, retirement enlarged the pool of pension and health care beneficiaries. According to population experts, this trend is likely to continue at an accelerated pace in the next decades. Moreover, the number of young Germans continues to shrink because of extraordinarily low birthrates, especially

in the eastern states. Experts warn that unless policies are put into place to remedy these tendencies, the workforce of the future will be sentenced to bear unprecedented burdens to support the ever-growing number of pensioners or to reject the system.

Taken together, the changed economic conditions accompanied by high unemployment rates, the astronomical costs of integrating East Germans into the Federal Republic's socioeconomic system, and the dramatic demographic shifts have affected literally all of the Federal Republic's social programs and the positions staked out in the social policy debate of the 1990s.

Opposing Views and Conflicting Interests

Debating the future of the expansive social safety net is by no means a new phenomenon in the reunited Germany of the 1990s. When the era of full employment ended and unfavorable demographics surfaced in the 1970s, reform proposals and policy adjustments were fairly common ingredients of West German politics. But the calls for reforms have become more frequent and urgent in the 1990s. Hardly anyone has questioned the need to reconsider the social welfare state as a whole or in part, but consensus is much harder to achieve with respect to the scope and direction of efforts to restructure the social safety net.

The most extreme reform approach, while not at all new and original, has been pushed more forcefully than ever by free market advocates in business, politics, and the social sciences. Their argument is economic in nature with some moral reasoning and justification thrown in. Pointing to the exploding social costs of the aging German society and their adverse effect on the economy, the free market school has proclaimed the expansive welfare state a failure. These critics have argued that the so-called riskfree society represented Germany's greatest risk for the future. The high non-wage labor costs, so the argument goes, discourage investments and innovation that would result in robust economic growth, greater global competitiveness of Germany's industry, and, most important, full employment. Just as American supply-siders, these German reformers have presented their ideas as benefitting everyone economically. They want to do away with what some of them call the "self-service" mentality that they link to the excesses of welfare-state policies in order to unleash individual energies, initiatives, and moral strength that would serve the common good.

While much of this sounds like Reaganomics with a touch of American anti-welfare state agitation in the name of moral renewal, even the most radical German reform proposals have been far more modest than those favored and already enacted in the U.S. And even the most fervent among Germany's free marketeers have not advocated the wholesale dismantling of the welfare state. Also, unlike welfare state opponents in the United States, they do not mount all-out attacks on social assistance but concentrate on large social-insurance programs. Not surprisingly, these sorts of reform plans have been especially popular among employers, including some of the leaders of influential organizations, the fading liberal party, the FDP, and segments of the CDU/CSU. Other reformers embrace the idea of the welfare state whole-heartedly: they want only to weed out or soften those features that reinforce the unequal distribution of income and wealth in the German society. For example, instead of linking the insurance-based social safety net to each individual's employment and earnings history, these reformers advocate plans calling for minimum old-age pensions or a guaranteed income for all regardless of one's employment and earning records.

In theory the idea of a guaranteed minimum income and the abolishment of most other social programs with the notable exception of health insurance appeals to virtually all ideological camps in the Federal Republic—from free-market champions in the FDP and CDU/CSU to welfare-state defenders in the SPD and the Greens. This solution promises to make much of the current bureaucracies, especially those dealing with unemployment and welfare benefits, obsolete. It has been suggested that the tax agency could administer one simple program that would guarantee everyone a modest income. Some critics have expressed fears that a guaranteed income would negate the incentive to work for one societal segment. Voices in the SPD and the labor unions, on the other hand, suspect that the introduction of a guaranteed minimum income or, as its proponents call it, "citizens' money" would simply serve as a clever vehicle to shrink the welfare state at the expense of low and middle-income people for the benefit of high-income individuals, corporations, and other advantaged groups.[18] For these critics, the guaranteed minimum income concept would work only if enacted simultaneously with a repeal of tax-breaks for privileged groups and individuals so that the level of "citizens' money" would compare well to the benefits of the proven welfare state.

Last but not least, there are those who have opposed systemic changes without denying that severe problems exist and will probably worsen.

Instead of redesigning the social security scheme completely, they are more comfortable with reforming each program separately and over time in a step-by-step fashion. This has been the approach most governmental decisionmakers and the most influential interest groups have preferred so far and are most likely to support in the foreseeable future. More important, a careful readjustment of the existing social state remains probably the only approach with a chance to find the, albeit grudging, acceptance of the electorate.

A number of major issues and conflicts between distinct interests surfaced in the ongoing debate about the future of the welfare state. These contradictory interests, some experts warned, would eventually pit group against group, especially:

- Contributors and beneficiaries of the generational contract;
- Persons with children versus childless persons;
- Mandatory insured persons versus those exempted from compulsory social insurance membership;
- Employers versus employees;
- Working contributors to the social insurance plans versus non-working recipients of unemployment or welfare benefits;
- The federal government, which mandates social policies, versus local communities that pay for one increasingly expensive unfunded mandate: social assistance.

The Generational Contract

The most sensitive questions touch on an implicit generational compact which is crucial for the survival of the pay-as-you-go social insurance scheme and thus the German-style welfare state itself. While three employed persons supported one pensioner in the 1960s, today only two workers finance the public pension and much of the health care of one senior citizen. Moreover, experts have predicted that the German society is moving rapidly toward a situation in which every employed person will have to support at least one retiree. While a trend in this direction exists in the United States as well, it is far less drastic than in the Federal Republic. Given these dramatic changes in German society, the so-called generational contract can be kept alive only by hikes in the already high social insurance contributions of those holding jobs or essential benefit cuts or both. In any case, the very people who now and in the near future support their elders' "golden years" will not enjoy the same generous benefits in their own retirement, when the working strata will not be large enough to support their elders in the contemporary fashion. The pensioners of the future must either work significantly longer or accept substantially lower benefits.

Under these circumstances, the working generations of the future may not be willing to bear the heavy contributory burden to support the carefree lives of millions of pensioners, many of them not yet 60 years old. As one expert observer put it, "How long is the 48 year old family man willing to pay for the world travels of the 58 year old early retiree?"[19] In the 1990s, critics have described a "Republic of the Old" where senior citizens are preoccupied with their youthfulness, excessive health care, and exotic vacations while ignorant of the burdens on the rest of society. Some have called this an exploitation of the younger generations.

Conservative reformers have talked about repealing the generational contract altogether and replacing it with a minimum income that would probably assure no more than recipients' subsistence. The individual wanting more would have to buy additional private insurance. While less generously provided for by welfare state programs than their German counterparts, senior citizens in the United States are also first in line, when it comes to social benefits. Americans over 65 are, for example, the only group enjoying universal health coverage (Medicare).

In the 1990s, according to one study, public spending in Germany for the over 65-year-old, nonworking population was three times higher than outlays for the benefit of the youngest generation under 25 years of age and still higher in comparison to the public benefits of any other group. This tremendous distributory advantage of the elderly has existed in spite of child and educational allowances and several other family-friendly benefits. For this reason even some welfare-state defenders have demanded a more even-handed distribution of social resources and a shift of resources from the oldest to the youngest generation. Unlike free marketeers who prefer leaving it up to each individual whether or not to take out private pension and health insurance, some of the social state adherents are willing to accept a gradual switch to a system with minimum public benefits for the aged as long as additional private insurance provisions are mandated. According to these reformers more public resources for the benefit of children, adolescents, and young adults are not only needed for reasons of societal fairness, but also for the survival of the generational contract and thus the welfare state itself.[20]

Families with Children Against Childless Free Riders

To raise two children up to age 18 in Germany in the 1990s, parents have to earn and spend several hundred thousand Deutschmarks—money that would be available as disposable income if they had no children. Yet, some time in the future, the two offspring are likely to contribute not only to the old-age pensions and the health care of their own parents but of childless retirees as well. While not carrying any of the financial burdens of child-raising, childless persons have always collected the same public pensions as parents with the same employment and earnings records and enjoyed the same public health benefits. This state of affairs was never intended by economist Wilfried Schreiber, who drew up the blueprint for the Federal Republic's postwar social security system in the 1950s. The design not only recommended a dynamic old-age pension, but a child- and youth-pension as well. The idea was that the employed strata would collectively support those who had left the workforce and those who had not yet entered the job-market. While the old-age pension became part of the initial social security system, the child- and youth-pension never did.

Although it is far more "family-friendly" than American public policy, critics in the Federal Republic have argued for a long time that their country's social policy is grossly unfair toward parents and their children and tilted in favor of childless free riders. But it took a 1992 ruling of the Constitutional Court to remind parliamentarians that they had not fulfilled the constitutional charge of protecting the family. Consequently, child- and educational allowances were raised as were tax-breaks for dependent children. The Court's ruling also nudged politicians to credit child-raising parents with three years worth of pension insurance for each child, a solution that has not satisfied parents and may ultimately not go far enough for the Constitutional Court either. As social and child-raising costs went up, more and more couples decided against having children. As the turn of the century approached, about half of all German households were childless.

Against this background, family policy has moved up on the Federal Republic's political agenda. Reformers have proposed increased child- and education allowances and burden-sharing schemes that would require childless taxpayers to pay surcharges or establish a children's fund to which everyone would contribute for the benefit of child-raising parents and their offspring. Conservatives, free-market liberals, and left-leaning politicians have found some common ground in the more radical proposals to share the burden, but have differed on the ways to redistribute it. Social Democrats have suggested the targeting of low- and middle-income families, while free market liberals have preferred non-means-tested child benefits. Regardless, Germans with and without children are on opposing sides in the social policy debate.

The Mandatory Insured Versus the Exempted

According to some critics, the Federal Republic's social insurance system could continue to manage quite well on its pay-as-you-go mode, if it were not for the government's decision to shift insurance funds into programs that should have been been financed with general tax revenues. Instead, these critics have pointed out, decisionmakers have financed all sorts of policies solely on the backs of insured employees, while the self-employed and career civil servants have gotten a free ride. For example, the costly retraining and subsidized job creation programs for the unemployed have been funded by unemployment insurance and thus by contributors only. Even the highest earners among the self-employed (unless voluntary members of the social insurance) have not contributed to these programs nor did civil servants. Since ultimately society in general and the business sector in particular benefit from these programs, critics have argued that general tax revenues must be used for these programs, and if needed raised.

More far-reaching in this view was the government's decision to raid the social insurance funds in order to finance a big chunk of reintegrating East Germans into the Federal Republic's socioeconomic system. Up to 1996 more than 200 billion Deutschmarks were transferred from the public unemployment and old-age pension funds in West Germany to the eastern states. Thus, the mass of employees in West Germany paid for an endeavor that was certainly not solely in their interest. By reaching into the social insurance funds decisionmakers avoided for a while the steep income tax hikes that would have hit the privileged groups as well. But in the process, according to critics, the political leadership has contributed, if not caused, what they themselves have come to characterize as a crisis of the social security system.

Employers Versus Employees

Employers' perennial complaints about the high non-wage labor costs and especially their share of the increasing social insurance contributions have never been as loud and shrill as during the economic restructuring in the 1990s. As we described in the previous chapter, the high wage and mandated social costs in Germany's industry have made it increasingly difficult for the industrial sector to compete with rivals producing in countries with significantly lower labor costs. Still, employees and their labor unions have come to suspect that employers and their organizations have exaggerated the impact of social insurance costs on productivity and competitiveness in order to land heavy blows against the welfare state. Infights between employers and employees are nothing new, not even in the consensus-oriented German labor relations model, but this time around hardline employers have utilized a credible threat: Unless the social insurance costs at home were contained, more plants and jobs would be relocated abroad.

Those Who Work and Those Who Don't

In Hartford, Conn., Ava Bilbraut and her 16-year-old son bring in about $253 a week and spend about a third of that to rent a two-bedroom apartment. The energetic 33-year-old mother hasn't any health insurance; indeed, she has been sued by a local hospital for failure to pay a bill.

In Berlin, Germany, Klaus Beilisch, a thin 30-year-old with wavy black hair, brings in the equivalent of $277 a week. Next month, he, his wife and their 16-month-old son are to move into a rent-free apartment. When Mr. Beilisch was hospitalized for six days last June with a circular problem, his health insurance picked up all but the $6.50-a-day tab for food. One more thing: Ms. Bilbraut, the American, works seven days a week behind the counter at a Cuban bakery. Mr. Beilisch, the German, has been unemployed since last May.

In early 1994, these were the opening paragraphs of a front page story in *The Wall Street Journal*. The following exposition provided American readers with a powerful comparison between their own and Germany's employment and social policies.[21] No reader could miss the point that the unemployed German worker was clearly better off than the hardworking American who held a low-wage job. But since the article focused on job creation and unemployment policies in the industrialized world, it did not mention that inside Germany some experts and many ordinary people had begun to compare the incomes and lifestyles of Germans who worked for a living and others who received unemployment or welfare benefits. In Germany not only critics of the welfare state but even some of its defenders have expressed misgivings over the diminishing distance between the pay of workers at the lowest end of the wage scale and the jobless worker collecting unemployment insurance, unemployment assistance, or welfare benefits.

Since then, a multitude of much-debated reform proposals in the 1990s—many of them pushed by ministers in the Kohl government—have suggested cuts, slower growth-rates, and tougher qualification standards in unemployment and welfare benefits with the need to reestablish stronger incentives to work. "Work must pay," has become a favorite slogan of those who want to reenergize the once-strong German work ethic. The central argument here is that the rewards for work must always be higher than social insurance benefits (i.e., unemployment benefits) while social insurance benefits must be more generous than social assistance.

This was the situation in the mid-1990s: In real terms, salaries and wages had grown very modestly for more than a decade, but social assistance benefits had gone up three times as much as wages. In some cases, the difference between the earnings of workers in the lowest wage bracket on the one hand and welfare benefits on the other had disappeared. Moreover, unless a jobless person was single, social assistance was typically higher than unemployment support. Also, the level of unemployment cash benefits plus rent subsidies and health insurance was not conducive to accepting job offers, especially when part-time work was available in the underground economy.

In the 1990s welfare state opponents, reform-minded politicians, and some segments of the mass media began to publicize extreme examples of people abusing the welfare state. As a result, the growth of a small but costly strata of nonworking people, who seemed content with social benefits that would be considered quite comfortable in poorer countries, has affected the views of many Germans. Working people have come to resent nonworking freeloaders—especially if foreign asylum seekers, refugees, or ethnic Germans returning from former Eastern bloc countries. And while hardly anyone has attacked welfare programs in general, an overwhelming majority of Germans have supported stricter enforcement of the requirement that able-bodied welfare recipients must either accept community jobs or face cuts in their benefits. However, not even the most radical German reformers have proposed anything that resembled the U.S.-style "ending-welfare-as-we-know-it" campaign and legislation.

Local Communities Versus the Federal Government

While local communities must provide social assistance to the needy in their jurisdictions, the nature and levels of welfare benefits are set by federal policies and therefore uniform throughout the country. The changing economic conditions and the influx of a large number of asylum seekers from abroad in the early 1990s doubled the number of welfare recipients and exploded the social budgets of most cities and counties. Without essential tax revenues of their own, many communities have complained increasingly that they simply lack the resources for mandated obligations that transcend the traditional role of localities to care for the needy. Indeed, the social costs of local communities have grown disproportionately in comparison to the social budgets of federal and state governments.

Welfare is the best example here. Local governments—especially larger cities with the greatest influx of asylum seekers and the largest numbers of unemployed workers—have protested their skyrocketing welfare expenditures without asking for changes in the fundamental welfare model itself. In the United States, on the other hand, where the Aid to Families with Dependent Children program left it to the individual states to set the level of welfare support, the welfare reform initiatives of the mid-1990s were to a large degree carried by governors and others in the states who wanted complete jurisdiction over the handling of social assistance. Neither localities nor federal states in Germany have ever asked for such jurisdictional changes. Nor have they suggested to cut, limit, or discontinue welfare benefits as American states and local governments have done. Rather, they have pressured the federal level to adopt policies promising to keep the long-term unemployed, who simply cannot find jobs, off the local welfare rolls, granting them instead unemployment benefits dispersed by the federal unemployment insurance fund. Lower level governments in the Federal Republic have neither called for nor supported federally mandated workfare arguing that the obligation to create public jobs would add to their expenditures without alleviating the underlaying problem—unemployment. The federal government has taken the initiative and supported a German version of workfare that is far less punishing than proposals and enacted policies in the U.S.

All in all, the substantive issues and positions in Germany's debate over basic welfare policies and funding modes were very different from—and free of—the ideological bent of the unfunded mandate discourse in the United States of the 1990s. One telling example here was the attitude toward noncitizens. Although by 1995 about one third of all German welfare recipients were asylum seekers, neither political leaders nor the public demanded that social assistance simply be scrapped for these foreigners. This was at a time when political leaders in the United States struck a cord with large segments of the public when they suggested denying social assistance not only to illegal immigrants but to legal immigrants as well.

The Politics of Retrenchment and the Case of the 1993 Health Reform

Given the already existing and likely future predicament of the German welfare state as we have sketched it in the preceding pages, the most important remaining question is an obvious one: Can the Federal Republic cope with the changed socioeconomic conditions in the reunited country and maintain and reform the social welfare state without upsetting proven political, economic, and social arrangements? We believe that social policy reforms in the late 1980s and the early 1990s offer some clues as to whether or not Germany's political system can cope with necessary adjustments that impose losses on the vast majority of voters. For this reason, we examine the case of the 1993 health care reform:

At the beginning of 1993 Germany implemented a statutory health insurance reform designed to bring the sharp increases in health-care costs under control initially for a period of three years (At the time, a more comprehensive health-care reform to be instituted in 1996 was already under discussion.). Although employees' and employers' contributions to the public sickness funds had been rising rapidly, the funds had been plagued by significant deficits. Prior to the 1993 reform, sickness funds and health providers had periodically negotiated fees and budget caps collectively and for whole regions or, in the case of hospitals, separate for each institution. But without the force of laws and sanctions behind them, these targets had been without teeth. In a radical change, the 1993 reform imposed for the first time mandatory global budgets for whole health care sectors, namely for physicians, hospitals, the dental care and the pharmaceutical sector, and tied cost-hikes to the rate of wage increases and thus to the revenue gains of the sickness funds.

Key features of the controversial reform were mandatory reductions in physicians' fees and prescriptions, in fully or partially reimbursed dental and other medical services, and in the price of prescription and over-the-counter drugs. At the same time patients' copayments were increased. The reform provided for sanctions in the form of financial penalties against individual health providers (for physicians exceeding average service volumes and prescribing levels) as well as top-level organizations of physicians and the pharmaceutical industry (in case of noncompliance with global budget caps).

The health care sector reacted angrily even before the reform was adopted and implemented. Dentists threatened to deny treatment to patients who were members of public sickness funds. Physicians and pharmacists accused the reformers of taking away their livelihood. Hospitals went public with plans to eliminate some of their most costly services. Health-care workers and their unions protested. But all of these interests, said to be among the most influential in the Federal Republic, failed to prevent the adoption of the reform package that they opposed so vigorously. Why was the Kohl government able to enact a major health care reform against the will of powerful interests even though the new provisions curtailed also some of the health care benefits of most Germans? The answers are found in several distinct characteristics of the Federal Republic's political setting, namely

- the deep-seated commitment to the social state,
- the inclusive decisionmaking process,
- the nongovernmental character of the public insurance funds, and the social institutions that implement social policy, and
- the key role of political parties.

The 1993 health care reform was adopted with the support of the parties of the governing coalition (CDU/CSU and FDP) and the major opposition party (SPD). Crucial was that there was no disagreement over the precarious financial situation of the sickness funds and the need to assure their fiscal soundness. In comparison, the fiscal status of the government-run social insurance funds in the U.S. is customarily questioned, often even after bipartisan commissions examine and report on the financial situation and outlook of one or the other insurance fund.

While social security, medicare, and unemployment insurance in the United States are completely under the control of the federal government,

Germany's major social insurance funds are independent public corporations that implement the policies established by law. To attack the management of mandatory health or other public insurance as yet another example of Big Government's inefficiency does not make sense and cannot be used for partisan advantages in the Federal Republic. After all, important constituents of the major parties are involved in running the funds. It is true that the government regulates the funds rather closely and that the public health insurance plans (with the exception of the sickness funds, which have some leeway in setting their particular level of services and membership contributions) are restricted to matters of self-administration. But each fund is directed by an equal number of labor union and employer representatives who are chosen in periodically conducted so-called social elections.[22] Since representatives of labor and business control the management of the social insurance funds, the two contributory sides with often contradictory interests and different partisan alliances nevertheless have first-hand knowledge and identical facts about each fund's balance sheets. This gives data and analyses about the social funds' financial predicament far more credibility than the sort of information compiled by the government about the government-run social insurance funds in the United States.

Moreover, the corporatist arrangement that by law and custom involves the major organizations in the decisionmaking process and leaves them to implement public policies (see chapter 5) is even more pronounced in the social- than in the economic-policy realm. When it comes to health care, for example, all major players and interests are represented through their top-level organizations in the concerted action assembly which was established by law and meets twice a year at the invitation of the health ministry to develop broad guidelines for the public health-care system. In addition, an eight-member expert council—with an equal representation of physicians and economists—contributes comprehensive analyses, studies, and recommendations to facilitate the concerted-action process. While this mechanism in itself is no guarantee for consensus building, as the process leading up to the 1993 health care reform demonstrated, it provides a forum for bringing all important interests together and assures an exchange of all kinds of views and arguments.

In addition, the major players in the health care sector have the same ties and access to the federal government, especially the ministerial bureaucracy, the federal diet, and state governments. Given this involve-

Republic the proposed reform was neither as prominently covered by the media nor as fiercely battled by health-care providers as Clinton's health reform plan was by the insurance industry in the U.S. As a result, the German public was far less informed about the details of the proposed changes and far less subjected to propaganda campaigns by supporters and opponents than was the American populace. While more West Germans accepted than opposed the suggested increase in patients' copayments, an overwhelming majority of East Germans labeled the suggested increases in out-of-pocket expenses as too severe. But in either part of the country public opinion was unequivocally supportive of reform features that were vehemently opposed by health-care providers. More Germans in East and West favored than opposed the proposed cuts in physicians' fees and in prescription and nonprescription drugs. This clear-cut public sentiment strengthened the hands of the reformers and their backers while weakening the opposition's case.

After initially resulting in impressive cost-control successes, the 1993 reform failed to contain health-care expenditures for three years as the reformers had anticipated. But this policy revision, following a less ambitious cost-cutting initiative four years earlier, contained several changes to be enacted in 1996 only. One of those delayed reform provisions allowed the sickness funds to compete for members. The expectation was that competition would force the public health insurors to adopt more efficient administrative methods, negotiate better fees with health-care providers, and offer members either more services or lower contribution rates. Beyond that, the 1993 reform was from the outset perceived as a provisional precursor of a far more comprehensive reform that was supposed to establish a viable public health-care model for the future. Indeed, government preparations for a more ambitious health-care reform and interest-group lobbying campaigns against further cost controls and other fundamental systemic changes began immediately after the enactment of the 1993 version. In the following years, more—albeit modest—reforms were adopted.

The Future of the German Welfare State

Dismantling the social-welfare state or major parts thereof, as it was debated in the United States of the 1990s, is not in the cards for the Federal Republic. Not only has the West German public consistently and strongly been in favor of the existing arrangements, but also newcomers to the system (i.e., East Germans, ethnic Germans from eastern Europe) with votes to be counted have been even more impassioned in their support for a comprehensive social state. Under these circumstances, German elites of all political persuasions have been well aware that they must be very cautious in any efforts to alter the social safety net. After all, in Germany the commitment to social security has spanned a period of more than 100 years and very different political systems from constitutional monarchy and dictatorship to democracy. The postwar social state was expressly put together with the lessons of the Weimar Republic's turbulent times in mind, and its ultimate goal was to safeguard social peace and thus the democratic system itself. Several decades later, whenever changes in the social welfare scheme are debated, the repercussions for the nation's "social peace" and "political stability" come up, with memories of Weimar thrown in.

But just as this consistent climate of public and elite opinion forecloses the dismantling of the welfare state, it also fosters a willingness among political decisionmakers to do what is needed to assure the survival of the basic system, even if that means imposing costs on many voters and the most influential groups. An ironic shift has occurred in the last decades of the twentieth century with respect to German and American welfare-state politics: partisan discourse and decisionmaking have been mostly characterized by pragmatism in the traditionally more ideological German setting while becoming highly ideological in the customarily more pragmatic political process in the U.S.

In the Federal Republic, decisionmakers' determination to preserve the integrity of the social state has been stronger than all other motivations and interests regardless whether a party to the right or left of the political spectrum has been the senior partner in the federal coalition government. The SPD-led government of Chancellor Helmut Schmidt initiated reforms in social programs (i.e., cancelling the scheduled increases of age pensions) in the 1980s as did the CDU-led government of Chancellor Helmut Kohl in the 1980s and 1990s. In the past, typically, the support of all major parties was sought and won. And this may well be the only feasible pattern for the future.

For as long as all political parties remain committed to the major pillars of the social state, and they have been thus far, they are likely to mediate between the multitude of organized and unorganized interests that already exist or are likely to emerge. When needed, decisionmakers in the party state can override even the most influential organized interests in the name of saving the social system without alienating the rejected interests irreparably.

In the Federal Republic all interests, whether organized or not, stand or fall according to the degree to which at least one of the major parties embraces their causes. Contrary to the American setting, where special interests bypass the political parties and strive for cozy relationships with influential individuals in both the legislative and executive branch, the road to political influence in Germany leads straight through the political parties. To concentrate on gaining access to individual decisionmakers and reward or punish individual politicians at the ballot box does not work in Germany's strong party state as it does in the American setting with its weak party system. For this reason, the predictions that the electoral power of Germany's growing number of senior citizens would eventually force politicians to align consistently with the aged against the young in an upcoming free-for-all distribution struggle ignore the role of the parties as arbitrators between conflicting interests.

The country's long-standing support for the principles of the welfare state, the continued influence of the ghost of Weimar, and, most of all, the political arrangements in the strong party state that have emphasized conflict-resolution and consensus remain potent indicators that the Federal Republic continues to be well-suited to adopt meaningful reforms and is unlikely to perform drastic surgery on the proven social security net.

Chancellor Kohl's 1996 "austerity plan" was a case in point: Even before the federal diet voted on his proposal, which went further than previous reforms and was attacked by critics as an assault on the welfare state, the Chancellor signaled his willingness to compromise. Postponing some of the original plan's provisions, he continued to insist on a number of cuts in social benefits such as a reduction in sick pay and unemployment benefits, additional charges for prescription drugs, and less time in health spas paid for by mandatory health insurance. Opposition leaders and a variety of interest groups did not question the need for spending cuts but called for policy changes assuring "social justice" and "fairness." In spite of their considerable differences, both sides agreed on the need for change in efforts to adapt welfare-state policies to the realities of the 1990s and, more important, to the likely challenges of the twenty-first century.

7

Germany Abroad
The Politics of Foreign Policy

On the 15th of December 1995 the front page of *The New York Times* featured a photograph of the huge German chancellor, flanked by the American and French presidents on his right and the British and Russian prime ministers on his left, looming over three Balkan leaders as they signed the Dayton agreement for peace in Bosnia. Chancellor Kohl's outstanding position in the picture was more than physical—it was symbolic. The Bundestag had just authorized him by a vote of 543 to 107 to contribute 4,000 German soldiers to the multinational force that was to implement the agreement. In the United States, in contrast, the Congress gave President Clinton much less emphatic support for the dispatch of 20,000 American troops. A substantial number of senators and representatives did not care for the notion of an innovative joint European-American peacekeeping mission in the Balkans—a concept that had won over Social Democratic and Green Bundestag deputies who had heretofore opposed any form of German military involvement. While members of the Congress and most Americans did not see why the leading global power should become entangled in a "European civil war," members of the Bundestag and most Germans felt that the leading European power could not but join the effort to enforce an end to the conflict.

The one-sided vote in the Bundestag attracted next to no attention in the United States, but a lot in the Federal Republic. It was clearly a pathmark in German politics, a far-reaching move on the road from Bonn to

Berlin that party leaders had previously shunned. However, where it would lead was by no means clear. Some observers feared that it might signal the beginning of a "remilitarization" of German foreign policy, others considered it a decisive step toward "normalization" in the conduct of foreign affairs following the disintegration of Communist Europe and the restoration of one Germany in the center of the European continent. But it was and still is really too soon to go beyond the standard "time will tell" assessment of the impact of obviously very complex developments.

In the Federal Republic of the Cold War era the politics of foreign policy—what should be done and what could be done—were a lot simpler than they are now. West Germans in a divided Germany in a divided Europe were for decades confronted by circumstances that allowed their leaders little room for maneuver. The preeminence of Soviet-American relations, the trade dependency of a fast-growing economy, and still vivid memories of the disastrous Third Reich limited the available options in foreign policy to an exceptional degree. The argument of governing leaders that they had done the best possible to promote German interest under these conditions was convincing. Time and again it cut the ground from under the opposition in elections dominated by foreign policy issues.

In those years policymakers learned to maintain their political footing at home and abroad by following three rules for secure navigation in foreign relations: (1) Always proceed cautiously and slowly; (2) never go it alone but keep the company of friends who can help you along; (3) don't swagger and keep a low profile. Close observance enabled CDU Chancellor Konrad Adenauer in the early years of the Federal Republic to boost his country's position in world affairs slowly by its inclusion in the European Economic Community, the North Atlantic Treaty Organization, and major international economic organizations over opposition from the Social Democrats. Later on it allowed SPD Chancellor Willy Brandt, in turn, to improve relations gradually with the Soviet Union, the East German Democratic Republic, and the rest of Communist Europe over opposition from Christian Democrats and Christian Socialists.

Abroad as at home, political stability was all important for the Federal Republic. And for the main players in the international affairs of the Cold War era German unification was not in accord with it. As long as that was evidently considered destabilizing by Soviet as well as Western leaders it was out of the question. Unification seemed accordingly pretty much of a lost cause until it came suddenly and unexpectedly in 1990 by German action. The Soviet Union withdrew entirely from East Germany and the United States, along with Britain and France, gave up what powers they had retained from the days of their occupation of West Germany.

But though a fully independent Federal Republic had been freed of the Cold War fetters on its sovereignty and radically changed—and more uncertain developments promised more influence in international affairs—the goals and conduct of the new Germany's foreign policy appeared to be essentially unchanged. American observers found that policy to be as reliable and predictable as before and German policy-makers just as cautiously restrained, if not altogether passive. The Bonn Republic's political leaders were not ready to venture further than in the past. They avoided joining the United States in the conduct of the 1991 Gulf War and then would not join other European countries in the United Nations force in the former Yugoslavia. Defense issues played no part in the 1994 federal election. The victorious Christian Democrats under Chancellor Kohl were for the most part not much more ready and willing than the opposition Social Democrats and Greens to follow President Clinton's call for "a more aggressive effort to solve the problems within Europe, like Bosnia, and beyond Europe's borders."[1] But scruples yielded to necessity when the Bundestag took the potentially far-reaching step to commit armed German soldiers to NATO's first "out of area" operation in the former Yugoslavia.

Social Democrats and Greens who supported the move held that it was meant only to put an end to the slaughter of the innocents in the former Yugoslavia—an exceptional action to deal with an exceptional case. But it was really more than that. After several years of groping and stumbling along the way, the political leaders of united Germany showed that they had found common bearings for dealing with unsettling situations in once-Communist Europe by military means if need be.

Beyond their partisan disagreements on particular policy questions, Germans remain committed to stability in international as in domestic politics. That shows in their political relationships with the United States, with other European countries, and with the rest of the world.

The American Connection

Relations with Germany play little or no role in American politics, whereas relations with the United States matter in all sorts of ways in

German politics. In recent years, for instance, the closing of most of the military installations the United States had located in Germany for almost half a century caused political problems in communities all at once deprived of a long-reliable source of income. The contemporary political system of united Germany bears the marks of the decisive American role in the creation and consolidation of a new political order for West Germany after the fall of the Nazi regime. For more than half a century German politics have seen furious battles on particular aspects of the American connection, but little disagreement on the need to keep it generally close and friendly.

In the Cold War era West Germans fought over the extent of military collaboration with the United States. As soon as the Federal Republic had been established under American sponsorship, its Christian Democratic Chancellor, Konrad Adenauer, agreed with the Eisenhower administration to end the postwar disarmament of West Germany and set up a new military establishment under NATO auspices. It was not a popular move and at first the Social Democratic opposition would have none of it. But with American backing Adenauer got it to support the necessary constitutional changes and to accept armament and NATO membership as necessary and desirable elements of military security arrangements with the United States. On that point practically all of the leading political figures were thereafter pretty much of one opinion—as they were not in other NATO countries. In the early 1980s Chancellor Schmidt of the SPD as well as Chancellor Kohl of the CDU thus agreed to let the United States put more powerful nuclear missiles in the Federal Republic despite mass protest demonstrations by a popular "peace movement" led by the new Green party.

With the end of the Cold War and the unification of Germany the military aspects of the American connection have come to take on a new meaning posing new questions. The argument that the Federal Republic must have vast American forces armed with devastating nuclear weapons on its soil to deter and, failing that, to stop a Soviet invasion is now meaningless. Defense policies shaped by NATO arrangements that put the control as well as the employment of German combat troops under American command have to be redesigned in the light of an entirely new situation. Contemporary Germany is not threatened by any country and threatens none. But its role in the new Europe still requires the protection of American nuclear weapons and the presence of American troops, according to leading politicians and military men in the Federal Republic.

The Germans have no nuclear weapons of their own and, by all indications, want none.[2] The argument of American, British, French, and Chinese leaders that a country needs a costly nuclear arsenal to give it prominence in international affairs is not heard in the Federal Republic. Its leaders hold instead that in return for renouncing a "nuclear option" it must have assurance of a credible American deterrent against threats of nuclear blackmail from whatever quarter.

Of all the European allies of the United States the Federal Republic has still the largest number of men under arms. But what for? That was the question when the *Bundeswehr* held a traditional Prussian military ceremony with torches, bands, and prayers before some two thousand prominent guests led by Chancellor Kohl in Bonn in the Fall of 1995. "It would be good," noted a leading German paper, "if the *Grosse Zapfen-streich* were loud enough to awaken the public and the policy makers so that they might begin to consider which direction this army should be marching in."[3] Soon after the Bundestag set a signpost with its endorsement of German participation in the international peacekeeping mission for Bosnia.

Set up originally to provide most of NATO's "conventional forces" for a war with the Soviet Union, Germany's defense establishment now faces some touchy political problems concerning the mission, structure, and cost of the Bundeswehr in the years ahead. Most important, particularly for relations with the United States, is whether, when, and how the Federal Republic should use force or the threat of force in dealing with other countries. That it would do so on its own except in self-defense—as its American, British and French NATO allies have done—is politically out of the question. That it would do so under all circumstances to honor its mutual defense commitments under the NATO and Western European Union treaties is more open to question, but far-fetched. The Bosnian venture, however, made Germans face up to the question of Bundeswehr participation in international military operations outside the NATO area.

Until then the German public and its leaders had been unwilling to go beyond providing some unarmed soldiers for UN operations in far-off African and Asian lands and "checkbook contributions" for American-led operations in the Gulf war. But the savage Balkan conflict in a region so much nearer to home and among people with historically close ties to Germany was different. American and European leaders demanded more than just another financial contribution for an allied operation. More important for domestic politics was that graphic media accounts of savage ethnic cleansing and the coming of tens of thousands of desperate refugees from the former Yugoslavia overcame opposition to sending German soldiers back to where Hitler's armies had ruled in World War II. After the Constitutional Court had cleared the way, the Bundeswehr got its first "out-area" assignment under NATO auspices by the precedent-setting vote of the Bundestag in December 1995.

By now most Germans generally go along with government policies that let combat aircraft, naval vessels, and ground troops of the Bundeswehr participate in more than defensive operations of the NATO alliance. However, the new military tasks of the armed forces have also underscored political questions regarding their makeup. As "an alliance army," the Bundeswehr must be ready "to contribute at short notice to managing likely international crises" according to a policy paper of CDU Chancellor Kohl's Government.[4] That calls for highly trained professionals. But the German armed forces, unlike those of the United States, consist in large part of draftees conscripted for less than a year of basic training to defend their country, not to carry out foreign policy missions.[5]

When the Bundeswehr was formed in 1955, West German political leaders wanted it to be made up of "citizens in uniform" from all sectors of society to ensure that peace and democracy would not once again be subverted by a professional force like the *Reichswehr* of the Weimar republic. That has been achieved. But it has become harder to justify conscription on military grounds than in the days of the Cold War. The unification treaty of 1990 provided for a smaller Bundeswehr and more and more of the young men subject to the draft have not wanted to be part of it. In the mid-1990s one out of three preferred to substitute mandatory alternative duties in social welfare organizations, though that involved serving longer. Conscription is not only unpopular, but for military purposes evidently less cost efficient in this day and age than an all-volunteer force like that of the United States.

But Christian Democratic leaders especially insist that Germany must nevertheless continue to have conscription.[6] They have left it to the military leaders to arrange for the consequently unavoidable segmentation of the Bundeswehr. Conscripts and reservists now form a relatively poorly trained defense force of "citizen soldiers" without a specific, meaningful mission. Career professional soldiers make up the elite units of a smaller, but much better equipped "rapid reaction force" that is designed to give German governments more strength and flexibility than before to employ military means in the conduct of foreign policy.[7]

But never alone and always in close cooperation with the United States, according to the people responsible for the conduct of German foreign policy these days. Not only in NATO, but in world-wide intergovernmental organizations like the UN the Germans have made it a rule to collaborate closely with the Americans. The notion of a German-American "partnership in leadership" for peace and security in Europe advocated by U.S. Presidents Bush and Clinton has been very much to the liking of the Kohl government. It wants Americans to consider the Federal Republic their most important and reliable European ally. It holds that German diplomacy needs the backing of American military power to be effective in seeking stability in Eastern Europe and the former Soviet Union. And it insists that more unity in the foreign policies of European Union countries cannot be at the expense of Germany's military ties to the United States.[8]

These ties, however, are rooted in the past and whether they will matter all that much for German foreign policy in the future is doubtful. New leaders and new conditions on both sides of the Atlantic are already transforming the character of the relationship. The time is past when close personal ties between influential German and American proponents of a so-called Atlantic Security Community provided strong links for the American connection. Military ties, in fact, now matter less and economic rivalry more and the interests of the United States and the Federal Republic in international politics are therefore becoming less compatible and more divergent. In American politics the focus of foreign policy interests—such as it is—has shifted from transatlantic relations with NATO allies to transpacific relations with such countries as Japan and China. In German politics the value of the American connection has been diminished by more economic integration among European Union countries and more competitition with the United States in world markets. Future German policymakers are by present indications likely to be not so much against but rather not so much with their American partners in the conduct of foreign relations.

The European Dimension

In years past West Germany's semi-independent Bonn Republic was pictured as a giant in European economic affairs and a dwarf in European power politics. In years to come united Germany's Berlin Republic will in all likelihood still be an economic giant but hardly a political dwarf among the countries of Europe.

Unification certainly changed Germany's position in Europe, but just how much and to what effect on domestic and international politics is by no means clear. At first some German and foreign commentators predicted that, for better or for worse, the expanded Federal Republic was bound to go the way of the German Reich and throw its weight about on the strength of its dominant geopolitical position in the middle of the continent.[9] Indeed, when Yugoslavia fell apart in 1991, Germany took the lead in formally recognizing the independence of breakaway Slovenia and Croatia and then got its more reluctant partners in the European Union to follow suit. But that unilateral action by the Kohl government proved to be a striking exception to the common precept of German politicians that their country should maintain a low profile in European affairs and not strike out on its own. "United Germany is number one in Europe," said Chancellor Kohl in a 1995 television appearance, but "we ought not to advertise it and better not talk too much about it."[10]

Looking backward to times past for geopolitical clues to the road ahead is not instructive when it slights the significant changes in German politics and foreign relations. For, other than in the days of the Second Empire and Third Reich, the European policies of contemporary Germany are not shaped by autocratic leaders concerned with questions of military strategy but by elected politicians wrestling with domestic economic problems.

First Among Unequals

The European dimension in German politics is set out first and foremost by the Federal Republic's role in the European Union, as we noted in chapter 1. In Germany EU membership has not, as in Great Britain and Norway, been a divisive partisan issue. Politicians of all stripes agree that on the whole it is is a good thing for their country to be in partnership with Europe's well-established democracies. And they share the view that German diplomacy should tread softly in the Union and not give credence to voices in other member countries who see it succumbing to the thrust of overwhelming German economic power.[11]

Since the EU is not a federal union—like the United States and Germany—but an international organization of independent states, its authority in the member countries depends on how far these are willing to forego sovereign rights and voluntarily comply with the decisions of EU bodies. In Germany that question has never been put directly to voters—as it has been in France and other European countries—but only to their parliamentary representatives. And these, by endorsing intergovernmental agreements to increase the authority of supranational EU bodies, have subscribed to limitations on national sovereignty that would be totally unacceptable in the United States.

The Basic Law of the Federal Republic has been amended so that any action by German authorities is now unconstitutional if it conflicts with the terms of EU agreements accepted by a two-thirds vote in the federal parliament. That means, for example, that the Bundestag may not make it more difficult for foreigners from EU countries to work and do business in the Federal Republic than for its own citizens. Accordingly, the European Union's Court of Justice in 1992 could nullify legislation supported by all the parties in the chamber which required truckers from other EU states to pay as much tax as their German competitors for the use of German roads. That would force up their costs of operation in Germany, said the Court, and put them at a competitive disadvantage in violation of European Union rules.

While such legally binding commitments to European supranationalism affect the lives of practically all Germans—in paying a EU sales tax on goods and services, for instance—they have become so much a part of daily living that most people fail to make the connection unless it is called to their attention in the media. Few knew and few cared that some politicians in Bavaria sought to deny foreigners from other EU countries their right to vote in local elections some years ago. Not many took notice when the European Court of Justice invalidated the preferential promotion of women in the public services of the state of Bremen under its affirmative action law. But a far more complex ruling by their own Constitutional Court that any EU agreement relating to the stability of the German currency required another constitutional amendment drew a good deal more public attention when it was featured in the media.

The state governments have gotten much more of a say in foreign policymaking than in the United States through Germany's membership in the European Union. And as economic issues have become more and military ones less important for the Federal Republic, politics in the states have become more intertwined with politics in the Union. For in Germany the federal government is bound by the constitution to take the particular regional and partisan interests of diverse state governments into account on European Union matters.[12]

Back in in the 1950s, when the recently established Federal Republic was just beginning to make its way in international politics, the famed German novelist Thomas Mann hoped that the road ahead would lead to a "European Germany" and not a "German Europe." The former meant a country joined to others in a peaceful continental community, the latter a continent dominated by the most powerful of hostile nation states. This distinction has been made time and again, at home and abroad, by German policymakers pushing for the tight and irreversible integration of the Federal Republic into a closely knit European Union. According to Chancellor Kohl that will forever put an end to the aggressive nationalism and bar a recurrence of the continental wars of the past. Others have looked more to the future. As they have it, a European Germany will give all of the countries in a closer Union more strength for dealing with the uncertainties of global power politics.

Before unification such German arguments for less national sovereignty in the European Union came easily to prominent politicians in a country that was not fully independent like Great Britain and France. But even after the former occupation powers gave up the last vestiges of control, the leaders of reunified Germany continued to advocate a "deepening" of the Union beyond its economic elements. Kohl's Christian Democrats and President Roman Herzog called for a European federation along German lines. While the opposition parties were not prepared to go on record to the same extent, they readily endorsed the Maastricht Treaty of 1992 for more a closer union.[13]

But it was soon evident that the Treaty's provisions for a single currency, joint foreign and security policies, and more common legal and socioeconomic measures were not liked as much in other EU countries. Referenda, elections, and policy statements showed less willingness to surrender sovereignty to the Union, to give up national vetoes over major decisions, and to diminish the "democratic deficit" by giving more power to the supranational European parliament. And there was clearly a good deal of concern in Britain and elsewhere that, fully implemented, the Maastricht Treaty would lead to the establishment of a German Europe under the guise of a European Germany. Norwegian voters chose to stay out of the Union entirely, against the advice of their government, and in Denmark and France opponents of the Treaty came close to rejecting it at the polls.

German Europeanists like Chancellor Kohl had to recognize that their plans for a tighter political union had gone too far. The European Unions' utter failure to settle the ethnic conflict in Bosnia on its own, without the United States and NATO, and its lack of popular support brought out that it was far from becoming some sort of United States of Europe. For the foreseeable future it seemed unlikely to go much further than to give political and big business leaders in Germany as well as other member countries more supranational means for the promotion of national economic interests.

Among ordinary Germans the unexpectedly severe impact of unprecedented economic problems for the Federal Republic raised new doubts about whether the benefits of more European integration would indeed outweigh what it might cost them, as they had been told. Most people felt that they did not have enough influence in the Union as it was and doubted that they would have more if it were to become a democratically governed federation.[14] But popular resistance to a tighter European Union did not amount to much until Germans were faced with giving up their treasured Deutschmark for a "Euro" of uncertain value in a monetary union with economically weaker countries. That did not sit well with many German voters and some leaders of the Social Democratic opposition to the Kohl government, desperate for an election issue, sought to turn such sentiments against the Christian Democratic Chancellor. Most SPD leaders stood with Germany's top business managers in backing the Kohl government's drive for monetary union by the end of the century. However, popular resistance at home let that government take a stronger position abroad despite foreign fears of a German Europe. It insisted that other European governments had to take the same political risks of unpopular budget cuts as the German if they wanted the economic benefits of merging their currencies with one of the three strongest in the world. That this was easier said by the one than done by the others was shown by the British government, which would have none of it, and the French, which did its best to meet German terms.

For policymakers in the Federal Republic good relations with their counterparts in France has been the key component of European integration from its start in the early 1950s. During the Cold War that involved sometimes quite difficult diplomatic efforts to strike a balance between the French connection to their country's most important economic partner and the American connection to its most important military one without alienating either. Since then there has been a decided shift in emphasis for the politics of German foreign policymaking that is obscured by official declarations to the contrary. Influential party leaders have hinted and more outspoken business leaders have made it plain that the Federal Republic no longer needs so much to be the junior military partner of the United States in NATO as the senior economic partner of France in the European Union.

While relations with the United States and European countries occasionally enter into German politics, developments in Eastern Europe have had remarkably little impact. Germans, as some have it, need be more concerned than other Europeans and Americans because they live in such close proximity to politically unstable lands in former Communist Europe. In this view, chaotic conditions as in the former Yugoslavia are likely to send a vast wave of refugees from Eastern Europe toward Germany that would produce great tensions and even Weimar-like political cleavages there. As the President of the Federal Republic, Roman Herzog, put it in the mid-1990s: "If we do not stabilize the East it will destabilize us."[15]

Thus far, at least, such admonitions have not made much of an impression on ordinary Germans. For many their principal concern regarding Eastern Europe is the loss of jobs to countries there as, for instance, through the building of Volkswagens in the Czech Republic. Providing for stability in Eastern Europe does not rank high on the agenda of leading policymakers who seem not at all sure what they could do if they would. They have been not been particularly eager to acknowledge with appropriate actions that for post-Cold War Eastern Europe Berlin is taking the place of Moscow as the center of power in the region. Far from seeking German hegemony, political and economic elites have proceeded with utmost caution into as yet comparatively uncharted areas for German foreign policy. In accordance with its well-established multilateral principles, they maintain that Germans cannot and will not undertake to safeguard stability in Eastern Europe on their own. And acting as if the position of the Federal Republic had not changed drastically in the region since reunification, they endeavor to keep its old low profile in the new relationship with former Communist countries in neighboring near Eastern Europe and more distant middle and far Eastern Europe—above all Russia. They do not wish to step on toes still sensitive from the tread of German boots in Hitler's days.

For Germans, as for Americans, predicting what will occur in Russia is very much a guessing game. In the Federal Republic close observers agree pretty much that resurgent Russian military power might pose a security threat but that steady Russian economic growth could provide great business opportunities. While Germany is already Russia's largest trading partner uncertainties about the future of the Russian economy have discouraged its bankers from investing in risky ventures. Political turmoil in Russia always causes a weakening of the German Mark in global markets. German policymakers hope that more stability will lead to closer economic bonds and, consequently, closer political ties between the two largest countries in Europe.

The efforts of neighboring Poland, Hungary, and Czech Republic to get into NATO and the European Union are not disputed among Germans. For those who care, membership in NATO is to be welcomed for extending Germany's military security umbrella well beyond its eastern borders while membership in the EU can be expected to further boost a German stake in surging East European economies that already exceeds that of other Western nations.

The Global Reach

When Germany's leading position as a continental power was based on military might commerce would follow the battle flag of its armies across Europe. These days international trade takes the flag of German economic power across the globe. And whereas then German leaders would to stay close to home, they now move about the world promoting German products and investments. Especially since the end of the Cold War, foreign policy concerns have become not only more demilitarized than in the United States, France, and Britain, but also more commercialized.

In a country that is second only to the United States in the volume of international trade, exports have long been more important economically and less controversial politically—and all the more so with the increasing Europeanization and globalization of German commercial interests. Europeanization has moved most German exports of goods and investments—like German vacationers—to other countries on the continent, while globalization has taken taken most of the rest to markets in North and South America. But that proved not to be good enough to sustain German prosperity in the 1990s. Urged on by the Kohl government, leading exporters like Siemens and Daimler-Benz set out belatedly to catch up with Japanese and American competitors in expanding Asian markets. The government provided economic assistance, such as insurance coverage for exports, and diplomatic support—most notably by wooing Asian autocracies like Indonesia, Iran, and China in spite of public demonstrations and Bundestag resolutions condemning them for violations of human rights.

The Kohl government has not let such criticism at home get in the way of a trade policy designed to win friends and avoid political friction in Asian markets. Instead of joining the American embargo on trade with Iran, the Federal Republic has sent more exports to that country than other Western nation as its policymakers have asserted that their efforts for a "critical dialogue" with the purported sponsors of international terrorism was a better way to change their ways than isolating them. And as Germany has come to be China's biggest European trading partner and the most successful competitor of the United States for access to its promising markets, leading members of the governing Christian Democrats like President Roman Herzog have argued that harmonious trade relations with China promote political "change through rapprochement" in that country as it had in those of Communist Europe.[16]

But such ingenious arguments cannot disguise the fact that in the view of current German policymakers commercial considerations come first and political differences must not be allowed to undercut profitable economic partnerships. And since the opposition to the governing coalition of Christian and Free Democrats has on the whole gone along with that position, it is likely to be maintained under a different government. Faced with mass unemployment and ailing export industries, Social Democrats and Greens have pretty much overcome their scruples to accept, if not entirely embrace, the argument that Germany's great stakes in international trade do not allow it to antagonize governments that can block access to promising global markets on political issues such as human rights.

What Roles for Germany in Twenty-First–Century World Politics?

The politics of foreign policy are concerned with how people inside a country deal with matters on the outside. In democracies like the United States and the German Federal Republic that may call for controversial decisions by elected officials subject to public scrutiny, approval, and criticism at home about what they do or do not do abroad. Germans thus credited Chancellor Kohl's personal diplomacy in the Soviet Union with the rapid withdrawal of Soviet forces after unification and then blamed him for slighting their economic concerns in negotiations for European Monetary Union. But playing the statesman usually gets more attention abroad than at home, especially when the voters do not relate domestic pocketbook issues to international developments. Since the end of the Cold War foreign policy issues have by and large been neither particularly prominent nor controversial in German politics.

Contrary to the fears of some and the hopes of others outside of the Federal Republic, Germans have been neither ready nor willing to take on more active roles in international affairs than before their unification. Accustomed to parochial politics when they lived in separate states, prominent as well as ordinary people have been slow to expand their vision since coming together in one. For 640 leading politicians, business managers, journalists, trade unionists and churchmen in a 1996 elite survey the most important policy problems facing their country were domestic ones—lagging economic growth, rising unemployment, and the persistent split between East and West Germans.[17]

German politicians, like most of their American counterparts, are literally more at home in local and regional party politics and more attuned to short-term electoral considerations than to long-range international developments. They leave that mostly to people in and out of government who make it their business to offer advice on foreign affairs—diplomats, bankers, journalists, and specialists in universities and think tanks. But since the spectacular failure of supposed experts on military security and foreign relations to anticipate the fall of the Iron Curtain and the enormous changes that followed—most notably German unification—their views have commanded more respect outside than inside the Federal Republic.

Generally speaking, Germans certainly do not want their country to engage in power politics as in the past. Opinion polls still show, as they have for more than half a century, that some naive souls wish that the Federal Republic could just be a big Switzerland, staying clear of entangling commitments while making lots of money abroad. Most everybody knows that this is out of the question, but practically nobody seems to have more than a vague sense at best where the Federal Republic is headed in its international relations. The country appears to be "muddling its way through world affairs," as one observer has it. "No real or new consensus has yet emerged on the ranking of new priorities . . . and . . . the appropriate means and institutions. Below the superficial level of continuity, policies and actors are drifting."[18]

To provide Germans with a better sense of potential directions in foreign affairs their political leaders have to give some key questions a thorough public airing in parliament and the media. For instance, to what extent is control over Germany's foreign relations slipping out of the hands of its government and how much will it have for pursuing particular German policy objectives in specific areas? What are are the options and realistic choices facing German policymakers at crossroads in European, transatlantic, and global relations? Germans should return to a "natural" assertion of national interests, according to Lothar Rühle, Minister of Defense in the Kohl Government.[19] But what those interests might be in particular areas and on particular occasions remains an open question in the contemporary politics of German foreign policy.

Neither government nor opposition leaders have been keen to bring questions like these before the public. They have preferred to stick instead to customary noncontroversial generalizations about the promotion of democracy, stability, and open markets for free trade throughout the world. The ideological cleavages and passions that once animated the politics of foreign policy in the Bonn Republic have given way to a bland interparty consensus on the need for lasting military security arrangements with the United States, for European integration, and for global trade.

That may very well change in the transition from the old politics of the Bonn Republic to new ones of the Berlin Republic. Clearer but potentially also more devisive redefinitions of distinctive German interests seem unavoidable in a world where "normal" countries like the United States have no inhibitions about aggressively promoting their own. At home and abroad German leaders are likely to find it more difficult to keep to policies designed to keep Germany "everybody's darling," like being the only member of the European Union to go with both the French desire for a tighter organization and the British for a larger and looser one.[20] A new generation of rival party leaders for top government positions may continue to abide by the general rules of German foreign policy that we noted at the outset of this chapter, but be more insistently outspoken and assertive on specific issues such as the promotion of German trade and investments within and beyond Europe.

Conclusion
The Road Ahead . . .

In the late 1990s, when an array of giant structures arose in the heart of Berlin on what was Europe's and perhaps the world's largest construction site, officials in Germany wondered if they could meet the timetable for relocating the federal government. Whether completed by the year 2002, as planned, or at a later date, chances were that the physical move from Bonn to Berlin would not end the period of transition in German politics that began with the reunification of the two Germanys. Commenting on the Federal Republic's glorious economic past and the severe problems of the late 1990s, one American observer noted that the Germany entering the year 2000 would be a very different place from the Germany of 1990. Others suggested that nothing less than Germany's particular brand of democracy was on the test stand since the successes of the Bonn Republic had been linked to West Germany's prosperity and generous social system.

But if the Federal Republic has arrived at a crossroads, as conventional wisdom has it, a fundamental change of direction is just as unlikely as the notion that the Berlin Republic will simply be a carbon copy of the Bonn Republic.

As described in the preceding chapters, the constitution and the institutions that served West Germany very well for forty years have remained in place after unification, as has the intricate system of arrangements, rules, and conventions characteristic of the Federal Republic's political process. And the attitudinal characteristics that tempered politics in West Germany have not dissipated in the years following reunification. But there have been changes as well—especially in the party system, in the mass media, in the demographic make-up, and in the influence of the European Union on traditionally domestic matters—that affect politics and policymaking in the post-unification years. At the threshold of a new century and millennium observers inside and outside Germany have wondered whether the predominantly old and the limited, but not insignificant, new features in the political realm will help or hinder in finding a balance between the continuity that most Germans cherish and the change that the country's immense socioeconomic problems demand. Could Germany's leaders inside and outside the government adopt effective reforms without upsetting political stability and social peace?

As we write this concluding chapter, the verdict as to these and similar questions and thus to the ultimate outcome of Germany's passage from the Bonn Republic to the Berlin Republic is not yet in. But the signs along the road already traveled provide some clues as to the system's ability to adapt to far-reaching changes inside and outside the country.

To be sure, some of the most pressing problems Germans are facing in the late 1990s and beyond are similar to the difficulties Americans wrestled with. Both countries try to maintain prosperity in an ever more competitive global economy with increasingly aggressive players, especially in the emerging markets of central and eastern Europe, Asia, and Latin America. Both countries are under pressure to educate, train, and retrain their workforce for the rapidly changing post-industrial economy. Both countries struggle with the need of controlling government spending, shrinking social programs, coming to terms with vast societal changes, and redefining foreign and security policies in the post-Cold War world. To suggest, however, that Americans can learn from Germany's successes and failures, as some U.S. observers have, ignores the important differences in politics here and there that exist side by side with many similarities.

To begin with, the three unique features that distinguish politics in Germany from politics in America and similar democracies, namely the consequences of reunification, the geographical location in the heart of post-Cold War Europe, and the legacy of the Weimar and Nazi past are important influences in the 1990s and likely to remain important factors in the years to come. In one way or another these elements will continue to influence how Germany deals with the problems at hand.

Contrary to expectations in the early 1990s, the aftermath of reunification has remained an important factor throughout the decade and chances are that the East-West cleavage in public attitudes and voting behavior, in the party system, in labor relations, in the politics of economic and social policymaking will continue to affect the political process in many ways. Whether the distinct differences between East and West Germans favor continuity or change depends on the issues involved. While the East can be a catalyst for change in some areas (and already has been, for example, with respect to increased flexibility in the traditionally rigid collective bargaining system), East Germans seem far less inclined than West Germans to accept significant cuts in the generous social welfare state that the Federal Republic can no longer afford. To the extent that the PDS, the successor organization of the German Democratic Republic's ruling communist party, concentrates on exploiting these sentiments in the East of the country, the only genuine East German political party could become a thorn in the hide of the mainstream parties and their preference for consensus in major issues.

The political significance of reunited Germany's preeminent position in Europe remains unclear. Obviously, a lot depends on unpredictable foreign developments beyond the reach of German policymakers, notably in Russia and other parts of the former Soviet Union. But the biggest question now facing Germans is how they will fare in a European Monetary Union. Just a few years before the projected replacement of national currencies by the Euro, German political leaders' unwavering support for the Maastricht Treaty and ordinary Germans' strong preference for their beloved German Mark has not triggered a vigorous public debate. Nor has there been a public discourse about the European Union's expanding authority and how this will affect the German people's control over their own domestic and foreign policy. Take, for example, the strict standards for membership in the Monetary Union. While putting pressure on Germany as on other countries to cut public spending and trim programs that need reforms with or without membership in the Monetary Union, the tough criteria have handcuffed national governments in fiscal matters. Although not quite as restrictive as the proposed balanced budget amendment to the U.S. Constitution, the conditions for membership, on which the Kohl government has insisted most vehemently, could have troublesome restraining effects on the German government's (and other member governments') leeway for deficit spending during crisis situations.

As the projected demise of the German Mark as well as the waning influence of the highly respected Bundesbank approach and the impact of the European Union on decisionmaking in Germany becomes more transparent, one wonders whether the deepening and widening of Europe's integration will become sooner or later a major issue in German politics. This seems not very likely as long as most leaders in the establishment parties show no desire to question their country's commitment to a common European currency—if only for fear that rejecting the Monetary Union could throw the European Union into turmoil and question the reliability of the reunited and strengthened Germany with respect to the political, military, and economic integration of Europe.

Still, the Federal Republic's unwavering dedication to ever greater European integration could become a political issue in the face of increasing economic difficulties. Already a growing number of economists, historians, journalists, and politicians have rejected the need of the European Monetary Union outright or suggested a postponement. Some have criticized Germany's strong commitment to European integration as "an unnatural and 'typically German' tendency to want to be different."[1] This latter group has argued that fifty years after the end of World War II Germans must once again be a "normal" nation and pursue their national interest. While for the time being simply a debate in elite circles, some observers have wondered whether sooner or later the "normalcy issue" could be exploited by populists to rally the public around a "return to nationalism" agenda.

So far, the enduring memories of the Third Reich and its Weimar prelude have prevented the return of "normalcy" to German politics. While a waning influence in day-to-day politics, the legacy of the past continues to linger beneath the surface—ready to emerge as a factor in the face of incidents and developments at home or abroad. Indeed, the tendency to refer to the Holocaust, World War II, and the Weimar years has increased in the mid- and late 1990s after seemingly subsiding in the preceding years. The most obvious explanation is that the fears of upsetting the highly esteemed social peace and political stability have never been greater in the Federal Republic than in the 1990s, when the country has been struggling with severe economic problems. The violent reactions on the part of some Germans to the recent influx of foreigners and reunited Germany's enhanced status as the economic colossus of Europe have bolstered the notion that the best way of mastering contemporary problems is not to forget the past. As a result, Weimar and the Third Reich are invoked in contemporary German politics in support of both continuity and change depending on which one of these values is seen as most likely to safeguard social peace and stability. For example, when in 1997 the rate of mass unemployment for the first time rose to what it had been just before Hitler came to power, commentators pointed to the consequences then in debating whether it would now be better for social peace and stability to maintain or reduce entitlements. In foreign affairs the memories of the past have made Germans squeamish about sending their military forces abroad as when German troops joined the NATO-peacekeeping mission to former Yugoslavia.

Two generations of Germans have for the most part been effectively immunized by schooling and mass media against a recurrence of the mass opposition to democracy in the Weimar era and the mass support for totalitarianism under Hitler. A small number of neo-Nazi hoodlums seeking and getting media attention have conveyed a distorted image to the outside world. Germans are on the whole less complacent about anti-democratic right-wingers than Americans and more willing to let government authorities curb their civil liberties as long as such measures comply with the constitutional precepts.

Important as they are, the extraordinary German aspects alone can neither explain German politics nor determine the country's ability to cope with giant-size problems. The institutional and procedural arrangements, the formal and informal rules of the game, and the underlying societal values matter a great deal. While the Federal Republic's democracy was modeled in more than one aspect along the lines of the American system, the differences between German and American politics are nevertheless more distinct than the similarities.

To begin with, the German system's deliberate tilt in favor of compromise and consensus and the American system's intentional bias in favor of adversary and conflict result in quite different brands of politics and political outcomes. Students of American politics have long recognized that the founding fathers did not really design a system of neatly separated powers but one of shared prerogatives. However, these power sharing schemes between the executive and legislative branches and between the federal government and the states are far more explicit and intertwined in the Federal Republic than in the United States. As a result, German politicians are more compelled than their American counterparts to search for common ground rather than dwell on conflict. The most important aspects here are the direct representation of the state governments in the upper chamber of the federal legislative branch and the predominant role of the political parties in the German system. Furthermore, the institutionalized features that cast German employers and employees in the roles of "social partners," not adversaries as in the United States, and incorporate all major societal interests into the governmental process are designed to bridge differences.

Also, the electoral system in the Federal Republic is less inhibiting and punishing than the American one, when politicians and their parties make tough decisions that inflict pain on the majority of voters. Because all members of the U.S. House of Representatives are elected for two-year terms and one-third of the members of the U.S. Senate is up for reelection every second year, elections are never far from the minds of legislators in Washington. Members of the Bundestag, on the other hand, have more time to act without thinking of the next election because they serve concurrent four-year terms. More important, unlike American voters the electorate in the Federal Republic tends to hold political parties and not individual lawmakers accountable for whatever policies they support or reject. In systems that separate neatly between governing and opposition parties voters reward or punish the party or parties in power for their performances. But in the Federal Republic's special brand of cooperative federalism it is less clear to what extent voters will reward or punish the governing or the opposition parties for their initiatives or the lack thereof. This is one more reason why the major political parties have an incentive to search for common ground on major issues.

Finally, while the American tradition holds individualism and self-reliance in high esteem, Germans value most of all social tranquility and collective responsibility for basic social welfare. These conflicting values inform economic and social politics and policies in both countries. In the past the basic agreement on a strong social component in the Federal Republic's market economy transcended the ideological and partisan differences of the Cold War era. More recently, reform debates in Germany focus even more on fiscal problems and solutions while lacking the moral and ideological fervor of comparable discussions in the U.S.

Because the described systemic features and societal attitudes add up to a strong incentive for compromise and consensus, students of politics in the Federal Republic have long questioned whether the system is flexible enough to adopt more than incremental changes if circumstances demand meaningful reforms. Splitting the difference in conflicts is seldom the stuff for substantial transformations and reforms. As the economic problems have mounted in the 1990s and the viability of important social insurance programs have seemed at stake, some observers in Germany have wondered about their system's capability and the political parties' will to enact reforms.[2] Some have blamed the tendency of the governing coalition and the opposition parties to meet behind closed doors and "forge compromises for which nobody is visibly responsible" for the lack of resolute actions.[3]

But the very features of German politics that work in favor of continuity and incremental changes in normal times have at the same time the attributes needed for adopting major reforms in the face of extraordinary problems. Toward the end of the 1990s some politicians have come to believe that the magnitude of the problems in Germany's economic and social system calls for bold solutions that only a "grand coalition" government of the two large parties (CDU/CSU and SPD) can work out and adopt. Others have preferred joint problem-solving in the influential conference committee charged with mediating differences between the two legislative chambers or in case-by-case concerted actions.

In the future, politics in Germany may come to resemble American politics more than now; they will, however, never be the same. Some of the differences that we have noted throughout this book may diminish, but most are profound enough to continue. That raises a question: how much do these differences matter when it comes to managing the common challenges? Above all, one wonders, whether Germans are politically better or less well equipped than Americans to deal with extraordinary problems in a democratic as well as effective manner. Germans are less self-assured on that score, but in our view their system is at least as suited for coping with major problems as that of the United States.

All of this is not to say that contemporary German politics are without bitter conflicts and confrontations. On the contrary, the enormity of the problems and the dimension of the needed reforms have led to a sharpening of inter- and intra-party divisions between conservatives and liberals, friends of labor and friends of business, those emphasizing the "social" and others stressing the "free market" part in Germany's brand of capitalism.

Most ordinary Germans support meaningful changes to preserve the socioeconomic arrangement—even if that means sacrifices—but they have very different views about specific reform measures and how they should affect various societal groups. This presents German politicians with a need for consolidating public opinion and opportunities for taking the lead. There are plenty of far-reaching media facilities for placing the pros and cons and potential consequences of various policy proposals before an interested public. But that has yet to happen. On the whole German leaders are not yet quite as media-savvy as many of their American counterparts.

When the reform debates heated up in 1997, one German politician compared his country's problems and the political in-fights they triggered with the disarray at the giant construction site in the heart of Berlin. But what looked like a wasteland in the capital city would soon be the new center of Berlin, with new government and corporate buildings and traditional structures like the Reichstag side by side. This transformation was perhaps a good omen for Germany's struggle to cope with the challenges of today and tomorrow—although restructuring the country's economic and social system will be far more cumbersome and time-consuming than preparing Berlin for housing the federal government.

Notes

Introduction

1. Paul Goldberger, "Christo's Wrapped Reichstag: Symbol for the New Germany." *The New York Times*, June 23, 1995.

2. The most obvious change was the disappearance of the Berlin wall. Built by East German communists in 1961, the wall ran just behind the eastern facade of the *Reichstag*. Gone, too, was the hammer-and-sicle flag hoisted by Soviet troops high over the Reichstag as a symbol of Nazi Germany's defeat.

3. John Rockwell, "New Germany's State of Mind." *The New York Times*, May 6, 1994.

1. "German Questions"—Old and New

1. Renata Fritsch-Bournazel, *Europe and German Unification* (New York/Oxford: Berg, 1992), p. 205.

2. Actually, individuals were entitled to exchange 4,000 East Marks at 1–1 and the rest of their savings at a still very favorable 2–1 rate.

3. According to an Emnid poll, for example, 67% of East Germans believed this in June 1995. See, "Stolz aufs eigene Leben." *Der Spiegel*, No. 27, 1995, p. 41.

4. See, for example, "Allensbacher Monatsbericht Juli 1994," *Frankfurter Allgemeine Zeitung*, Aug. 10, 1994.

5. "Stolz aufs Eigene Leben." *Der Spiegel*, no. 27, 1995.

6. According to Emnid polls. See, "Stolz auf Eigene Leben." *Der Spiegel*, no. 27, 1995, p. 49.

7. According to the *Allensbacher Jahrbuch der Demoskopie 1984–1992* and the "Allensbacher Umfrage zum Geschichtsbewusstsein," Frankfurter Allgemeine Zeitung, May 3, 1995, 87% of the public in East Germany and 82% in West Germany believed in April 1995 that uniting the two Germanys was the right decision. Three years earlier, in March 1992, 73% of the East German and 66% of the West German population expressed such support.

8. The migration of Russian Jews, who are freely admitted under special arrangements, substantially increased this number in recent years.

2. Representative Democracy: Roots of the System

1. Kurt Sontheimer, *The Government and Politics of West Germany*. (New York: Praeger, 1973), p. 95.

2. Willy Brandt, *People and Politics: The Years 1960–1975* (Boston: Little, Brown, 1976), p. 55.

3. For Better or for Worse: More Participatory Democracy

1. In the United States social scientists have traced a relationship between "negative" media coverage of Congress and low public esteem for the legislative branch. See, for example, Thomas E. Mann and Norman J. Ornstein, *Congress, the Press, and the Public* (Washington, D.C.: American Enterprise Institute and The Brookings Institution, 1994). In the Federal Republic a similar relationship is said to exist. See, Werner J. Patzelt, "Das Volk und seine Vertreter: eine gestörte Beziehung." In *Aus Politik und Zeitgeschichte* March 18, 1994.

2. Robert Putnam has identified the spread of television as one of the reasons why Americans' civic engagement declined in the last several decades. See, Robert D. Putnam, "Bowling Alone." *The Journal of Democracy*, Jan. 1995.

3. Wolfgang Donsbach, "What Part Did the Media Play?" *The Public Perspective*, vol. 6, no. 1, 1994.

4. To trace the attitudes of the general public and of elites in the Federal Republic we consulted a multitude of public opinion polls conducted by the Konrad-Adenauer-Stiftung, Emnid and the Institut fuer Wirtschaftsforschung Halle (as published in *Der Spiegel*), the Institut fuer angewandte Sozialwissenschaft, Forschungsgruppe Wahlen, the European Commission's *Eurobarometer* as well as elite and public opinion surveys conducted by the Allensbach Institut fuer Demoskopie for the business journal *Capital*.

5. "Wann moechten Sie sterben?" *Der Spiegel* 39/1994, pp. 65–90.

6. The right to privacy, too, is limited by the liberal use of wire tapping by law enforcement agencies in order to protect the state.

7. Peter J. Katzenstein, "West Germany's Internal Security Policy: State and Violence in the 1970s and 1980s" (Western Societies Program Occasional Paper number 28, Center for International Studies Cornell University 1990).

8. Conrad Schnippen is quoted by Hermann Meyn, *Mass Media in the Federal Republic* (Hamburg: Wissenschaftsverlag Volker Spiess, 1994).

9. This finding was contrary to conventional wisdom and the expectation that parties matter more than personalities in the parliamentary German party system. For more on television's influence on the 1990 election see Hans Mathias Kepplinger, Hans-Bernd Brosius and Stephan Dahlem, *Wie das Fernsehen Wahlen beeinflusst. Theoretische Modelle und empirische Analysen* (Munich: Verlag Reinhard Fischer, 1994).

10. Wolfgang Donsbach, "What Part Did the Media Play?" *The Public Perspective*, vol. 6, no. 1, 1994.

11. Donsbach, Ibid. For recent analyses of campaign reporting in the U.S. and its impact on American politics see, for example, Thomas E. Patterson, *Out of Order* (New York: Alfred Knopf), 1993; Matthew Robert Kerbel, *Edited For Television: CNN, ABC, and the 1992 Presidential Campaign* (Boulder: Westview Press), 1994.

12. These numbers are mentioned in Christina Holtz-Bacha, et al., "Political Television Advertising in Western Democracies: A Comparison of Campaign Broadcasts in the United States, Germany, and France." *Political Communication*, vol. 11, no. 1, 1994.

13. According to Christina Holtz-Bacha et al., ibid., 32% of German campaign ads during the 1990 federal election campaign were negative versus 49% of the campaign advertising in the 1988 presidential election.

14. Forschungsgruppe Wahlen e.V., for example, conducts surveys for the second television channel ZDF, the Emnid Institut polls for the newsweekly *Der Spiegel*.

15. After World War II the Social Democrats were able to reclaim their daily newspapers dating back to the Weimar era but lost one after the other for financial reasons. The SPD still owns shares in several newspaper publishing corporations in West Germany. After unification the SPD was awarded partial ownership in two East German newspapers in response to the party's claim on SPD-owned presses that had been taken over first by the Nazis and later by East Germany's Communist Party. For more on the past and present German media see Hermann Meyn, *Mass Media in the Federal Republic*.

16. Ben H. Bagdikian, *The Media Monopoly*. Boston: Beacon Press, 1983, p. 93.

17. Meyn, *Mass Media in the Federal Republic* pp. 72–73.

18. In 1997 the monthly fee for radio and television was 28.25 Deutschmarks or about $18.80.

19. Larry Sabato has described the political consequences of the modern media's "feeding frenzy" tendencies. See, Larry J. Sabato, *Feeding Frenzy: How Attack Journalism Has Transformed American Politics* (New York: The Free Press, 1991). For the U.S. press's appetite for scandals, see Suzanne Garment, *Scandal: The Culture of Mistrust in American Politics*. New York: Times Books, 1991.

4. *The Impact of Societal Change*

1. The postwar baby boomers make up a larger proportion of today's electorate than in the United States since in Germany the older generations are comparatively smaller due to heavy losses in the Second World War and the younger due to a declining birthrate.

2. From 1955 to 1981 the proportion of secondary school students with at most nine years of a basic pre-vocational education declined from 72% to 47%, the proportion receiving a longer preparatory education for university studies went up from 15% to 27%. By 1992 the number of students at institutions of higher learning was almost seven times as great as in 1960.

The rapid pace in the expansion of formal schooling made for correspondingly much sharper generational differences in levels of education than in the United States.

3. Critics of these arrangements hold that they are outmoded as well as unpopular, but the 1994 report of the Constitutional Reform Commission saw no need to change them.

4. That showed up in a 1994 international opinion survey which asked people whether they thought religious authorities had a good rather than a bad influence on the way things were going in their country. Three-fourths of the American respondents, but only one-fourth of the German considered the clergy benevolent. See, *Public Perspective*, vol. 5, no. 6 (Sept–Oct. 1994), p. 92.

5. *Der Spiegel* 25/1992, p. 44.

6. When Germany was reunified less than 70% of the people in East Germany had been baptized and less than 20% of the families had any ties to a church. Since then baptisms have not increased in the East and are diminishing in the West.

7. In the 1950s surveys showed roughly that one out of three West German adults were going to church at least once a week. By the 1960s that had dropped to one in four, but only one in ten never went at all. However, polls taken after unification found that now it was only one in ten adults who did attend services every Sunday and that no more than that considered religious faith a very important part of life; for one in three religion was of no importance. In the United States, on the other hand, polls taken about the same time found that almost half of the people questioned attended church several times a month and that only one out of ten considered religion not very important. Whereas in 1967 more than two-thirds of West Germans told pollsters that they believed in God, twenty-five years later more than half of reunited Germans said they did not. Just 26% of all the adults questioned and merely 13% of those under thirty considered Jesus the son of God. In sharp contrast, simultaneous polls in the United States found that 80% of the respondents embraced this basic Christian principle and 95% believed in God.

8. Germans who are willing to do without the religious services provided by the established churches find this the best way to lower tax payments that cannot, as in the United States, be reduced by moving to another state: for taxes are

the same in all the Länder of the Federal Republic. Catholics who fail to pay the surcharge are excommunicated by their church and that may help explain why its membership has not fallen off as much as that of the Protestant Church.

9. In 1994 the CDU put a prominent member of the small Jewish community in Germany on its national executive committee

10. Renate Schmidt, who headed the Social Democratic ticket in the Bavarian state legislature election in 1994, found it advisable to start once more paying a church tax she had not paid for three decades.

11. In the early 1970s and—following unification—once again in the the early 1990s, large majorities in both houses of the federal parliament disregarded strong objections from the Protestant and, even more, the Catholic clergy in voting for highly popular reforms of the law on abortions—only to have them thrown out by the Federal Constitutional Court.

12. Gerd Heinrich, Vice President of the Nordelbische Evangelisch-Lutherische Kirche, was quoted in "In "Feiertage sind ein kulturelles Gut von hohem Wert . . . für das Leben in unserem Volk." Der Spiegel 15:23, 1994, p. 96.

13. Kölner Stadtanzeiger, March 7, 1994.

14. By the 1980s young women on the average had at least as much secondary schooling as men and by 1991 they made up four out of nine graduates in higher education. And women's share of doctoral degrees awarded in the Federal Republic shot up from 6% in 1980 to 27% in 1992.

15. No more than one out of ten marriages ended in a divorce. "It was," as one recent account has it, "an era when one was expected to get married and have children."

16. Allensbach Jahrbuch 1947–55, p. 18

17. The proportion of married women with jobs increased from about one out of three in 1970 to close to a half in 1990.

18. From board room through middle management German women held less than 6% of all positions in the mid-1990s. Though their share of middle management positions—such as office manager—has gone up in recent years, it remains well below the 40% level reported for American women in the 1995 Report of the U.S. Glass Ceiling Commission. But it is above all top management that remains far more of a male preserve than in the United States. In 1995 women occupied only about one in ten chief executive positions in Germany, mostly in trade and services and next to none in industry. The number of women on the boards of the 626 largest firms in the Federal Republic went up from just two to twelve between 1982 and 1993. But that was still only 0.5% of the membership, whereas in the United States close to 6% of the seats on the boards of Fortune's top 500 corporation were held by women.

19. However, when a male civil servant in the city-state of Bremen complained to the European Court of Justice that he had been unfairly passed over in promotion in favor of a less qualified female, the Court ruled in 1995 that German authorities had violated the equal opportunities law of the European Union which they were bound to obey.

20. In the federal election of 1994 gender differences were on the whole of no importance in the distribution of the votes. That of the women, however, showed greater generational differences than that of the men. The victorious Christian Democrats received more than half of the votes cast by women over 60, but less than a third of those under 34. The Social Democrats, on the hand, did exceptionally well among young women in the 18 to 34 age group. They got 40% of their vote but only 30% of that of the men.

21. According to the latest available figures, the female membership of the two leading parties almost doubled with the entry of the baby boomer women in the 1970s and then leveled off. (CDU 19% in 1976, 23% in 1988, 25% in 1994; SPD 20% in 1976, 27% in 1988, 27% in 1994.) And while in the exceptionally conservative Christian Social Union (CSU) the proportion of women has increased very little (11% in 1976, 14% in 1988, 15% in 1994), it has increased above all in the emphatically egalitarian Green movement (from 38% in 1988 to 50% 1994).

22. The Greens have gone the farthest with a nation-wide quota that requires at least half of their office holders to be women and the Social Democrats are well on the way to meeting a 40% set-aside target. In 1997 the Christian Democrats adopted a quota that promised at least one-third of party offices and parliamentary seats of the CDU to women during the following three years. Some of the most vocal resistance has come from women who maintain that a special quota deprecates the achievements of women politicians who gained prominence in spite rather than because of their gender.

23. Before the Weimar Constitution of 1919 gave women the right to vote in all German elections a few nonpartisan organizations of mostly upper-middle-class women had fought apart from the political parties for their enfranchisement. But thereafter separate women's groups wielded little or no influence in German politics for half a century, especially during the Nazi regime. After its fall a special Women's Affairs Division of the American military government could not get West German women to unite in an independent political organization of their own to fight gender discrimination. It took another twenty years and a new generation of baby-boomer feminists to engage a substantial number of women in a common campaign for gender equality in the Federal Republic.

24. Unification did not bring militant feminists in West Germany additional strength, as some expected in view of the widespread demonstrations by East German women demanding a new deal in the final days of DDR. In the Summer of 1990 some 40,000 of these had attended a meeting called by a new Independent Women's Movement that after unification proved to lack firm mass support. While women in the new states have wanted the same easy access to abortion they had under Communism, they have no use for the radical feminists' approach to reform. Militant feminists, for their part, have found it difficult to relate to the past experiences and present concerns of women in the East who lack their own sense of female solidarity and feminist consciousness.

25. It has particularly close ties to the Federal women's Ministry which sponsors conferences for the coordination of common actions for equal rights and whose chief is a keynote speaker at the annual congresses of the Council.

26. In West Germany the birthrate declined by 59% between 1964 and 1993 and by 70% between 1985 and 1992. Nine out of ten women now past 60 had children, but among their baby boomer daughters about three out of four have none. In East Germany the birthrate fell by 36% between 1988 and 1993 and by 80% between 1989 and 1993. "Eastern Germany's adults appear to have come as close to a temporary suspension of child bearing as any large population in human experience . . . such a precipitous decline in fertility is virtually outside the experience of the industrial world." See, "Living and Dying in a barren Land." *The Economist*, 4/23/94, p. 54.

27. According to widely cited 1993 estimates by Carl Haub of the Population Reference Bureau in Washington, Germany's population will fall by eight percent over the next three decades

28. By last count 16% of the people in Germany were under 15 years old, compared to 22% in the United States.

29. This was the title of a 1993 feature story in *Der Spiegel*, Germany's leading weekly on public affairs. Just who belongs to this "Republic of the Old" is is not self-evident in these matters. As in the United States, the distinction between minors and adults is a lot more clear cut in law than that between the middle-aged and the elderly in politics. German opinion polls—like American ones—have long lumped together anybody past sixty-five—the retirement age set for social security pensions when people normally did not live as long as the do now. In present-day Germany that takes in one out of five adults, according to census figures, but most people now retire in their fifties. To an increasing extent social statistics about the so-called old include "young-old" senior citizens along with their "old-old" parents.

30. Heidi Schüller. 1995. *Die Alterslüge: Für einen neuen Generationenvertrag* (Berlin: Rowohlt, p. 47).

31. Federal Ministry of the Interior. Survey of the Policy and Law Concerning Foreigners in the Federal Republic of Germany. July 1993, p. 9.

32. This restrictive, so-called blood-right entitlement to citizenship over generations goes back to the large-scale German emigration of Germans to the United States and other countries in the nineteenth century. Adopted by Bavaria in 1818 and then incorporated in the immigration and naturalization law of the German Reich in 1913, it has been retained by governments and courts in the Federal Republic as consonant with a special provision in its constitution granting automatic citizenship to all who had had been "denaturalized" by the Nazi regime, to refugees from Communist East Germany, and to people of "German stock" (*Volksdeutsche*) from other Communist countries.

33. In 1993 only 21% were over 60 and 58% were under 45

34. Quite a few of the framers who put that provision into the Basic Law in 1948–49 had fled abroad from Nazi persecution and come to value political asylum very highly.

35. In 1973 only about 5,000 people and in 1983 some 20,000 had requested political asylum. In 1992, however, there were more than 430,000 applicants coming not just from former Communist countries but faraway places like Sri Lanka.

36. And might be flown out again at government expense, like seven Sudanese who in 1995 were denied political asylum when they landed at the Frankfurt airport and sent back home after the Constitutional Court refused to stay their deportation.

37. Federal Ministry of the Interior, 1993, p. 84.

38. In 1967 only 4.4% of the children born in the Federal Republic had been aliens; by 1993 that had increased to 13%. Almost half of non-German households but only a third of German ones included at least two children and among women with a Turkish passport the birthrate was three times as high as among women with a German one.

39. By last count (1993), 16% of total population but as much as 25% of its non-German component are under 18 years of age while only 3% of the aliens but 16% of the Germans are more than 64 years old.

40. According to various, not entirely consistent sources the ratio of contributors to beneficiaries was in the mid-1990s roughly 4:1 among aliens and less than 3:1 among Germans.

41. By current estimates of the Federal Government about one in ten of the resident aliens now in the country will be of pensionable age—that is, over 65—by the end of the decade. But that does not mean they will get a pension. For example, in 1994 less than a third of some two million Turkish nationals were employed in jobs that earned them and their spouses a social security pension.

42. Federal Ministry of the Interior, 1993, p. 6.

43. Ibid., p. 26.

44. In Frankfurt and other major cities with large Turkish populations as much as a quarter of the population consists of aliens who do not have the right of European Union nationals to run and vote in local elections like Germans. When two state legislatures sought to extend that to all aliens in 1990, the Constitutional Court ruled that they were not entitled to privileges granted by the Basic Law to "the German people."

45. In close to a quarter of a century, from 1970 to 1993, less than half a million non-Germans were naturalized. Since then somewhat less restrictive federal legislation has allowed for aliens that have resided for 15 years in the Federal Republic to be naturalized if authorities in the states where they live consider it "in the public interest."

46. As put in the 1993 Report on the Commission on Constitutional Reform: "The integration of aliens does not come from letting them vote. The right to vote depends rather on their integration and consequent naturalization."

47. However, German naturalization laws have always allowed dual citizenship for German emigrants naturalized in the United States.

48. A 1994 survey found that more than six out of ten Turkish nationals and seven out of ten of people from the states of former Yugoslavia wanted dual citizenship. Some have found a way to get it in Berlin by renouncing their Turkish nationality until they are naturalized and then withdrawing that renunciation with the consent of Turkish and the connivance of German authorities. See, "Drinnen vor der Tür." *Die Zeit*, June 11, 1993; also, *Frankfurter Rundschau*, October 13 1993.

49. And that is taken by some to include ethnic German *Aussiedler*, who conservatives hold to be fellow members of one homogeneous German cultural family and, therefore, socially and politically easily integrated. In fact, surveys show that while these newcomers may have come to live as Germans among Germans, many have not been given a homecoming welcome by native Germans but have rather encountered a good deal of hostility as outsiders. The citizenship entitlement formula that lumps all of them together, no matter where they came from, evidently conceals "multicultural" differences among them that set them more or less apart from native Germans. The strange ways of an ethnic German from Kazakhstan, for example, has seemed as alien to them as those of an asylum seeker from Sri Lanka or refugees from Bosnia.

50. In the words of Kurt Biedenkopf, the CDU governor of Saxony, it "threatens the cultural substance of the German nation and just those spiritual [*geistige*] qualities that can help to unite the country and integrate migrants from abroad ("Biedenkopf Papier." *Der Spiegel* 25, 1995, p. 17).

5. Capitalism with a Human Face

1. Kohl made his remark at a CDU conference in October 1995 in Karlsruhe. See, Peter Gumbel, "Kohl Criticizes Germans for Losing Their Work Ethic," *The Wall Street Journal*, Oct. 17, 1995.

2. The bill passed in the Federal Diet , but failed to make it through the Federal Council.

3. The new law grants presidents line-item veto authority in order to rescind any spending item contained in appropriation bills, targeted tax breaks, and new or increased entitlement spending unless Congress passes a "disapproval bill" that would be subject to presidential veto.

4. See David Marsh, "Die Bundesbank. gefesselt von Europa." *Die Zeit*, no. 25, 1992 (Sept. 25), p. 15.

5. In the mid-1970s a member of the SPD (Herbert Ehrenberg) introduced an amendment in the Federal Diet designed to commit the Bundesbank to add economic growth and unemployment to its primary goals. But this futile initiative did not take aim at the Bundesbank Act of 1957 and its provision that in exercising its delegated powers the *Bundesbank* "is independent of instructions from the Federal Government."

6. Under pressure from Rep. Gonzales and other members of Congress the Federal Reserve agreed in 1994 to a more timely release of Open Market Committee deliberations.

7. Roland Vaubel of the Mannheim University conducted this particular study. Susanne Lohmann of the Univerity of California found also evidence for pre-election effects in the *Bundesbank's* monetary policy. See, *Der Spiegel*, Sept. 26, 1994, pp. 104–5.

8. President and vice-president of the *Bundesbank* and the five additional members of the central bank's directorate are appointed by the federal government. The state governments appoint the presidents of the regional central banks—eleven before the German reunification and nine after a reorganization of the regional central bank system in the early 1990s.

9. In early 1997 about two-thirds of the German public did not like the idea of replacing their Deutschmark with the European currency (Euro) according to a survey conducted by the Forschungsgruppe Wahlen e.V., Mannheim published in *Politbarometer*, Jan. 1997: 75% of the German populace feared that the common European currency would not be as strong as the German Mark.

10. In 1995, for example, after the Constitutional Court ruled unconstitutional a provision in Bavaria's school ordinance mandating that all classrooms in public schools be equipped with a crucifix, leaders of the state's governing Christian Social Union denounced the decision angrily as intolerant. The chairman of the party, Theo Waigel, called for reforms in the appointment procedure for new members of the Constitutional Court.

11. In fact, the DBB is formally not a labor union like the others because of the special status of civil servants in Germany. While enjoying many extraordinary benefits in terms of job security, health care, taxation, and pensions, they are prohibited by law from striking.

12. By the mid-1990s several DGB unions considered mergers in the face of their shrinking membership. A similar development occurred in the United States, where one merger united the steelworkers and rubberworkers in one labor organization.

13. ÖTV-Gedankenspiele: Tarifleistungen nur noch fuer Mitglieder?" *Deutschland Nachrichten*, Jan. 13, 1995, p.4.

14. "Kämpfen und Kungeln." *Der Spiegel* 43, 1993, pp. 50–68.

15. William Lewis, "The Secret to Competitiveness." *The Wall Street Journal*, Oct. 22, 1993.

16. Craig R. Whitney, "West European Companies Head East for Labor." *The New York Times*, Feb. 9, 1995, p. D3.

17. "Germans Strike Less," *The Week in Germany*, May 7, 1993. According to this account, among industrialized countries only workers in the Netherlands, Austria, and Switzerland were still more restrained than their counterparts in the Federal Republic. Even in Japan the average annual strike days per 1,000 workers were with 64 higher than in West Germany.

18. John Ardach, *Germany and the Germans* (London: Penguin Books, 1991), p. 128.

19. This is the major reason why Saxony more than any other region has become the testing ground for innovations and departures from the entrenched labor relations model.

20. Quote in "Labor Leader Calls for Reform of Wage." *The Week in Germany*, March 28, 1997, p. 4.

21. In 1996 this led to a bitter conflict between the two German building industry associations (*Hauptverband der deutschen Bauindustrie* und *Zentralverband des Deutschen Baugewerbes*), who pleaded for minimum wages for all workers at German construction sites, and the Confederation of German Employers' Associations BDA, who opposed such a measure. In protest, the construction industry's associations revoked their membership in the BDA.

22. Those who successfully completed their apprenticeship became journeymen and the best of them eventually had the opportunity to become masters. This system is still in place today in that those who train apprentices still must be masters in their field or otherwise licensed.

23. Some apprenticeship programs require one and a half days of vocational school attendance each week. And in some occupations apprentices alternate between working and attending school for several weeks or months at a time.

24. The fast food tax, which was challenged by two McDonald's restaurants and two vending machine operators, imposes significant extra costs—about 30 cents for each paper plate, 6 cents for each plastic eating utensil, 25 cents for each can or bottle.

25. In some instances banks vote 90% or more of the shares; this is for example the case at Siemens, Mannesmann, VEBA, Hoechst, and BASF.

26. In 1995, for example, the three largest banks voted 42% of the VEBA shares, 41.7% of Bayer, 40.4% of BASF, 38.8% of Mannesmann, 34.5% of Siemens.

27. Peter Gumble, "West German Program to Salvage East Shows Signs of Paying off." *The Wall Street Journal*, Dec. 9, 1994, p.1.

28. Take for example the legislation adopted in 1994 that makes it less costly for employers to hire staff on a temporary basis for up to 18 months. The old law had discouraged firms from hiring temporary workers for fear of colliding with labor law provisions and works councils when they had to lay off employees. In another attempt to fight unemployment, a law that prohibited mandatory retiring at age 65 was rescinded.

29. For instructive polls see, *Politbarometer*, Feb. 1995.

6. Social Welfare State Under Pressure

1. In the United States the federal government's role in the area of social welfare did not begin in the New Deal era as is often assumed. The U.S. government installed a first social welfare program following the Civil War in form of a pension system for aging Union veterans and their survivors that was far more comprehensive than the initial Bismarckian programs. Perpetuated in the late nineteenth century by a Republican Party eager to win and maintain the loyalties of Union veterans, the pension system was created and upheld for the benefit of a group that could not have been more deserving in the eyes of the victorious side—men who fought to preserve the very state that could go on to reward them. But as the generation of these veterans passed away, so did the federal government's

involvement in social welfare. For a detailed account see Theda Scocpol, *Protecting Soldiers and Mothers: The Political Origin of Social Policy in the United States* (Cambridge: Harvard University Press, 1994).

2. Robert Y. Shapiro and John M. Young. "Public Opinion and the Wellfare State: The United States in Comparative Perspective." *Political Science Quarterly* 104:59–89.

3. In 1989 the top 1% of American households held 39%, the top 20% close to 85% of the nation's wealth according to a 1995 Twentieth Century Fund Report by Edward N. Wolff, "Top Heavy: A Study of the Increasing Inequality of Wealth in America." In comparison, 10% of German households possessed 50% of the country's total wealth in the early 1990s according to *The Week in Germany*, June 4, 1993.

4. In 1994, according to the Organization for Economic Cooperation and Development, total tax revenues in the Federal Republic amounted to 46.1% of the overall domestic economy (GDP) versus 31.6% in the United States. This was before hefty (ca. 10%) tax hikes effective January 1, 1995 that included among other measures a "solidarity surcharge" of 7.5% on the income tax for the reconstruction of East Germany, an additional 1% income tax increase for the new nursing care insurance as well as hikes in the wealth and insurance taxes.

5. Since the Bonn government imposed a 30% tax withholding on interest income in 1993, especially wealthy Germans deposit their money in bank accounts in neighboring Luxembourg which are beyond the reach of the German tax authorities. This way, many billions of Deutschmarks are sheltered from tax revenues every year. This is the closest Germans have come to revolt against their high taxes.

6. A December 1994 poll by Forschungsgruppe Wahlen e.V., Mannheim, for example, revealed that 50% of the respondents (42% in West Germany and 79% in East Germany) expressed the need for more social security; 25% in the West and 11% in the East opted for the existing scope of the welfare; 22% in the western and 9% in eastern Germany preferred greater reliance on free market solutions and individual responsibility.

7. Traditionally, the Federal Employment Office has handled the vocational training and retraining of those who do not meet the pension funds' qualifying requirements.

8. Unemployed persons under 42 years of age received unemployment insurance benefits for one full year, if they had been employed for at least 2 years in the 7 years prior to losing their jobs. If an unemployed person was 54 years or older and had worked at least 5 years and 4 months during the last 7 years, the unemployment insurance paid benefits for 2 years and 8 months.

9. In certain cases, employers received up to 70% of such wage subsidies.

10. In 1993, for example, the Labor Office in Hamburg calculated that an ABM-job cost 42 000 Deutschmarks a year, an unemployed person 38 000.

11. In 1992, for example, more than 394 000 East Germans but less than 80 000 West Germans worked in ABM jobs.

12. According to *The Week in Germany* (January 13, 1995), the 1991 per capita spending on health care in Germany was 40% below U.S. expenditures.

Similarly, in the early 1990s, the Federal Republic spent close to 10%, whereas the United States more than 13% of the GDP on health care.

13. Calculated as a percentage of earnings, health-care contributions amounted on average to 13.4% of wages in the early 1990s. Following the reforms implemented in 1993, there was a modest rollback of contributions to 13.25%

14. As long as unemployed persons collected unemployment compensation benefits, their health insurance premiums were paid by the Federal Labor Office; welfare agencies enrolled the recipients of social assistance in statutory sickness funds; pensioners paid reduced premiums to the funds they belonged to before their retirement.

15. The 1993 study was conducted by the Institute of German Business according to *The Week in Germany*, April 2, 1993.

16. If a state does not abolish one work-free holiday, employees must pay the entire insurance premium (1.7% of earnings as of Jan. 1996).

17. 4.6 million persons received social assistance in 1994.

18. There were other reservations as well, for example, that a uniform minimum income would not take into account the special predicaments and needs of the disadvantaged or those living in high-cost metropolitan areas.

19. Ursula Lehr according to "Ausbeutung der Jungen," *Der Spiegel*, 16/1995, p. 101.

20. Heidi Schüller, a member of SPD's shadow cabinet during the 1994 federal election campaign, is one of the most outspoken advocates of restructuring the welfare state and drawing a new generational contract at the expense of the old and for the benefit of the rest of society. See, Heidi Schüller, *Die Alterslüge* (Berlin: Rowohlt, 1994).

21. David Wessel and Daniel Benjamin, "Looking for Work: In Employment Policy, America and Europe Make a Sharp Contrast." *The Wall Street Journal*, March 14, 1995, pp. 1, A5.

22. When unions and employers agree on candidate slates that simply fill the open positions, a common practice, no elections are held.

23. In this respect the hands of the dominant welfare institutions were forced, for example, by the provisions of the newly introduced nursing care insurance. By giving beneficiaries an option between provided nursing care or monthly cash payments, the new insurance opened the door for beneficiaries and their families to make nursing care arrangement with for-profit providers.

24. The U.S. Senate passed a softer version designed to withhold federal funds from organizations explicitly devoted to lobbing and advocacy.

7. Germany Abroad: The Politics of Foreign Policy

1. Quoted in *The Wall Street Journal*, July 13, 1994.

2. The 1955 treaty providing for the rearmament of West Germany barred the Federal Republic from the club of nuclear powers and the 1991 treaty providing for the unification of Germany maintained the exclusion.

3. *Badische Zeitung* quoted in *The Week in Germany*, Nov. 3, 1995.

4. Federal Ministry of Defense, *White Paper 1994*, pp. 83–85

5. Since the mid-1960s some 160,000 men thus joined the Bundeswehr involuntarily every year.

6. When French President Jacques Chirac announced in 1995 that conscription no longer served a purpose and would be abolished in France, German political leaders would not agree.

The Kohl government as well as the Social Democratic opposition in parliament held that in their country the draft remained an essential component of democracy. What is rarely mentioned is that as more and more draftees have opted for alternative civilian service, Germany's officially "recognized" large welfare agencies have come to depend increasingly on conscription for an indispensable free and reliable supply of involuntary manpower for their social activities on behalf of the state.

7. If all goes according to plans, this new force will take in about one out of five members of the Bundeswehr by the late 1990s.

8. They have thus resisted French efforts to loosen Germany's NATO ties through the creation of a separate military establishment of the European Union countries.

9. "Germany got back its historical continuity. We are back in the Germany Bismarck created in 1871. . . . The new situation facing the country—and the continent—after 1990 resembles much more the constellations of the late nineteenth and earlier twentieth century than the European structure of the last four decades." Baring, "Germany What Now?" 1994;9.

10. Quoted in *The Economist*, May 27, 1995

11. In Great Britain opponents of membership in the European Union have thus argued that the Germans exercise undue influence in its councils, as when the continental members of the EU placed an embargo on British beef products in the 1996 "Mad Cow Disease" episode.

12. Not only constitutional amendments, but also all federal legislation concerning European Union issues require a two-thirds vote by the state governments in the *Bundesrat*. Moreover, recent changes in the constitution provide governments of the Länder with more opportunities to bypass the federal government—or pressure it—by attending to their interests in direct negotiations with EU authorities. Some East German states have thus lobbied with the EU Commission in Brussels for economic aid under regional development programs of the Union.

13. The Social Democratic leader Oscar Lafontaine hailed it for repudiating the nation state of old in favor of a commitment to the "European nation" of the future

14. Opinion polls of the mid-1990s found that more than two-thirds of ordinary Germans did not share the view of top business managers and political leaders that German national interests were properly looked after in the European Union. And most had not been convinced by Chancellor Kohl that German influ-

ence would be even greater if it became a democratically governed federation. (cf., e.g. *The Economist*, Jan. 13, 1996, p. 48; *Focus*, 21/1996)

15. *Politische Meinung* I/1995, p.1

16. See *The Week in Germany*, Nov. 22, 1996. There is a certain irony in Herzog's unacknowledged use of a terminology that his Christian Democrats had denounced early in the 1970s when it was introduced by the government of SPD Chancellor Willy Brandt for a policy of more harmonious relations with Communist East Germany.

17. "Umfrage." *Focus* 21/1996, pp. 70–71

18. Josef Jannings, "A German Europe—a European Germany? On the Debate over Germany's Foreign Policy." *International Affairs*, Jan. 1996, p. 33.

19. Karl Kaiser and Hanns W. Maull. *Deutschlands neue Aussenpolitik Band I: Grundlagen* (Munich: Oldenbourg).

20. The term comes from: Christian Meier, "Deutschland zwischen der Bonner und Berliner Republik.." *Zeitschrift für Politik* 3 (1994): 275.

Conclusion

1. See Inter Nationes, "European Monetary Union: German Viewpoints," May 1996, p. 4

2. In early 1997 the news magazine *Der Spiegel* wrote, for example, that the controversies surrounding changes in the tax system and in the old age pension insurance put the reform capability of the German society and the political parties' will to reform on the test stand. See, " Auf Kosten der Jungen." *Der Spiegel*, Feb. 3, 1997, p. 26.

3. From an editorial in the *Saarbrücker Zeitung* (Jan. 29, 1997) reprinted in *The Week in Germany*, Jan. 31, 1997.

Bibliography

Afheldt, Horst. 1995. "Ausstieg aus dem Sozialstaat?" In *Aus Politik und Zeit-geschichte*, 16 June, 3–12.

Alber, Jens. 1992. *Social and Economic Policies and Older People in Germany.* Konstanz: Report for the Commission of the European Community.

———. 1993. *Social Integration of Older People in Germany.* Konstanz: Report for the Commission of the European Community.

Anderson, Christopher and Carsten Zelle. 1995. "Helmut Kohl and the CDU Victory." In *German Politics and Society* 13(1):12–35.

Andres, Gerd. 1992. "Einwanderungsland Deutschland." In *Einwanderungs-land Deutschland.* Transcript, Tagung der Friedrich-Ebert-Stiftung 14–51, May.

Ardagh, John. 1991. *Germany and the Germans.* London: Penguin Books.

Ash, Timothy Garton. 1994. "Germany's Choice." *Foreign Affairs* 73(4):65–81.

Atkinson, Roy. 1994. "Worried Germany Grapples with Shortage—of Germans." *The Washington Post*, March 2, 10C.

Baaden, Andreas. 1993. "Interkulturelle Projektarbeiten zur Integration von Aussiedlern." In *Aus Politik und Zeitgeschichte* B48.

Baden, Klaus. 1994. "Immigration and Social Peace in United Germany." In *Daedalus.* 123(1):85–106.

Bäcker, Gerhard. 1995. "Sind die Grenzen des Sozialstaates überschritten?" In *Aus Politik und Zeitgeschichte.* June 16, 13–25.

Bagdikian, Ben H. 1992. *The Media Monopoly.* Boston: Beacon Press.

Baring, Arnulf, ed. 1993. *Germany's Position in Europe: Problems and Perspectives.* Oxford-Providence: Berg.

Becker, Ulrich et al. 1992. *Zwischen Angst und Aufbruch: Das Lebensgefühl der Deutschen in Ost und West nach der Wiedervereinigung*. Düsseldorf: Econ.

Bergedorfer Gesprächskreis. 1992. *Wege zur inneren Einheit: Was trennt die Deutschen nach Überwindung der Mauer?* Hamburg: Koerber Stiftung. Protokoll no. 94.

Bergner, Jeffrey. 1991. *The New Superpowers: Germany, Japan, the United States and the New World Order*. New York: St. Martin's Press.

Bergsdorf, Wolfgang. 1993. "Orientierungsnöte in der säkulari-sierten Gesellschaft. Unpublished lecture (April 22).

Berg-Schlosser, Dirk and Ralf Rytlewslki, eds. 1993. *Political Culture in Germany*. New York: St. Martin's Press.

Berschin, Helmut. 1995. "Migrationsland Deutschland." In *Politische Meinung* 303(Jan.):11–14.

Bertram, Barbara. 1993. "Zur Entwicklung der sozialen Geschlechterverhältnisse in den neuen Bundesländern." In *Aus Politik und Zeitgeschichte*, 5 February.

Betz, Hans-Georg. 1991. *Postmodern Politics in Germany: The Politics of Resentment*. New York: St. Martin's Press.

Brähler, Elmar and Horst-Eberhard Richter. 1995. "Deutsche Befindlichkeiten im Ost-West Vergleich." In *Aus Politik und Zeitgeschichte*, September 29, 13–20.

Braunthal, Gerard. 1995. "The Perspective from the Left." In *German Politics and Society* 13(1):36–49.

Brinkmann, Heinz Ulrich, ed. 1990. *Wirtschaftspolitik*. Bonn: Bundeszentrale fuer politische Bildung.

Bürklin, Wilhelm. 1988. *Wahlverhalten und Wertwandel*. Leverkusen: Leske & Budrich Verlag.

Burnstein, Daniel. 1991. *Euroquake: Europe's Explosive Challenge Will Chance the World*. New York: Simon & Schuster.

Cartellieri, Ulrich. 1994. "Arbeitslosigkeit in der Bundesrepublik Deutschland: Ansatzpunkte zur Behebung der Arbeitsmarktprobleme." In *Aus Politik und Zeitgeschichte*, March 25, 3–8.

Conradt, David P. 1993. *The German Polity, Fifth Edition*. New York: Longman.

Conradt, David P. et al., eds. 1995. *Germany's New Politics*. Tempe, AZ: German Studies Review.

Cook, Fay Lomax and Edith J. Barnett. 1992. *Support for the American Welfare State*. New York: Columbia University Press.

Dalton, Russel J. 1993. *Politics in Germany*, Second Edition. New York: HarperCollins.

Dalton, Russell J. et al. 1995. *Germany's New Politics*. New York: Longman.

Dalton, Russel J. and Wilhelm Bürklin. 1995. "The Two German Electorates: The Social Bases of the Vote in 1990 and 1994." In *German Politics and Society* 13(1):79–99.

Deeg, Richard E. 1992. "Germany's Länder and the Federalization of the European Union." Paper for the Annual Meeting of the American Political Science Association, Chicago, Sept. 3–6.

Deutscher Bundestag. 1993. *Bericht der Gemeinsamen Verfassungskommission.* Bonn (November 5).

Deutsche Bundesbank. 1989. *The Deutsche Bundesbank: Its Monetary Policy Instruments and Functions.* Frankfurt: Deutsche Bundesbank Special Series No. 7.

Donsbach, Wolfgang. 1994. "What Part Did the Media Play?" *The Public Perspective* 6(1).

Edinger, Lewis J. 1986. *West German Politics.* New York: Columbia University Press.

"Ein Einig Volk von Blutsbrüdern." 1993. *Der Spiegel* 11(March 15):50–70.

"Ein radikaler Umbau des deutschen Sozialleistungssystems." 1993. Frankfurter Rundschau, May 27.

Faist, Thomas. 1994. "How to Define a Foreigner: The Symbolic Politics of Immigration in German Political Discourse, 1978–1992." In *West European Politics* 17(2):50–71.

Faul, Erwin. 1992. "Gegen die Multikulturisten." *Politische Meinung*, March 27, 4–11.

Federal Ministry of Health. 1993. "The Statutory Health Insurance Reform Law." Press release.

Federal Ministry of the Interior. 1993. *Survey of the Policy and Law Concerning Foreigners in the Federal Republic of Germany.* Bonn (July).

Federal Minister of Labour and Social Affairs. 1991. *Co-determination in the Federal Republic of Germany.* Bonn (November).

———. 1992. *Social Security.* Bonn (February).

Ferree, Myra Mars and Brigitte Young. 1993. "Three Steps Back for Women: German Unification, Gender, and University 'Reform.' " In *Political Science and Politics* 26(2):199–205.

Fichter, Michael. 1993. "A House Divided: German Unification and Organized Labor." In *German Politics* 2(1).

Flynn, Gregory. 1993. "Germany and the New Europe." In James A. Cooney et al., eds. *German-American Relations Yearbook 2.* Frankfurt/New York: Campus.

Förster, Peter and Walter Friedrich. 1992. "Politische Einstellungen und Grundpositionen Jugendlicher in Ostdeutschland." In *Aus Politik und Zeitgeschichte*, September 11.

Fritsche-Burnazel, Renate. 1992. *Europe and German Reunification.* New York: St. Martin's Press.

Fulbrook, Mary. 1994. "Aspects of Society and Identity in the New Germany." In *Daedalus* 123(1), Winter.

Garment, Suzanne. 1991. *Scandal: The Culture of Mistrust in American Politics.* New York: Times Books.

Geissler, Heiner. 1992. "Die Gesellschaft von morgen." In *Politische Meinung* July: 21–27.

Gellner, Winand. 1992. "The Integration of East Germany Into the West German Interest Group System: Problems and Possibilities." Paper for the Annual Meeting of the American Political Science Association in Chicago, September 3–6.

Germroth, David S. and Rebecca J. Hudson. 1993. *Beyond the Cold War*. Owings Mills, MD: American Literary Press.

Glos, Michael. 1994. "Zukunft gestalten, Bewährtes erhalten, Stabilität sichern." In *Aus Politik und Zeitgeschichte*. April 15, 8–13.

Glotz, Peter et al. 1992. *Die planlosen Eliten*. Munich: Edition Ferenczy bei Bruckmann.

Glouchevitch, Philip. 1992. *Juggernaut: The Keys to German Business Success*. New York: Touchstone.

Göckenjan, Gerd. 1993. "Alter—Ruhestand—Generationsvertrag?" In *Aus Politik und Zeitgeschichte*, April 27.

Goodman, John. B. 1992. *The Politics of Central Banking in Western Europe*. Ithaca: Cornell University Press.

Graf, William D. 1992. *The Internationalization of the German Economy*. New York: St. Martin's Press.

Grosser, Dieter, ed. 1992. *German Unification: The Unexpected Challenge*. New York: St. Martin's Press.

Gunlicks, Arthur B. 1986. *Local Government in the German Federal System*. Durham: Duke University Press.

Haftendorn, Helga. 1994. "Gulliver in der Mitte Europas." In Karl Kaiser and Hanns W. Maull. *Deutschlands neue Aussenpolitik Band I: Grundlagen*. Munich: Oldebourg.

Hanrieder, Wolfram. 1989. *Germany, America, Europe: Forty Years of German Foreign Policy*. New Haven: Yale University Press.

Heitmeyer, Wilhelm. 1993. "Gesellschaftliche Desintegrationsprozesse als Ursachen von fremdenfeindlicher Gewalt und politischer Paralysierung." In *Aus Politik und Zeitgeschichte*, January 9.

Helm, Jutta. 1985. "Codeterminism in West Germany: What Difference Has It Made?" In *West European Politics* 9:32–53, January.

Hendriks, Gisela. 1991. *Germany and European Integration: The Common Agricultural Policy: An Area of Conflict*. New York: St. Martin's Press.

Henzler, Herbert A. and Lothar Spät. 1995. *Countdown für Deutschland*. Berlin: Siedler Verlag.

Hesse, Joachim Jens. 1987. "From Cooperative to Joint Policy-Making." In *West European Politics* 10:68–87. October.

Hetlage, Robert and Karl Lenz. 1995. *Deutschland nach der Wende*. Munich: Verlag C.H. Beck.

Herzog, Roman. 1996. "Ende des Trittbrettfahrens." In *Politische Meinung*, January, 27–35.

Hoffmann-Lange, Ursula. 1992. *Eliten, Macht und Konflikt in der Bundesrepublik*. Opladen: Leske + Budrich.

Holz-Bacha et al. 1994. "Political Television Advertising in Western Democracies: A Comparison of Campaign Broadcasts in the United States, Germany, and France." In *Political Communication* 11(1).

Horstkotte, Hermann. 1993. "The Economic Principles of Social Security in Germany." In *Social-Report* of Inter Nationes, Bonn, 1st Quarter.

Hülshoff, Michael G., Andrei S. Markovts and Simon Reich. 1993. *From Bundesrepublik to Deutschland*. Ann Arbor: University of Michigan Press.

Hüser, Francis. 1995. "Fremdenfeindlichkeit in Deutschland." In *Aus Politik und Zeitgeschichte*, November, 24, 22–28.

Hradil, Stefan. 1992. "Die 'objektive' und 'subjektive' Modernisierung: Der Wandel der westdeutschen Sozialstruktur und die Wiedervereinigung." In *Aus Politik und Zeitgeschichte*, July 10, 3–14.

Hubel, Helmut. 1992. *Das Vereinigte Deutschland aus internationaler Sicht: Eine Zwischenbilanz*. Bonn: Forschungsinstitut der Deutschen Gesellschaft für Auswärtige Politik.

Hüpphauf, Bernd, ed. 1993. "United Germany and Europe Towards 1990 and Beyond." In *European Studies Journal* 10(1–2).

Jacoby, Wade. 1994. "Industrial Relations in Western Germany: The Politics of Imitation." Paper delivered at the American Political Science Association Annual Meeting, New York, September 1–4.

Jacobs, Lawrence R. and Robert Y. Shapiro. 1995. "Don't Blame the Public for Failed Health Care Reform." *Journal of Health Politics, Policy and Law* 20(2):411–423, Summer.

Jesse, Eckhard and Armin Mitter, eds. 1992. *Die Gestaltung der deutschen Einheit*. Bonn: Bundeszentrale für politische Bildung.

Jesse, Eckhard and Armin Mitter, eds. 1992. *Die Gestaltung der Deutschen Einheit: Geschichte—Politik—Gesellschaft*. Bonn: Bundeszentrale für politische Bildung.

Julitz, Lothar. 1993. "Ohne Zuwanderung schrumpft die Bevölkerung in Deutschland." *Frankfurter Allgemeine Zeitung*, April 9, 16.

Kaiser, Karl and Hanns W. Maull, eds. 1992. *Die Zukunft der deutschen Aussenpolitik*. Bonn: Forschungsinstitut der Deutschen Gesellschaft für Auswärtige Politik.

———. 1993. *Deutschlands neue Aussenpolitik, Band I: Grundlagen*. Munich: Oldenbourg.

Katzenstein, Peter. 1987. *Policy and Politics in West Germany*. Philadelphia: Temple University Press.

———. 1990. *West Germany's Internal Security Policy: State and Violence in the 1970s and 1980s*. Ithaca: Western Societies Program Occasional Paper number 28 Center for Social Studies Cornell University.

Kepplinger, Hans Mathias et al. 1994. *Wie das Fernsehen Wahlen beeinflusst. Theoretische Modelle und empirische Analysen*. Munich: Verlag Reinhard Fischer.

Kerbel, Matthew Robert. 1994. *Edited For Television: CNN, ABC, and the 1992 Presidential Campaign*. Boulder: Westview Press.

Kirchner, Emil and James Sperling. 1992. *The Federal Republic and NATO*. New York: St. Martin's Press.

Kitchelt, Herbert. 1991. "The 1990 German General Election and National Unification: A Watershed in German Electoral History." In *West European Politics* 14(4): 121–148, October.

Klug, Wolfgang. 1995. "Mehr Markt in die Freie Wohlfahrt?" In *Aus Politik und Zeitgeschichte*, June 16, 34–43.

Koch, Burkhard. 1992. *Germany's New Assertiveness in International Relations*. Stanford: Hoover Institution.

Koller, Barbara. 1993. "Aussiedler in Deutschland." In *Aus Politik und Zeitgeschichte* B 48.

Kommers, Donald. 1989. *Constitutional Jurisprudence in the Federal Republic of Germany*. Durham: Duke University Press.

Koretz, Gene. 1993. "The Upside of America's Population Upsurge." *Business Week*, August 9, 20.

Kriesi, Hannspeter. 1989. "Neue soziale Bewegungen: Auf der Suche nach ihren gemeinsamen Nenner." *Politische Vierteljahresheft* 28(3):315–334, September.

Kuechler, Manfred. 1992. "Framing Unification: Issue Salience and Mass Sentiment 1989–1991." Chapter draft for Russel Dalton, ed., *Germany Votes 1990: Reunification and the Creation of a New German Party System*. London: Berg.

Kühnhardt, Ludger. 1994. "Multi-German Germany." In Daedalus 123(1): 193–210.

Kutz-Bauer, Helga. 1992. "Was heisst frauenspezifisches Lernen und Handeln?" In *Aus Politik und Zeitgeschichte*, June 12.

Landua, Detlef and Roland Habich. 1994. "Problemgruppen der Sozialpolitik im vereinten Deutschland." In *Aus Politik und Zeitgeschichte*, January 21, 3–14.

Langfried, Christine. 1985. "The Impact of the German Constitutional Court on Politics and Policy Output." In *Goverment and Opposition* 20:522–542, Autumn.

Lapp, Peter Joachim. 1992. Ein Staat—*Eine Armee: Von der NVA zur Bundeswehr*. Bonn: Friedrich-Ebert-Stiftung.

Lauk, Kurt J. 1994. "Germany at the Crossroads: On the Efficiency of the German Economy." In *Daedalus* 123(1): 57–83.

Lehr, Ursula and Joachim Wibbers. 1995. "Gesunde Alte—weniger Kosten." In *Politische Meinung*, April, 57–62.

Lindemann, Beate, ed. 1995. *Amerika in uns*. Mainz: Haase & Köhler.

Mann, Thomas E. and Norman J. Ornstein. 1994. *Congress, the Press, and the Public*. Washington, D.C.: The Brookings Institution.

Markovits, Andrei S., ed. 1982. *The Political Economy of West Germany*. New York: Praeger.

Markovits, Andrei S. and Russel J. Dalton. 1995. "Spin Doctors and Soothsayers: The Bundestag Elections of October 16, 1994." In *German Politics and Society* 13(1):1–11.

Marsh, David. 1992. *The Most Powerful Bank: Inside Germany's Bundesbank*. Ithaca: Cornell University Press.

McFalls, Laurence H. 1995. "Political Culture, Partisan Strategies, and the PDS." In *German Politics and Society* 13(1):50–61.

Mehrländer, Ursula and Günter Schultze. 1992. *Einwanderungskonzept für die Bundesrepublik Deutschland.* Bonn: Friedrich-Ebert-Stiftung.

Meier, Christian. 1994. "Deutschland zwischen der Bonner und Berliner Republik.." *Zeitschrift für Politik* 3: 261–279.

Meier-Braun, Karl-Heinz. 1995. "40 Jahre 'Gastarbeiter' und Ausländerpolitik in Deutschland." In *Aus Politik und Zeitgeschichte*, August 25.

Melzer, Wolfgang. 1992. *Jugend und Politik in Deutschland.* Opladen: Leske + Budrich.

Mensing, Friedhelm and Helmut Nagelschmitz. 1994. "Ohne Städte ist kein Staat zu machen." Paper published by Inter Nationes, Bonn. SO 7.

Mertes, Michael. 1994. "Germany's Social and Political Culture: Change Through Consensus?" In *Daedalus* 123(1):1–32.

Meyn, Hermann. 1994. *The Mass Media in the Federal Republic of Germany.* Berlin: Wissenschaftsverlag Volker Spiess.

———. 1996. *Massenmedien in der Bundesrepublik Deutschland.* Berlin: Wissenschaftsverlag Volker Spiess.

Müller, Steven. 1994. "Democracy in Germany." In *Daedalus* 123(1):33–56.

Neuhaus, Rolf. 1979. *Social Security: How It Works in the Federal Republic of Germany.* Bonn: Friedrich-Ebert-Stiftung.

Oberndörfer, Dieter. 1992. "Vom Nationalstaat zur offenen Republik." In *Aus Politik und Zeitgeschichte*, February 21.

Patterson, Thomas E. 1993. *Out of Order.* New York: Knopf.

Padgett, Stephen. 1993. "Party Democracy in the New German Polity." In *German Politics and Society* 23 (Spring)

Patzelt, Werner J. 1994. "Das Volk und seine Vertreter: eine gestörte Beziehung." In *Aus Politik und Zeitgeschichte*, March 18, 14–23.

Risse-Kappen, Thomas. 1991. "Public Opinion, Domestic Structure, and Foreign Policy in Liberal Democracies." In *World Politics*, July, 479–512.

Ristau, Malte und Petra Mackroth. 1993. "Latente Macht und neue Produktivität der Älteren." In *Aus Politik und Zeitgeschichte* 44, 27–38.

Roberts, Geoffrey. 1991. "Emigrants in Their Own Country: German Reunification and its Political Consequences." In *Parliamentary Affairs* 44:373–388, July.

Rohrschneider, Robert and Dieter Fuchs. 1995. "A New Electorate? The Economic Trends and Electoral Choices in the 1994 Federal Election." In *German Politics and Society* 13(1):100–122.

Rüttgers, Jürgen. 1994. "Erneuerung aus der Mitte." In *Aus Politik und Zeitgeschichte*, April 15, 3–7.

Rupier, Herman-Josef. 1991. *Der besetzte Verbündete: Die amerikanische Deutschlandpolitik von 1949–1955.* Opladen: Westdeutscher Verlag.

Sabato, Larry. 1991. *Feeding Frenzy: How Attack Journalism Has Transformed American Politics.* New York: The Free Press.

Scheuch, Erwin K. and Ute Scheuch. 1992. *Cliquen, Klüngel und Karrieren.* Hamburg: Rowohlt.

Schröder, Karsten. 1994. "Das System der gesetzlichen Krankenversicherungen: Fundament des deutschen Gesundheitswesens." In *Social-Report*, Inter Nationes, Bonn, 3rd Quarter.

Schüller, Heidi. 1995. *Die Alterslüge: Für einen neuen Generationenvertrag.* Berlin: Rowohlt.

Schulz, Werner. 1994. "Politik der Reformen und Reform der Politik." In *Aus Politik und Zeitgeschichte*, April 15, 27–32.

Schultze, Günter. 1992. "Anmerkungen zum Verständnis der 'multikulturellen' Gesellschaft. In *Multikulturelle Gesellschaft.* Bonn: Friedrich-Ebert-Stiftung.

Schuster, Thomas. 1995. *Staat und Medien: Ueber die elektronische Konditionierung der Wirklichkeit.* Frankfurt-on-the-Main: Fischer Taschenbuch Verlag.

Seffen, Achim. 1995. "Umbau des Sozialstaates unter Sparzwang." In *Aus Politik und Zeitgeschichte*, June 16, 26–33.

Shapiro, Robert Y and John M. Young. 1989. "Public Opinion and the Welfare State: The United States in Comparative Perspective." In *Political Science Quarterly* 104:59–89.

Siebert, Horst. 1994. *Geht den Deutschen die Arbeit aus?* Munich: Bertelsmann.

Smyser, W. R. 1993. *Germany and America.* Boulder: Westview.

———.1992. *The Economy of United Germany.* New York: St. Martin's Press.

Spieker, Manfred. 1986. *Legitimitätsprobleme des Sozialstaats: Konkurrierende Sozialstaatskonzeptionen in der Bundesrepublik Deutschland.* Berne: Paul Haupt Verlag.

Spittmann, Ilse. 1995. "Fünf Jahre danach—Wieviel Einheit brauchen wir?" In *Aus Politik und Zeitgeschehen*, September 15, 3–8.

Statistisches Bundesamt. *Datenreport 1992.* Bonn: Bundeszentrale für politische Bildung.

Stern, Susan. 1991. *Meet United Germany.* Frankfurt: Frankfurter Allgemeine Zeitung GmbH.

Szabo, Stephen F. 1992. *The Diplomacy of German Unification.* New York: St. Martin's Press.

Thaysen, Uwe. 1994. *Der Bundesrat, the Länder and German Federalism.* Washington, D.C.: American Institute for Contemporary German Studies.

Thränhardt, Dietrich. 1995. "Die Lebenslage der ausländischen Bevölkerung in der Bundesrepublik Deutschland." In *Aus Politik und Zeitgeschichte*, August 25.

———. 1992. "Eine Zuwanderungspolitik für Deutschland am Ende des Jahrhunderts." In *Einwanderungsland Deutschland.* Transcript, Tagung der Friedrich-Ebert-Stiftung 14–51, Mai.

United States General Accounting Office. 1994. "German Health Reforms: Changes Result in Lower Health Costs in 1993." GAO/HEHS-95–27.

United States General Accounting Office. 1993. "1993 German Health Reforms: Initiatives Tighten Cost Control." GAO/HRD-94–2.

Veen, Hans-Joachim and Jürgen Hoffmann. 1992. *Die Grünen zu Beginn der Neunziger Jahre*. Bonn: Bouvier.

Veen, Hans-Joachim and Elisabeth Nölle-Neumann, eds. 1991. *Wählerverhalten im Wandel*. Paderborn: Schöning.

Vester, Michael. 1993. "Das Janusgesicht sozialer Modernisierung." In *Aus Politik und Zeitgeschichte*, June 25.

Von Beyme, Klaus and Manfred Schmidt, eds. 1985. *Policy and Politics in the Federal Republic of Germany*. New York: St. Martin's Press.

Watson, Alan. 1992. *The Germans: Who Are They Now?* Chicago: edition q, inc.

Weaver, Kent R. and Bert A. Rockman, eds. 1993. *Do Institutions Matter? Government Capabilities in the United States and Abroad*. Washington, D.C.: The Brookings Institution.

Wessel, David and Daniel Benjamin. 1995. "Looking for Work: In Employment Policy, America and Europe Make a Sharp Contrast." *The Wall Street Journal*, March, 14, 1, A5.

Wilke, Manfred and Hans Peter Müller. 1991. *Zwischen Solidarität und Eigennutz: Die Gewerkschaften des DGB im deutschen Vereinigungsprozess*. Nelle: Verlag Ernst Knoth.

Wingen, Max. 1992. "Grenzen der Zuwanderung." In *Politische Meinung*, June, 37–45.

Wittkämper, Gerhard W. 1992. *Medien und Politik*. Darmstadt: Wissenschaftliche Buchgesellschaft.

Young, Brigitte. "The German Political Party System and the Contagion from the Right." In *German Politics and Society* 13(1):62–78.

Index

Note: Illustrations are on unnumbered pages that are given in the index as i(1) through i(11), Illustrations appear as a group after page 000. References to notes are indicated by an "n" following the page number, e.g. 262n7. When identically numbered notes in several chapters appear on one page, the chapter number is given in parentheses, e.g. 262n1(ch.3).

Compiled by Fred Liese